# LIONS OF IRELAND

MAINSTREAM SPORT

# LIONS OF IRELAND

## DAVID WALMSLEY

MAINSTREAM
PUBLISHING

EDINBURGH AND LONDON

**For Max, the littlest Lion**

First published in Great Britain in 2000 by
MAINSTREAM PUBLISHING COMPANY (EDINBURGH) LTD
7 Albany Street
Edinburgh EH1 3UG

ISBN 1 84018 484 1

This edition 2001

A catalogue record for this book is available from the British Library

Typeset in Bembo and Giza
Printed and bound in Great Britain by Cox and Wyman Ltd

# ACKNOWLEDGEMENTS

MANY THANKS ARE DUE to all those whose advice and assistance has made the writing and production of this book possible. Thanks first to all the players who took the time to recount their experiences of life with the Lions and also to those who opened their personal scrapbooks and photograph albums; particularly Harry McKibbin, Syd Millar, Robin Thompson, David Irwin and Tom Kiernan. Thanks also in this regard to Johnny Brennan at the Rugby Museum, Limerick, and Paul Collins at *Munster Rugby News*.

Special thanks also go to Donal Lenihan for kindly agreeing to contribute the foreword, to Barry O'Driscoll and Feidlim McLoughlin for their invaluable help with the detective work and also to Ollie Campbell for 'librarian duties'. No thanks to the man on the door at Jury's who didn't know who Fergus Slattery was. Sorry, Fergus!

Thanks as well to everyone else who offered expert knowledge and assistance: Cliff Morgan, all at *Rugby News*, Howard Evans, and all at Mainstream Publishing, especially Bill Campbell and Elaine Scott. Special thanks to Dad and Mum for reading through the earliest drafts and to Penny and Allan for the 'office space'.

Finally, the biggest thank you of all is for Lucy and for Max, for all their help and support and mostly just for always being there.

Every effort has been made to trace and acknowledge the copyright holders of all photographs used in this book. Where this has not been possible the author would like to take this opportunity to apologise for any inadvertent omissions.

# CONTENTS

# FOREWORD
# BY DONAL LENIHAN

*Donal Lenihan was manager of the 2001 Lions in Australia in and went on two tours as a player, to New Zealand in 1983 and most famously as captain of the midweek side in Australia in 1989. A former captain of Ireland, he played 52 times for his country, appeared in two World Cups and most recently has been manager of the Irish national team.*

THE LIONS HAVE always been good for the Irish. But then, I would like to think the Irish have always been good for the Lions. As well as 70 Test players and almost 100 tourists, Ireland has given the representative side of the four Home Unions more captains and coaches than any of its partners. In return, the Lions have given Ireland's greatest individuals a chance to display the full extent of their talents; a chance they might never have received if restricted to playing solely for their country.

Irish rugby has always produced a lot of very talented individual players but as a team we have never been in the very highest class. When Ireland travelled to the southern hemisphere we always knew that we would be struggling against the odds. Thankfully, the Lions have always given the Irish a platform to go out with the very best and show that they are as good as them. Being part of the Lions set-up has given Irish players the opportunity to take on the best on an equal footing and they have always responded to that. The 1997 tour, to South Africa, was proof of the pudding in the contribution of the four Irish players on the panel, and in particular the three who played in the Tests. Paul Wallace came in as a late replacement and was one of the heroes of the Test team, while nobody would have tipped Jeremy Davidson to partner Martin Johnson in the second-row — and yet he ended up as the players' choice as player of the series.

Of those Irish Lions predecessors, Tony O'Reilly, Willie John McBride and Mike Gibson are the ones who really stand out for me. And of those, Willie John, with his five tours and his captaincy of the 1974 side, would be the first name most people think of when they think of the Lions – for his presence, his leadership and simply for the awe he still inspires. I attended a couple of receptions held as part of the 25-year reunion of that record-breaking 1974 side and I looked around at the great players who were involved in that golden age of 1971–4 – the likes of Gareth Edwards, J.P.R. Williams, world-class players every one of them – and I got the feeling that even now they would run through a wall for McBride. That is the finest testimony to his greatness.

McBride is one of eight Irishmen to captain the Lions to date, and when you add that figure to the number of players from Ireland who have been involved with the side, as well as those who have also coached and managed it, you can't help but think that for the smallest of the four countries this is a fantastic achievement, and a fantastic tribute to the character the Irish bring to the Lions' atmosphere. The different nationalities bring different traits to the side but perhaps the Irish bring the most important of all. The Irish are great mixers and have always been the ones who have pulled people together. It's part of the make-up and character of the Irish people in general and the Lions' environment provides the opportunity to develop that and bring it to the fore.

The Irish have always had character and being away on tour and being under pressure never creates a problem for them. I have never been on an Irish tour where people were homesick – a problem I've seen people from other countries struggle with. They tend to accentuate the positive. You never see Irish players complaining about hotels, training facilities or anything. They just get on with it. They are very adaptable and willing to take on any challenge, and that attitude is vital in the Lions' context, where you will find the going tougher than on probably any other tour.

Of course, Lions tours are very different now, the main change being that they are so much shorter, so much more compact. Because of the length of tours in the old days, the Lions haven't always had the best results; by the time the Test series came round there were so many injuries that the side selected was not always a true reflection of the strength of the party. Today's shorter tours should at least allow you to get your best team on the field in the Tests – although as we discovered in Australia in 2001, the nature and physical intensity of the modern game can still take a heavy toll.

Fewer games do not mean Lions tours have become any easier though, and the professional game has brought new pressures of its own. However, the focus and the high standards demanded on tour can push the younger players particularly through the steepest of learning curves. A Lions tour accelerates the development of the best young players, which is another reason why it is so important to all four Home Unions. Tony O'Reilly went on his first Lions tour at the age of 18 (he had his 19th birthday out in South Africa) and he said that one Lions tour was worth two years at university in what it taught him, not just about rugby, but about life. In 1997, having Jeremy Davidson training and playing with the Martin Johnsons and Doddie Weirs really brought out the best in him, and, with all respect, did so far quicker than his normal club and country environment could.

That experience, which I am sure he would not swap for the world, might have been denied him not so many years ago when rugby went professional and there was a lot of speculation over the future of the Lions. There was a rising tide of opinion that the whole idea had lost its relevance in the modern era, particularly in view of the growth and success of the Rugby World Cup. But Lions tours are special and in my view the coming of the professional age has cemented their place in the rugby calendar more firmly than ever. In the old days players from several countries were brought together for the Barbarians and representative sides quite regularly; a combined Ireland and Scotland played England and Wales in several centenary matches. But because of the demands on players today – not to mention the insurance implications – they very rarely get the chance of appearing with players from other countries. The Lions is one of the very few remaining vehicles with which a player can not only be recognised as the very best in his position but also play and live with players of other nationalities. While there were question marks over the future of the Lions, the 1997 tour put that talk well and truly to bed and kept the Lions at the forefront of world rugby.

The 2000 tour may not have enjoyed the same success in the Test series, but it generated more interest in rugby in Australia than any tour there had done in the past and confirmed the age-old value of Ireland to the Lions and of the Lions to Ireland. Irish players have used the Lions to confirm their greatness, to make their names and to take their game to new heights. In Keith Wood, Brian O'Driscoll and Rob Henderson, we had a Test performer in each of those categories. In return for their individual contributions, the Lions experience has always helped the Irish to improve collectively through the influence and example of those who toured, and I expect the legacy of Australia to be no different. The fact that we ended up with eight players on the tour must have a positive effect, as long as the players take on board the lessons that were there to be learned.

The tradition of the Lions of Ireland is intact and will, I hope, continue in New Zealand in 2005 and for many, many tours to come.

*Donal Lenihan*
*2001*

# INTRODUCTION

WHEN THE BRITISH LIONS set off for South Africa in 1997, the Test team was widely expected to bear more resemblence to an England XV than a representative side drawn from all four of the Home Unions. Some even suggested the Irish, Scots and Welshmen among the party were there as little more than cosmetic tokens. In the end, of course, they could not have been more wrong, with Neil Jenkins kicking the series-winning points, Allan Bateman and Alan Tait defying their age in the three-quarters and Gregor Townsend marshalling the back line from out-half. And up front, the series could not have been won without the massive influence of three Irishmen in the pack: Paul Wallace a cornerstone at prop, hooker Keith Wood, an explosive, all-action talisman in both the tight and the loose, and second-row newcomer Jeremy Davidson reigning supreme in the lineout. Had it not been for untimely illness, back rower Eric Miller would have ensured that 50 per cent of the Test pack carried Irish passports. In Australia four years later, the Irish still provided three of the stars of an ultimately ill-fated adventure in Keith Wood, Brian O'Driscoll and surprise package Rob Henderson.

Ireland's contribution to the history of the British Lions has been just as influential throughout their century-odd of involvement. The most-capped Lion? Ireland's Willie John McBride. Top Test try scorer? Irish wing Tony O'Reilly. Most internationals as captain? Ireland's Ronnie Dawson. Most capped Lions wing? O'Reilly again. Centre? Mike Gibson. Flanker? Noel Murphy. The list of great Irish contributions goes on and on. Four tours took place between 1938 and 1959; each party was captained by an Irishman. Later, Tom Kiernan led the side to South Africa in 1968, with Dawson as coach, while the greatest of all Lions sides, the 1974 vintage, was captained by McBride and coached by Syd Millar, who managed in 1980 alongside coach Noel Murphy. Ciaran Fitzgerald was the most recent captain, in 1983, although current Ireland skipper Keith Wood was close to following him in Australia in 2001, when another Irishman, Donal Lenihan, managed the tour.

And the Irish contribution off the pitch? Well, there's a book in itself. No other country can bring such a potent package to the touring table and without Ireland the Lions might lose less than a quarter of their playing resources but would see their collective strength sapped by far, far more. In his foreword to this book, Donal Lenihan has highlighted the qualities and traditions that have allowed the Irish to play such an important role in Lions history. From a relative outsider's perspective, Wales legend Cliff Morgan, who believes he played the best rugby of his career in Dublin with Bective Rangers, is equally insightful. He says: 'There was a time when the captain of the Lions was picked because they thought he could handle a team better than anyone else, and they were probably right in most of players they chose and probably right in picking more Irish captains than from any of the other countries. The Irish have great presence amongst people. When they walk into a room people instantly have respect for them and that is so important for a captain.'

All six surviving Irish leaders of the Lions recount their experiences in these pages among what is hopefully a broad, representative cross-section of their countrymen who have worn the jersey of the four Home Unions, from the royal blue of the pre-war tours to the sponsored blazing red of the 1997 victors in South Africa and the first Lions of the twenty-first century. Together I hope the players' words paint a picture of their rugby lives and times, and of the tours that were the times of their rugby lives. And, most of all, that they celebrate the great Lions of Ireland.

# 1

## SMILING SAM MEETS
## LAWRENCE OF ARABIA

AS SAMMY WALKER LED his Lions onto the Cape Town quayside in June 1938, one South African newspaper was informing its readers: 'Sixteen members of this British team are teetotal abstainers and the rest of them are pretty abstemious. What's more, they will get to bed early. On nights before matches they are in bed at 11 p.m., while midnight is the latest at any time.'

More than 60 years on, Harry McKibbin, the Queen's University centre and mainstay of that Lions back division, still smiles at the thought that anyone could have included Blair Mayne in that description. Of course, at that point the South Africans had not met him.

Mayne, the strong man of the tourists' pack, lived as he played: hard and fast. In a life likened by one former player to that of Lawrence of Arabia, he stood out as a fearless, dashing competitor in everything he did. He became a war hero in North Africa, where he helped found the Special Air Sevice, and died tragically in a road accident at the age of just 40. Yet the tall, lean, Northern Irish lock packed more into that brief lifespan than lesser mortals could cram into twice the time, not so much burning the candle at both ends as dousing its entire length in petrol and casually tossing in a match. As far as the newspaper image of the Lions as teetotal early-nighters went, they must have been referring to somebody else. Mayne, who went missing for four days in Pietermaritzburg, was a law unto himself. 'I don't think he had any rivals as a character on that tour,' recalls McKibbin with a wry smile.

McKibbin, now 84 and one of only three surviving pre-war Irish Lions, says of his fellow student at Queen's: 'He was a real wild man. He also disappeared the night before we were due to travel along the coast by ship and the next morning there was still no sign of him until we got to the boat. There he was, still in his dinner jacket, saluting us from the deck. He was also a very strong man. On another occasion I was in bed one morning when he burst into the room, squashed the bed up at either end with me in the middle and then piled all the furniture in the room on top so I couldn't get out.'

Like McKibbin, Mayne was heading for the legal profession and he went on to become president of the Belfast Law Society. Yet far from being an establishment figure, Mayne enjoyed a reputation as a maverick unafraid to take on authority, a trait that once landed him behind bars himself. As a wartime captain in the Royal Ulster Rifles, the heavyweight boxer was left languishing in the glasshouse after laying out a commanding officer whose conduct he disapproved of as their unit battled across the Litani River during the 1941 invasion of Syria. Then, like a scene from *The Dirty Dozen*, SAS founder David Stirling rescued him from detention to help set up his crack force to fight highly dangerous guerrilla actions behind enemy lines.

Mayne, imaginatively nicknamed 'Paddy' by his army comrades, was the perfect man for the job, a fearsome warrior of enormous physical strength and huge bravery with a superb, analytical mind. He was also a natural leader but had a notoriously short fuse. Fellow SAS man David Sutherland later recalled in his memoirs, *He Who Dares*: 'If he didn't like you, you had better watch out. I remember an evening at the officers' mess bar going out for a pee and returning to find a body on the floor and Paddy rubbing his right fist. "Oh, he bored me," was Paddy's laconic comment.'

Boredom was not a problem for Mayne on the battlefield, where he caused major damage to the German campaign in a succession of daring raids on desert airfields, single-handedly taking out 15 planes on one mission and tearing the mechanics out of some aircraft with his bare hands when he ran out of explosives. He rose to the rank of Lieutenant-Colonel and took command of the SAS on Stirling's capture in 1943, leading his unit through the invasion of Italy and then in action across most of northern Europe, winning four Distinguished Service Orders along the way. Jack Kyle says of his exploits: 'I understood that to win a Victoria Cross the act of bravery has to be in the presence of a superior officer and his exploits were carried out when he was in charge.

'He was an amazing character. I remember listening to Margot Fontaine and she said she felt most alive when she was dancing. Men like Blair Mayne were the same, tremendous men of action, they allowed all the energy within them to rush to the surface.'

But Mayne was also cucumber cool. Sutherland recalled congratulating him on the night he was awarded his first DSO and venturing concern that his risk-taking might get him killed. He recorded Mayne's response: '"Don't worry – that won't happen," and he turned over and went to sleep. Luckily for us and unluckily for the Germans, miraculously he survived the war.'

Sadly Mayne's luck did not follow him into peacetime and he died in 1955 when his sports car hit a lamp-post as he drove home in Newtownards one night. His name lives on in Blair Mayne Way in the town and in the memories of the Lions tour of 1938.

The tourists lost the Test series 2–1 but Mayne was part of an Irish contingent all of whom returned with their reputations enhanced. The rangy lock was among the Lions forwards who put on weight during the trip to counter the massive Springbok pack but he did so at no cost to his ability to get out among the backs, where his handling skills created several fine tries, none more important than the one he conjured up for Laurie Duff to secure victory in the third Test, the only time eight Irishmen – the entire 1938 quota – have appeared in a Lions team.

The other key man in the move that led to Duff's try was Sammy Walker, the captain of Ireland and now the Lions. Walker, a Belfast bank clerk who died in 1972, was a hugely popular figure on the tour with both his players and his hosts, with the latter dubbing him 'Smiling Sam' for his good humour and bonhomie. He was reckoned to have happily signed thousands of autographs on tour and also acted as choirmaster to the team, whose anthem had become 'A Tribute to Ould Ireland is MacNamara's Band'. One newspaper even declared him 'the man with the loudest and heartiest laugh in Ireland'. But he also earned respect for his leadership and performances on the field, where he played in all three rows of the pack, usually at prop but also in establishing a fine second-row partnership with Mayne.

Walker was the second Irish captain of the Lions, after Tom Smyth, the Ulster doctor who led the party to South Africa in 1910. Smyth, who played for Malone but was in a spell with Welsh giants Newport at the time of the tour, was educated at the Ballymena Academy that would later turn out Syd Millar and Willie John McBride. He played in every position in the scrum but was best as a wing-forward in the finest Irish traditions, a harrier of opposing half-backs and a fleet-footed, quick-thinking supporter of his outside backs. Although the Lions lost the series in the deciding Test,

Smyth gained a reputation as a shrewd tactician and a worthy pioneer for the long line of Irish Lions leaders that would follow.

Smyth's tour was the first of the modern Lions age, 1910 being the year in which the team became the official representative of the four Home Unions, but he was not the first of his countrymen to make their mark on the touring team. Two Triple Crowns in three years earned nine Irish players a trip to the Cape in 1896, where they helped secure a 3–1 series win in which Bective Rangers half-back the great Louis Magee and Wanderers prop Tom Crean were the outstanding performers. Crean was the party's vice-captain and led the side 14 times on tour, including two Tests, in the absence of injured skipper Johnny Hammond. Strongly built and six foot, two inches tall, the former sprint champion wowed the crowds with his power and pace around the field, scoring a total of five tries, including one in the second Test. A specialist in London's Harley Street at the time of his early death in the 1930s, he had settled in Johannesburg after the tour and later won a Victoria Cross in the Boer War, as did his fellow Wanderer and Irish Lion Robert Johnston. Another in the same tradition was the giant lock and master of the dribble George Beamish, a tourist to New Zealand in 1930 while playing for Leicester and the RAF. Standing more than six feet tall and weighing over sixteen stone, Beamish led Ireland to their first victory in Cardiff the following year and lived up to his reputation as the finest forward of his generation while wearing what was then the blue jersey of the Lions.

When Sammy Walker and his men arrived in South Africa in 1938 as the last Lions to play in blue, Crean's forwards of 1896 were still rated the best the country had ever seen. It is a tribute to the likes of Walker, Mayne and wing-forward Bob Alexander, all of whom packed down in the three Tests and were joined by Bob Graves at hooker in the third, that an eight originally considered both too tall and too disliking of hard work in the tight to match the Springboks in the scrum were finally considered in the same class as those predecessors. Walker admitted being impressed by South African forward play, saying: 'Your players study the game more than we do at home. They get down to elementary fundamentals, such as pushing in the scrums.' But he added that after switching from the standard 3-2-3 scrum formation to take on the hosts at their 3-4-1 game, 'Our forwards were able to develop as the tour went on.'

While Walker was determined to take the 3-4-1 scrum back to

Ireland with him, on the other side of the fence Arthur Marsberg, the 1906 Springbok full-back, was much taken with the versatility of the Lions eight. He wrote: 'One of the Irish forwards tells me that the Irish selectors do not pick a specialised pack. They select the best eight forwards available, one of which is always a hooker, and they pack down as they get to the scrum. I think all keen rugger men will have noticed the influence of this on the play of the brilliant Irish forwards in the British pack. They are accomplished in all phases of forward play. Some of them run with the ball like three-quarters, and yet they revel in the hardest mauls.'

Alexander, who was killed in Sicily during the Second World War, was perhaps the most versatile of those forwards, a real utility player who could fill almost any role. He kicked goals and scored six tries on tour, including a vital one in the last Test, with others coming in provincial matches when injuries required him to step in on the wing, a task he also performed with ease against the Springboks themselves.

Walker, too, was hugely versatile, both as a rugby player and a sportsman at large. A schools long-jump champion and a fine footballer, cricketer and swimmer, he had made his Ireland début against the Boks in 1932 at the age of just 18, acting as an emergency goal-kicker and with the Lions he regularly turned up as a support winger in second-phase play. That ability to operate as an outside back gave his team a crucial victory in the run-up to the first Test when they became the first tourists to beat Transvaal since 1896. Walker had one spectacular solo try disallowed but popped up in the three-quarters to take a scoring pass from England's Jimmy Unwin and end a 20-minute siege of the Lions' 22, prompting the normally reserved manager Major Jock Hartley to leap into the air furiously waving the tourists' mascot, a carved wooden lion on a long pole, given to them by the Rhodesian ladies' hockey team.

A bustling, energetic player, Walker was robust with it, playing in 20 of the 24 matches despite being knocked out in an on-field dust-up. And when he was sidelined, by a bruised thigh for the game against Western Transvaal, the Lions suffered their first defeat as they drifted without the clarity of his leadership. The idea of packing the third Test team with Irishmen was partly forced on him by mounting injuries and partly inspired by a conversation with one of the Springbok selectors on the boat journey from Port Elizabeth to Cape Town, but the victory itself was directly attributed to Walker's rallying cry as captain.

Springbok skipper Danie Craven, playing his final Test match, said of his opposite number's role: 'I believe Sam Walker told his men before they went on to the field that they had to win this match or the tour would be regarded as a failure, and he asked them to play as they had never played before, even if they had to leave Newlands in an ambulance.'

The Lions had lost the opening two rubbers, including Port Elizabeth's 'Tropical Test' played in 100-degree heat, and now, in what would end up one of the most exciting internationals in history, found themselves trailing 13–3 at half-time and staring a whitewash in the face. Walker repeated his exhortations as his men sucked on their half-time oranges and they responded in the do-or-die fashion he called for. The Lions stormed back to take the lead when Queen's University out-half George Cromey ghosted through a glint of a gap close to the scrum, drew the full-back and found Alexander flying up on his shoulder to dive over the line as three Springboks hurled themselves on top of him. The Boks retook the lead but the Lions still had fuel in the tank and pulled clear in the closing stages as Walker's pack went on the rampage. The final score was 21–16, the Lions had become the first team to score 18 points in one half against the Boks and the *Cape Times* declared: 'No captain ever led a team to victory more worthily than Sam Walker.'

The man himself said of his day: 'I do not think a more thrilling Test match could have been played anywhere. I asked a lot of my men and they responded magnificently, and at half-time, with the wind in our favour, I really felt we had a great chance to win the match. It was a tremendous thrill to bring it off at Newlands, but the biggest thrill of my career was when the final whistle went and Ben du Toit, Louis Strachan and others hoisted me onto their shoulders and chaired me off. That is real sportsmanship.'

There was one more official game to play on the tour after the third Test, and another little piece of history to be made. Against the Combined Universities, Walker dragged several tacklers with him over the line for a try that earned him the memorable headline 'Walker manages a try when festooned with Africans', but the day belonged to McKibbin who scored a record 16 points in the 19–16 win, including the nerve-racking penalty that won the game with its very last kick. McKibbin's feat also provided an insight into the place of rugby in South African society. As Europe slid unstoppably towards war, the *Cape Argus* decided those worthy of inclusion in its 'In the Limelight' column that week were beleaguered Czech president Dr Edvard Benes, former British foreign secretary Anthony Eden, who had stepped up his campaign for an international stand to be made against Nazi Germany – and one H.R. McKibbin, rugby footballer of Ireland and the Lions.

The compact, textbook tackler, who returned to South Africa as assistant manager of the 1962 Lions and was later president of the IRFU in its centenary year, was the star back of the tour even though he was only 22 when he and his fellow Ulstermen set off on the Heysham steamer to join the main party in England just hours after he had sat his final law exam. Another tourist also catching the boat at the end of a busy day was George Cromey, who had been licensed as a probationer for the Presbyterian ministry before setting off. At five feet tall and weighing a shade over ten stone, Cromey was the smallest man on the tour and was nicknamed 'The Little Minister'. A brave, reliable and clever performer, he was overlooked for the bigger, if more erratic, Jeff Reynolds after being shaken by some heavy tackling in the defeat of Free State Country but showed his value in the third Test when he and his experienced Ireland half-back partner, Clontarf's George Morgan, were finally given their head. The smart, tireless Morgan created one try, Cromey two others and the out-half kept his team going forward with a fine display of kicking from hand, using the wind shrewdly to keep South Africa on the turn. With Hadyn Tanner generally the preferred scrum-half, Morgan had previously been played out of position at full-back, where he was kicking the ball 60 metres from hand in the thin air of the veld, and many judges suggested that had the duo played in the earlier Tests the Lions might well have won the series.

McKibbin linked up with his compatriots smoothly, but he had done so with every set of half-backs he played outside on tour. Remarkably confident for a youngster with only one cap to his name – he even took over kicking duties when Vivian Jenkins and Russell Taylor were injured, scoring 30 points in the last three matches – McKibbin quickly matured into an incisive attacker and a top-class tackler. He had already caught the eye on his Ireland début that year by causing havoc against Wales and keeping the great Wilf Wooller quiet, and not for nothing did former Springbok captain Paul Roos dub him 'the storm centre' of the Lions backline. Another former South African Test star, the centre and famous coach 'Boy' de Villiers, rated the young Ulsterman and his midfield partners 'superior in every way to the All Blacks and Wallabies centres'.

McKibbin exploited any gap that appeared in front of him more through his eye for an opening than through raw pace, but he was also an intelligent kicker from hand. He tormented his hosts with the short punt behind the defensive line – which also discouraged the South African backs from their habit of coming up offside against Lions teams they believed could not kick the penalties their transgressions risked conceding – and with the accuracy of his cross-kicking, the effort that created a try for Bill Clement against Western Province Town and Country being rated the best ever seen at Newlands. McKibbin probably did not remember much about it as he left that contest on a stretcher, suffering concussion after being kicked in a ruck. He spent a week in hospital but returned on his twenty-third birthday against Craven's crack Northern Transvaal team to cement his Test place with an outstanding display capped by a flamboyant overhead miss pass that sent in Dublin University's Vesey Boyle for the final try.

Under Walker's leadership and with that Irish-inspired third Test victory to their name, the 1938 Lions left South Africa having altered many of the pre-tour perceptions that surrounded them. Given little chance against the unofficial world champions and playing against sides who by Walker's reckoning 'played 50 per cent above their normal form' when facing the Lions, they left with the best record of any touring side to the republic, scoring more points than even the 1928 All Blacks, then the only side even to draw a series there. And as they prepared to set sail on the Athlone Castle with a farewell party for the huge crowds that gathered to see them off, they may have shed the temperance society image in which they had been painted on arrival. The *Cape Times* reported euphemistically that 'conversational powers lessened considerably as the hour of departure drew near', and added: 'Many fond farewells were said and the majority of the younger members of the fair sex, and even some of the older ones, had lost a lot of their lipstick when they came ashore.'

# 2

## MASTER AT WORK

WHEN IT COMES TO scattering compliments, New Zealanders are not among the world's most natural confetti throwers, especially where rugby is concerned. They revere their own as sporting gods, from Pinetree and Fitzy to Zinny and the rest, but when it comes to those who bear an emblem other than that of the silver fern, acknowledging even the slightest superiority over any of the men in black remains a crime against the state. So when the *Rugby Almanack* of New Zealand named Ireland's Jack Kyle and Wales's Ken Jones among its five players of the year for 1950, and the editors did not find themselves up on treason charges, it was safe to assume they were indeed two of the greatest players the game has seen. They may be hard to please, but Kiwis are pretty good judges.

Jones, an Olympic sprinter, was the finest wing of his age. Kyle, the jinking, butter-coated Queen's University out-half, remains arguably the finest stand-off of all time. His hosts as a Lion in 1950 certainly had no doubts. And half a century on, during which time the likes of Barry John and Phil Bennett have travelled their shores, New Zealanders still refer to Kyle as the greatest player in his position seen in the country since the Second World War.

His team-mates certainly rated him as such. Jim McCarthy, the flying Dolphin flanker who got the closest view of Kyle in action as the playmaker's supporting outrider in Ireland's great sides of the immediate post-war era, says simply: 'Jack Kyle was the finest ever. I heard Bill McLaren say the best rugby player he ever saw was Mike Gibson – which was interesting because a lot of people would say Gareth Edwards – but for me Jack would have been the best. Apart from his speed over 20 yards, Jack was brilliant because he was unorthodox. You were never quite sure what he was going to do. It was never: Jack is going to go on the inside from the first scrum, Jack is going to go on the outside from the second scrum. There was a lot of freedom of expression that I don't think is there now. Today you rarely see a guy in a back movement, with the exception of France, selling a dummy, cutting inside, beating a guy on the outside for speed – which was Jack's forte – because the back row are out in the backs, especially from the rucks.'

The modest Kyle would colour at the use of the word genius, but that was the one on the lips of all those who saw him play. In their 1978 bestseller *Men In Black*, the New Zealand writers Rod Chester and Neville McMillan declared: 'The subsequent British teams all had very good fly-halfs, but none of them posessed the Irishman's genius, especially as a runner with the ball. It should also be remembered that loose forwards had much more latitude in Kyle's day than they now have and just how good this great Irish player would have looked under today's rules, one can only imagine.'

In his own era, under the threat of encroaching flankers who were not obliged to stay bound until the ball had left the scrum, Kyle was a colossus and the creative force behind Ireland's golden age of the late '40s and early '50s. As he is always swift to point out, the pack in front of him provided the best platform then available in European rugby but he drove that advantage home with more flair and technical brilliance than any of his rivals. An elusive, electric runner, a sweet tactical kicker from hand and a better tackler than he gives himself credit for, Kyle's was an all round talent. He won a world-record 46 caps over an 11-year international career that began in Ireland's first post-war international and ended with a season in which he was part of the first Irish team to beat a touring side, the 1958 Australians defeated 9–6 in Dublin.

He won three International Championships with – some would say for – Ireland, the first the only Grand Slam in their history, and the second built on another Triple Crown. Appropriately enough, northern rugby's greatest prize was captured in his native Belfast in 1948 with a 6–3 win over Wales in front of 30,000 fevered fans gathered for a game that more than 100,000 others had been clamouring to see. Captain Karl Mullen chose a game plan based on forward power and the inspiration of Kyle. The local boy did not disappoint, settling the nerves by setting up an early try with a perfectly timed pass for Barney Mullan to take at full tilt, and once prop John Daly had restored Ireland's lead in the second half, Kyle's educated boot worked the touchlines magnificently to run the clock down and play out time. Ravenhill went wild, stripping Daly of his shirt before he could escape the field. As in the course of almost every match he played, Kyle skipped away with his kit intact.

Ireland repeated the trick the following season, with the surgeon-to-be again sticking the knife into Wales, this time in Swansea where he made a blindside break before cross-kicking for McCarthy to catch and score in a 5–0 win. Two years later he was at it again, but this time in Wales. Kyle was as influential in defence as attack. Cliff Morgan, making his début opposite him, still marvels at the way the master 'took me right through the rugby curriculum' that day, scoring a brilliant solo try and pulling off a try-saving tackle on Ken Jones, then the fastest man in the game, to earn the 3–3 draw that regained the championship for Ireland.

Although his national side had drawn a collective blank the previous year, individually 1950 was another golden year for Kyle with the Lions in New Zealand and Australia. That party was the last to travel by sea and spent a full six months away from home, circling the globe in the process, heading out through the West Indies and Panama Canal and back via Ceylon and the Suez Canal to complete their circumnavigation. It began in the lowest possible key with Kyle's father, who was not a rugby man, spotting his son's name while reading the minor columns of his newspaper. The player recalls: 'When the team was announced, it was in the papers. That was how I found out. My father was reading *The Telegraph* and found the Lions team to South Africa way down the bottom of the page.'

Initially, the medical student was unsure if he would be able to go. He says: 'Three months of the tour were over the holidays but I still missed a term at university. My father asked me if I intended being a rugby player or a doctor. We calmed him down when I told him I could make up the term the following year.'

So Kyle was in, and in for the adventure of a lifetime. 'We met in London in April,' he says, 'and were addressed by the colonial secretary and told we were representing our teams and our countries and more or less to behave ourselves. Then we were given our blazers, two I think, which were the only things we were given. We were supplied with socks but not our own boots, we had to bring our own. I think we had to supply our own shorts too. OK, it was hard to get everyone boots because everyone had their own choice but they never offered to give us the money for them. People sometimes seem to think that it was always 'shamateurism' but I was never offered any money in my career. You even had to return your jersey after a game or be charged for it. When I first started with

Ireland we all played in our club socks and it was such a motley collection of reds and blues and almost every hue that the union eventually decided they had better supply us with the same colour.

'We set off with the Lions from Liverpool and sailed to Curaçao in the West Indies. We got off there and then sailed through the Panama Canal, which was an exciting experience, then across the Pacific which took another two weeks. We were hoping to stop at Pitcairn Island, where the islanders sold produce, but we passed at midnight and the captain decided he wasn't going to wait for dawn. We got a terrific reception when we arrived in Wellington because the last touring side had been in 1930, and we then crossed to Nelson on the South Island, a gorgeous spot. They told us about the famous dolphin called Jack who always met the ship as it left harbour and guided it across the sea between the islands, and he did turn up for us too.'

That, however, was where the fun stopped as after three gentle warm-up matches the Lions headed on into the dark heart of New Zealand rugby. Kyle says: 'We were beaten by Otago in Dunedin when we ran up against this tremendous rucking. Then we went down to Invercargill, which was where George Norton broke his arm, although he stayed on until they flew Lewis Jones out, and we were beaten by Southland. Our next game was the first Test so the outlook wasn't very good.'

The injury to Norton, Bective and Ireland's goal-kicking full-back, had provided an object lesson in New Zealand attitudes towards players lying on the ball. Norton was first to discover what happened to those who found themselves on the wrong side of the ruck. The risk of injuries had been something the selectors were very conscious of when they drew up the party, particularly in ensuring that Kyle would receive a ready supply of quality ball. The out-half explains: 'On the 1930 tour they had only taken one scrum-half and he had been injured so they were completely goosed because there were no planes to get a replacement out. So this time they took three scrum-halfs and of course none of them got injured.'

For the first international, Kyle lined up outside Scotland cap Angus Black at Carisbrook and says: 'For some reason we did a lot better than in the two previous games and drew 9–9.' That reason might have been the sublime form of the Lions out-half as Kyle scored one try himself, set up another for Ken Jones and put in the long kick that led to the penalty from which John Robins booted the Lions' other points. For Jones's try, Kyle demonstrated his punting accuracy by putting full-back Bob Scott in rare trouble for the Welsh wing to cash in on as the garryowen went loose. For his own score he showed off his talent for running in broken play, bringing the crowd to its feet after counter-attacking from a miskick, slicing through the All Blacks' rearguard, leaving the great Scott for dead with a high-speed swerve and then shrugging off a desperate high tackle to cross the line. His Lions and Ireland teammate Jimmy Nelson, watching this one from the stands, was not surprised that Scott, one of the All Black legends of his age, had not been able to get near Kyle. He says: 'Jack would push his behind out to one side so if you were chasing him you couldn't get hold of him. Because of his body shape you thought he was running in a straight line when actually he was edging away from you all the time.'

Like many of the most naturally gifted sportsmen, for Kyle, his brilliance was pure instinct. He said of that first Test try: 'Somebody kicked the ball into my arms. It wasn't from a set piece, it was done at a subconscious level as always. People say you scored this try and that try, but these things happened without you really knowing consciously what you were doing. You don't set off thinking "I'm going to beat this guy here then run round here", you just set off and hope something will work.

'I would think all things which are done well are done at a subconscious level. I play golf at a conscious level and I'm thinking too much about it. It's only when you stand up there and know that this ball will go where you want it to without having to think about how it will get there that it actually does so. It's an instinctive reaction. It's what tennis players have and it's what anybody who's done anything in rugby had. You could start talking about how I did this or that but really it was your body taking over and doing it for you.'

The Lions did not lose another provincial game on tour but lost the last three Tests, albeit by generally narrow margins. Nevertheless, the attacking three-quarter play that became their hallmark and which revolved around Kyle's quick thinking and range of talents earned its master his place on New Zealand's roll of honour for 1950. He says of his nomination among the five players of the year: 'That was very pleasing, especially in New Zealand where they are so good on their rugby knowledge. But then on a tour like that you are doing nothing but playing rugby, that was your whole job and you got fit playing two games a week.'

His team-mates were in no doubt as to what qualities earned him his bouquets. Nelson says of his playing days: 'Jack Kyle was the best by some way. Firstly, he had magical hands. Secondly, he was dynamite off the mark from a standing start. He wasn't fast over long distances but in those first few strides he was electric.'

The benefits of that speed off the mark were obvious to Kyle's captain Mullen. He says: 'Because he had that great acceleration over short distances he took the ball very close to the gain line so when he received the pass he accelerated right through it. Bleddyn Williams and Jack Matthews were given great opportunities because of way Jack played.'

Kyle jokes that his brother-in-law, centre Noel Henderson, once asked in a team-talk if the captain could tell him 'whether the out-half would be tackling his man today', but Nelson, following up from the pack, never worried if the stand-off was the last line of defensive cover. 'He could never tackle straight on but he was a magnificent tackler from the side. The back-row Ireland had at the time really suited his game, too. We made sure there was no one coming through on his inside, and on his outside Jack would have them.' And he adds: 'The Lions tour was probably the best part of his career because he was playing with better players. Ireland's only decent three-quarter at that time was Noel Henderson.'

Kyle was certainly in his prime in the early '50s but sees that Lions experience as the finishing school of his rugby education. He says: 'I probably learned more on that tour than anywhere else. We would run round the deck of the ship and do PT and in the afternoons we would go to a special room we had with a blackboard and talk rugby. I had never talked so much rugby in my life.'

In fact, Kyle recalls the length of the field try scored by Ken Jones in the final Test in Auckland, rated as one of the finest ever seen at Eden Park, as coming from just such a pre-arranged play. The speed with which Lewis Jones flew onto a hard flat pass from Kyle to make the initial 50-yard break suggested he had intercepted a ball intended for Bleddyn Williams, but the author of the move remembers differently. Kyle says: 'We lost 11–9 but the try we scored was a move which we had practised and came from a throw over the top of the lineout. We gave the wing the nod, threw the ball over the lineout and I was looking for it. Lewis Jones was playing at full-back and as I got the ball he was bursting through the middle. So I gave it to him, he burst through and gave it to Ken Jones, who had come in off the left wing. It was one of those spectacular tries.'

Not that Kyle, who captained Ireland six times, ever wanted the detail in the game plan modern players work with. He says: 'In American Football there are set moves; rugby is a game of spontaneity. The ball comes out, you get hold of it and if a gap appears you try and go through it. If that's not possible you let it out or kick it.

'The only training we did with Ireland – and never did this change in all the time I was with the Irish side – was to meet on the Friday and run out in the afternoon to do what you might call a little light training. It was only things like if you were playing with a scrum-half you hadn't played with before, just what signs will we use. And that was nothing too complicated; it was usually, if I'm going right I'll tap my right leg, if I'm going left I'll tap my left.'

It may seen strange in a modern game where the top players' seasons last for almost 12 months, but in Kyle's day being overplayed was seen as as big a danger as being overtrained. Today's international coaches would kill for what happened in the aftermath of the 1950 Lions tour: Kyle, who had scored seven tries in 19 matches down under, sat out three months of the club season to make sure he was fresh for the International Championship in January. He recalls: 'Because that tour started in April straight after our international season, when I came back in October the domestic season was starting again and people were saying to me, "Now you mustn't play. If you keep on playing through the season you'll be exhausted by the time the internationals come round." So I sat in the stand and tried to explain matches to my old man, who never played rugby. I watched matches for three months: October, November and most of December, when the Irish trials were coming up. I got back into training just after Christmas and this was the idea because otherwise I would go stale. It was something you just wouldn't believe these days.'

The rest cure obviously worked as Ireland were champions in 1951 and those who played straight through were soon feeling the effects. Jimmy Nelson, the marauding Malone lock who went on to become president of the IRFU and in 1950 was complimented on being the Lions forward whose style was closest to that of the magnificent Otago pack, was among the most played tourists and soon found himself suffering for it. He says today: 'I came back shattered because of the last 16 matches in New Zealand I played 13 of them and then all six matches in Australia. Out of the whole 30 matches I played something like 23 of them. When I came back I was fighting fit but I was shattered mentally for a whole season.'

When let loose against opposing defences once more, it was Kyle who continued to do the shattering, right up until his international retirement in 1958. Looking back at the history of clashes between the hemispheres, the great out-half laments the records of the British and Irish sides, both collectively and individually, believing they possessed the talent to have done much better. He says: 'All we can say about northern rugby is what Oscar Wilde said about the Irish: "we are a nation of brilliant failures".' Kyle, at least, should be exempt from his own assessment. Brilliant, always. A failure, never. Just ask the All Blacks.

# 3

# Mrs Clifford's
# Tuck Shop

THEY ARE PROUD OF Tom Clifford down Limerick way. Head
south from the city centre to the home of Young Munster and you
will soon be walking through the gates of Tom Clifford Park. Climb
the stairs of the pavilion, heading up towards the Tom Clifford
Room, and you will be greeted by the image of the man himself,
immortalised in oils and keeping a warm eye on the place from
inside the portrait frame that dominates his clubhouse wall. In
Limerick, rugby is king. And in Limerick rugby, Tom Clifford will
always hold the throne.

The heartbeat of every team he graced and the life and soul of
every party he enlivened, Clifford became the first son of Limerick
to be honoured by selection for the Lions. He never lifted the
Munster Cup but in his 14 appearances for Ireland he won a Triple
Crown and International Championship in 1949 and a second
championship in 1951. In between times, he wrote his name in the
Lions history books with his exploits on and off the field in New
Zealand and Australia. As a five foot and nine inches, fourteen stone
and seven pounds prop-forward, Clifford was renowned at home for
his valuable ball-handling and goal-kicking skills, but with both
Ireland and the Lions he proved his technical ability in the tight
against some of the world's hardest scrummagers, despite often
giving away more than half a stone to his opponents. Fearless and
uncompromising on the field, full of fun and good humour off it, he
befriended prime ministers and enjoyed the company of legends but
was never happier than with his beloved 'Munsters'.

Yet Clifford might never have been a rugby player, or indeed a
serious sportsman of any sort. His early career was interrupted by a
debilitating bout of pleurisy which left him inactive for two years
and forced him at one point to accept that he might never lace up

a pair of boots again. His spirit and desire saw that he did so at the very highest level, but had it not been for a chance introduction to rugby as a teenager it might have been in another code entirely.

Born in County Tipperary, Clifford moved to Limerick at the age of three and later attended the city's Christian Brothers School, where soccer and hurling were the compulsory sports. Young Tom excelled at the former, going on eventually to appear in League of Ireland sides, and made his rugby début purely by chance. Typically he went straight in at the deep end. Young Munster found themselves a man short as they prepared to set off for a match against Cork Constitution and roped in the reluctant 14-year-old as a makeshift full-back, promising they would look after him. They presumably did as Clifford's sole later memory of the occasion was falling asleep in the pub afterwards.

That episode did not make him an instant convert to the code and his main sport remained soccer until the early 1940s. Willie Allen, the Young Munster back rower who played five seasons with Clifford in the black-and-ambers' pack, including a number of appearances alongside him in the front row, recalls his team-mate's talents for all sports. 'Tom played in defence for the Limerick soccer team and he also played for a team called Wembley Rangers as a centre-forward. The opposing goalkeepers didn't like him coming in on top of them much. He was a natural, he could turn his hand to any sport, and he really had an unmerciful punt of the ball. Even the old leather ones he could drive two pitches away. He had a real belt of the ball. He used to take the place kicks and as well as his strength in the scrum he could run with the ball like a three-quarter. He was a tremendous all-round footballer and for a prop he was very lively around the field.'

Having made his début at full-back, Clifford soon moved into the pack, initially as a back rower, where he was good enough to be selected for Munster ahead of the great Jim McCarthy, and then as a lock and finally loose-head prop after putting on weight while housebound by his illness.

As with 'Munsters', his international début came about when Ireland also found themselves a man short, in a manner of speaking, after fellow Munsterman John Daly of Cobh defected to rugby league at the end of the Grand Slam season of 1948. Clifford began the ensuing campaign with a defeat against France, but Ireland went on to win the Triple Crown by beating Wales in the decider, a match he rated the highlight of his career. He was already one of the greats of Munster and Irish rugby but selection for the Lions tour to New Zealand and Australia the following year would confirm his legendary status.

From the moment the players assembled on the quayside in Liverpool, his team-mates knew that Tom was of a different breed. Jimmy Nelson, the Malone second rower who was another pillar of the tour, recalls: 'Tom arrived with three trunks when most of us had two suitcases. We thought the people in Limerick must have kitted him out, then one night about midnight, when we had had a drink or two, Tom says would anyone like something to eat? We said yes, but where from? Come on down to the cabin, says Tom, and when we get there he opens one of the trunks and it's stuffed with fruitcake and biscuits. "My mother said you're not to be going short of food, I'll give you this to tide you over," he says.'

After that Tom's cabin became the place to be, to such an extent that the players all wrote thank you letters to Mrs Clifford for keeping them so well fed. Jim McCarthy says of the routine: 'Tom was an ordinary guy from Limerick who would be having his tea at six o'clock, if you know what I mean. He wouldn't be a late-night diner and didn't go for these huge, fancy menus they had on these boats. But he had all this food his mother had made for the Lions and Tom decided that he would have his evening meal, or his tea as he called it, every night at six o'clock and that was where we would all gravitate to as well.'

Not that Clifford eschewed the ship's food entirely. He and his great friend Bill McKay would stage regular eating contests – which Tom would always win by the odd dozen courses – and on one occasion he munched his way through the entire menu to win a bet and received a signed menu card from the astonished chef to mark his achievement.

All the Lions put on a few pounds during their long voyage, partly through the quantities of food on offer from both the galley and Mrs Clifford's food parcels and partly through the lack of scope for exercise on board ship, where too much running on the hard decks could cause niggling muscle strains and pulls. But once they were training daily in New Zealand they became fitter than they had ever been. Clifford was among those to benefit most and in the shape of his life played more matches than any other front-row forward, making 19 appearances in total, including three Tests in New Zealand and both internationals against Australia.

Clifford's resilience and toughness helped him set that record and the latter quality also earned him the task of minder to the man alongside him at the coalface, captain and hooker Karl Mullen. The slaughterman turned aircraft refueller and the Dublin gynaecologist may have sounded an odd couple, but Mullen held his team-mate in the highest regard on and off the field, despite Clifford's teasing of his diplomatic captain that he would refuse to stand for the British national anthem. The Old Belvedere man says of their experiences together: 'Tom Clifford was the greatest. He had the heart of a Lion, he would take no nonsense from anybody. He wouldn't do anything dirty like kick a man on the ground, but if anyone, say, punched me in the scrum they wouldn't do it again, Clifford would be on to it straight away.'

Mullen often had need of Clifford's services, for as the outstanding hooker of his age few opponents could get the upper hand against him by fair means alone. Technically, he was a fine striker of the ball, particularly effective against the head, and a solid performer in the lineout, while his pace and ability to read the game made him a superb cover tackler. Like his fellow medical student Jack Kyle, he stood out in Irish rugby from an early age, making his representative début alongside the great out-half against the British army at the end of the war. Kyle says of their baptism: 'During the war years the British army played an Irish XV every year at Christmas. The Interpros were going on but no Irish side ever got together apart from then and caps weren't awarded. Karl and I were the same age, 19, and when the Irish side came out for the Christmas of '45 we were both in it.'

Mullen established himself as a fine technician during the 1947 campaign and revealed himself as a master tactician the following term. Still just 21, he captained Ireland to a Triple Crown at his first attempt (Ernie Strathdee had been in charge for the first, Parisian leg of that historic Grand Slam), added a second Triple Crown and championship the following year and completed his championship hat trick in 1951, his final year in charge. He played one more season, under Des O'Brien, whom Mullen had made pack leader on his début, before bowing out with a quarter-century of caps to his name. Kyle says of his leadership: 'I loved playing under Karl. He had quite a style of captaincy; he was a guy who would have certain ideas but would also say OK, play your own game.'

That was the style Mullen aspired to, chairing dressing-room discussion groups rather than holding one-man team-talks as a means of getting his players to think about their roles in the game plan and about the strengths and weaknesses of the opposition. He says of his methods with Ireland: 'The whole team discussed tactics. That was a procedure we always went through. Every man had his say and I thought that was a mark of a team that was strong in collective spirit.'

Mullen adopted the same council-of-war approach with the Lions and although one draw was all his side had to show from four Tests against the All Blacks, his captaincy attracted praise from all sides. Leading the Lions, he says today, was little different in essence to guiding his national side, although his duties on tour were far more onerous than with Ireland. 'I had been captain of Ireland for three years so I was used to talking to the boys and putting them through their plans of action. I was always one for before we went on the field every guy knowing exactly what they had to do in both attack and defence. And if we had a few weak spots we would try and cover them up.

'We had a manager who was a diplomat [Surgeon-Captain L.B. 'Ginger' Osborne] so I was really in charge and had to decide on how to get the boys fit on the five-week journey out to New Zealand. Luckily we had three PE teachers and we had a regime each day where we did workouts on the deck including sprinting, running laps of the deck and all kinds of gymnastics. And then we had a team-talk every day and discussed every aspect of the game from hooker to full-back, in every position, whether in defence or attack. We had all this documented so when we got to New Zealand we had all our plans already, let's say, loosely organised defensively and in attack. For example, if you were scrumming on your own line and were passing back, would you pass to the out-half, to Jack Kyle, or back to George Norton or Lewis Jones at full-back? We had all those moves worked out and agreed on. Having five weeks together was a great settling in time. There was no boredom and we had no disagreements. We were an unusual side from that point of view, there were no guys who were nasty and it was same on and off the pitch. We had a very well organised and disciplined team.'

The players working with him admired his efforts, particularly in view of the difficulties under which he had to work. Jimmy Nelson admits he did not always agree with Mullen's tactics as captain – and the skipper himself later admitted that he was forced to play more Barbarians-style rugby than he felt was prudent by his masters on the four Home Unions tours committee – but acknowledges: 'We had a very good manager who knew bugger all about rugby. He was a charming man but that was a real problem because we didn't have a coach. It was impossible for Karl to coach 30 people and be a captain at the same time. We trained hard enough but it was very basic stuff. We should have had a lot more technical training but there wasn't that sort of thing about then.

Jim McCarthy adds: 'Karl was a quiet captain. You probably wouldn't know he was captain unless you were told. He wasn't a bellower and a director, he was never a guy people looking in would be conscious was captain, but he was excellent at it. Firstly he was a very good player but he also had a quiet authority about him and he had the ability to get on well with everyone. When you think there were English, Scots, Irish and Welsh, a captain would want to be someone who had the ability to keep all the different factions happy and keep the team from becoming too clannish. Guys who make the Lions selection are all good players or they wouldn't be there in the first place. Discipline and organisation are important but there isn't that much you can tell them about playing the game.'

Mullen's team meetings were designed to draw on his team-mates' vast collective experience and he believes the 1950 Lions had the raw material to win the series once they had recovered from the shock of the New Zealanders' physical rucking game. He says: 'We started at Wellington and they usually give you a few easy matches but we went down to Otago in Dunedin and were then beaten again by Southland, which was the lowest point of the tour. We were really low after that because although they were extremely strong we shouldn't have lost. It was a real shock to us but that tough schooling probably did us a lot of good. We were trampled on up front but we learned a lot from it and we should have won the drawn-first Test, which was another tough forward battle. They certainly didn't spare us in the rucks but we didn't back away. We had a few tough men ourselves, though: Tom Clifford and Don Hayward and Bill McKay as well.

'We were never outplayed and we should have won the third Test too. We had it won but they put an extra man [injured captain Roy Elvidge, who returned to the field as a rover when loose forward Peter Johnstone had already moved out to cover for him in the backs] out in the middle of the field and we didn't counteract it enough. They played with seven forwards and the extra man in the backs scored, actually. He made the difference.'

Having played his best game in comprehensively outhooking his opposite number in the second Test, Mullen missed those final two rubbers after pulling a leg muscle in training. Being non-playing captain did not darken his invariably sunny disposition, nor did it ease the burden of being alone on the bridge. He says: 'It's kind of a lonely job if you're totally in charge. My duties would have been to arrange training, look after tactics, discipline and team picking, although I would ask Bleddyn [Williams] and the other national captains to sit in on selection. It was a big responsibility on and off the field. In those days we hadn't any coach, but it's surprising on Lions tours because the amount of competition is usually enough to get the boys extremely fit. If they weren't I would tell them so and put them in the Wednesday match. They were all very keen to get in the Test games.'

Despite the absence of Mullen and Clifford, who was dropped as one of eight changes to the side, the fourth Test was rated the most enterprising of the series and although the Lions were beaten 11–8 the tour finale provided its abiding memory as the fans clamoured to acclaim the tourists. Mullen recalls: 'All the crowd at Eden Park came on to the pitch and they circled the team and they sang "Now Is The Hour". That was the first time that was done there and it was very moving.'

The Lions left New Zealand having established a reputation as the best-loved touring party to visit the islands, with no one more fêted than Clifford. Nelson remembers: 'Tom was a huge personality and he turned out to be a great friend of the New Zealand prime minister, Sidney Holland. Tom was a slaughterman by trade, but he was the first person the prime minister always came to see.'

Mullen has similar memories of the Munsterman's popularity: 'We travelled by train through the South Island and every station we stopped at we had a full band to meet us and we all marched behind the band up to the hotel. That was part of the ritual. Tom Clifford always said this band was especially for him and he would march at the head of it. On the way back I wrote to the Lord Mayor of Limerick saying how proud they should be of Tom Clifford and mentioned the band. So when he got home and got off the train from Dublin, the Lord Mayor had arranged for him to have a different band in every street, and he was chaired to the town hall and made a freeman of the city of Limerick. It was a great occasion down there.' A crowd of more than 8,000 turned out to cheer the returning hero, who had ended his tour by being restored to the side for the final two Tests in Australia which the battle-hardened Lions won comprehensively, Nelson scoring twice in the second Test in what remains a unique feat for a Lion against the Wallabies. Later captains sometimes complained that a warm-up against the then relatively weak Australians left them unprepared for the trials of New Zealand but Mullen believes his side could have been better off going there first. 'We were really fit by the time we beat Australia and we trounced them,' he says. 'It might have been better if we had gone the other way and been fit when we got to New Zealand.'

That only left the long journey home, which as ever was enlivened by Clifford the joker and entertainer, who was at great pains to make sure his kinfolk would recognise him on his return after so many months away. McCarthy says: 'When he left Limerick he had an army kind of haircut, a little fringe on the front and then quite short, but he let the hair grow on the voyage out so he wouldn't look so funny out in New Zealand. And on the way back the last thing he did in Marseilles was to get the exact same haircut so he could go back to Limerick the way he left it.'

Clifford was recognised as the balladeer of the squad, with 'O'Reilly's Daughter' his party piece, although he did have a more extensive repertoire than that. His old club-mate Willie Allen remembers: 'He was a tremendous "ball-hopper", as we used to say. He was mad for a bit of fun, always one for a singsong. He had his little song, "When I was a wee wee tot, they put me on a wee wee pot, to see if I could wee or not . . ." When they went on the tour there was a fancy-dress party on the ship one night and for Tom they made a napkin out of a sheet and let him crawl around sucking on a Guinness bottle.'

Clifford, despite his love of taking the rise out of his team-mates, was a loyal friend who hated letting anyone down and sent Christmas cards to his old playing partners religiously right up until his death. Allen recalls him bringing the entire Welsh team to meet his Young Munster mates the day after an international in Dublin, while Kyle will never forget his final vocal performance on the 1950 tour. He says: 'On the last night of the trip before we arrived back in England we were having a farewell party. Tom hadn't been too well but someone said we would have to have "O'Reilly's Daughter" one last time, so some of the fellows went down to his cabin where he was lying on his mattress. They lifted the mattress up with him still flat out on it and carried him up all the decks to the party and put Tom and his mattress down on a big table in the middle of the room. Tom sat up in his pyjamas and dressing gown, sang "O'Reilly's Daughter" then lay straight back down again. The lads picked up the mattress again and carried him back down to his cabin. That was the sort of person Tom was; even though he was feeling unwell he would still do that for everyone.'

Clifford died in 1990 and was honoured by Young Munster when the club renamed their Greenfields ground Tom Clifford Park. With or without that memorial, his name and legend will always live on, from Limerick to Wellington and beyond.

# 4

## MISSING FROM ACTION

THERE WAS NO SHORTAGE of surprises in store for the Lions of 1950 as they fought their way across New Zealand and Australia. The fact that Bill McKay defied a badly broken nose and concussion to star in all six internationals and finish as top try scorer among the forwards was not one of them. That his Ireland colleague Jim McCarthy could not join him in the Test XV, and that the final member of their country's back row, Des O'Brien, did not make the party at all raised more than a few eyebrows at home, but that McKay withstood everything the All Blacks could throw at him was nothing less than expected.

McKay, a medical student at Queen's University in Belfast, had served in the Second World War as a commando in the British army, spending much of his time in high-risk operations, twice being sent behind Japanese lines in the jungles of Burma and on one occasion being among only a handful of soldiers to survive the mission. With the war over, rugby provided a less life-threatening outlet for his energy and he quickly established himself in what became arguably the best back row Ireland has seen. To many judges, he remains the finest loose forward the country has produced.

Supremely fit and brimming with determination, McKay was among the most uncompromising of opponents. An Irish champion in both boxing and 400-metre running, he combined the best of both disciplines to emerge as one of the fastest, bravest and hardest men on the Lions tour. The combative Ulsterman, who died in 1997, would always be the first to point out that the success of Ireland's back row in the glory years of the late '40s was a truly collective effort, but his team-mates were always aware of the contribution he made to the team. Karl Mullen, his captain with both Ireland and the Lions, cites his fitness, commitment and work rate as vital to the fortunes of both and adds: 'Bill McKay was very tough; a big man but very quick and he was a brilliant tackler.'

Jack Kyle, the principal beneficiary of the work of McKay, McCarthy and O'Brien with Ireland, also remembers the former's speed around the field, effectively giving the team two open-side flankers as McCarthy was every bit as quick. He says: 'Bill McKay was very fast, although he was actually a miler rather than a sprinter. He ran against Roger Bannister once and only lost by a yard. He was hitting the 4.4-minute mile, which was very good for a miler then. As my friends always used to say, the three of them did all my work for me. They were so quick they would get out on the out-half for me. The plan we had was if the opposing out-half was coming up on the outside I was responsible for him, but if he came on the inside the two wing-forwards were responsible. The only trouble we had was when Cliff Morgan used to come inside, then outside and give the ball to Ken Jones, who was an Olympic sprinter and would put it under the posts!'

Alongside O'Brien and McCarthy, McKay pioneered the art of the attacking back-row unit and laid down the blueprint for Irish loose forward play, based on good scrummaging technique combined with disruption of the opposing half-backs and rapid support play in the farthest reaches of the field. Like his captain Mullen, McKay had appeared 17 times for Ireland before being selected for the Lions, totals that made the duo the most experienced players in the pack. Both men wore the responsibility well, with McKay relishing close-quarters combat against the hard men of New Zealand and coming out with ten tries from fifteen matches to show who generally emerged on top. That tally indicated that, aside from his destructive capabilities, McKay was just as dangerous with the ball in hand, as did his displays in playing a half at centre against England in 1950 when Des McKee was injured, and on the wing for all but the first 15 minutes of the game against Scotland the following season after George Norton also had to go off.

For bravery, though, it was hard to top his efforts in the third Lions Test against New Zealand in Wellington. McKay had been forced off after 25 minutes of the previous international after suffering concussion and a badly broken nose at the bottom of a ruck. He recovered at the home of former All Black Maurice Brownlie, a member of the 'Invincibles' side of the 1920s, in Gisborne, on the North Island's east coast, where he later returned to settle on emigrating to New Zealand as a doctor. Given little chance of making the third Test three weeks after his injury, McKay defied the odds to appear at Athletic Park wearing a large facial harness to protect his damaged hooter. He made no concessions to the injury he was carrying and played his usual robust game but received little luck for his pains, conceding the penalty for offside which Bob Scott goaled to give the All Blacks a 6–3 series-clinching victory.

McKay had still made an impact on his hosts, ensuring a warm welcome on his return to live in the country that had described him simply as 'brilliant' on tour with the Lions. His only regret in 1950 was that the Kiwi public had not been able to reach the same verdict on his Irish back-row colleagues. Jim McCarthy was every bit as quick and incisive as McKay and went on to score more tries than any other Irish forward, but he was a relatively small player and that counted against him in New Zealand. As McCarthy himself explains: 'The New Zealanders then used to play ten-man rugby. The year before they had toured South Africa and were whitewashed 4–0 by the Springboks, who really introduced ten-man rugby, keeping everything tight and taking the ball up through the forwards, taking it up the touchlines. New Zealand then adopted that style themselves – they didn't play a good style of rugby but it was winning rugby.'

Mullen confirms the assessment of McCarthy as an attacking gem who was most effective as a forager and support player against more expansive sides. He says: 'Jim was very, very quick but not the biggest player. Whereas Bill was a big tackler, Jim was more of a back-up for Jack Kyle, he would always be right on Jack's inside shoulder. If Jack made a break he knew straight away that Jim would be on his inside and could take the ball on for him.'

Despite being muscled out of Test contention, McCarthy, who played for the Dolphin club in Cork, was still a valuable member of the party, for his contribution off the field as well as his efforts in the provincial matches. He certainly enjoyed himself, remembering it today as 'an extraordinary event'. He expands: 'Can you imagine asking your boss for seven months off now? The guys were all bankers, mine managers, schoolteachers, doctors, guys from the City; looking back there was extraordinary variation. Only about one or two couldn't get off and I think one chap actually gave his job up, saying I'm not missing a trip like this, I can get a job when I get home. Another fellow, I won't mention his name, his wife hadn't told him she had discovered she was pregnant before he left so when he got home and saw this huge bump, well, to say he was shattered would be an understatement!'

Although McCarthy scored four tries and enhanced his reputation against several of the stronger provinces, the selectors felt he was too slight to risk in the Test series itself. But O'Brien, the London Irish, Cardiff and Old Belvedere number eight, did not even get that close, being left out of the party altogether, a decision that shocked all those who knew and played with him.

Mullen admits to being 'very surprised' when he saw no O'Brien on the list of players he would lead, while the other Irish Lions were equally bemused by his omission. McCarthy says: 'I thought Des would get on that trip. Ireland were on a roll in that period but in that damned year 1950 there were a number of injuries. So we really played super rugby in '48, '49 and were beaten twice in 1950. Wales won the Triple Crown and the championship in 1950 and knowing Wales, everyone in Wales is the best that ever played. So Wales dominated that Lions squad, whereas if it had been the year before or even the year after, when we won the championship again and had a really good side, we would have provided the bulk of the squad. But that year the Welsh were the dominant part, they had 14 players on it. Of course, if Wales had really had their way they would have had 30 players on it.'

And he adds: 'Des, Bill and I played 14 times together, which was an extraordinary amount, but we were naturally good together. Des was a wonderful sort of a player, very knowledgeable about the game, a general who would roam about the back line. As a number eight his primary duty was to cover to the corner flag. I don't think that's the number eight's duty now. Bill used to go left all the time and I used to go right all the time. We never played open and blind at all and we didn't really plan anything, we just kind of knew our job.'

Second-row Jimmy Nelson goes even further: 'Des O'Brien wasn't physically big but he was always in the right place at the right time and, most importantly, knew what to do when he got there. I don't know why they didn't pick him for the Lions in 1950 and I could never understand why he wasn't a successful manager with the Lions in 1966. When I knew him, he was a man among boys.'

Fully half a century on, O'Brien freely admits that his omission still eats at him, particularly over the politics he feels influenced the selection process. He says: 'They told me I was too old. I was 31. But you see England had to get a representative in so I missed out. It was a pity because I would have loved that tour. We had a very good back line then and with the Welsh wing-forwards and Bill McKay as well – Jim McCarthy was a little bit light for New Zealand – that would have been a very good back row. I suppose if I had gone in '50 I wouldn't have gone in '66, but I would rather have gone in '50.'

Ironically, while that omission may have helped O'Brien win the manager's job when the Lions returned to Australia and New Zealand in 1966, in between times he might have been made an outcast for allegedly 'professionalising' himself. The lineout specialist explains: 'I was proposed by Sarsfield Hogan, who was the guru of the IRFU. He felt I had been very unjustly treated not being picked for the 1950 Lions, and then I was instrumental in the setting-up with Karl Mullen of the first coaching school in rugby, I think. It was in the Butlin's camp outside Dublin; they gave us the camp for a week and we set up a coaching school. That was in the late '50s, I think. The manager of Butlin's, Desmond Scaife, who was later secretary of the Leinster Branch, felt there was a course needed and gave us the camp free for a week. We got members of senior teams and schoolboys and coaches from Wales, Ireland, England, Scotland and France, but we were frowned on by the Rugby Union because they felt getting Butlin's camp was professionalism and they wanted to shut us down. But I think these two things combined and the Irish union proposed me.'

Indeed, by 1966 O'Brien's coaching school ideas had been recognised as ahead of their time, for two years earlier an identical project had been launched with union blessing – at the very same Butlin's camp in County Meath. However, the tour, captained by Scotland's Mike Campbell-Lamerton, was one of the least memorable Lions expeditions. They played badly enough to become the first visitors to be whitewashed 4–0 by the All Blacks, experienced the darker side of New Zealand rugby and gained a reputation for not being the happiest of ships, with discipline regularly under question. O'Brien told his interview panel that if they wanted a coach they would be appointing the wrong man in choosing him, but was assured that Welsh PE teacher John Robins, the 'Honorary Assistant to the Honorary Manager', would take charge of that side of the trip. The team struck trouble when Robins had to return home after rupturing his Achilles tendon, but O'Brien believes they were not helped by the objectives his masters set.

He recalls: 'I had put all my stuff down on paper and sent it in before the interviews. Top of my list of aims was winning four Tests in New Zealand, then playing Lions type of rugby and then enjoying it. They removed my number one and said, "Your top priority is not winning four Tests in New Zealand, it is bringing the traditions of Lions play to Australia and New Zealand," which is somewhat different from today.'

Nor did O'Brien have any say in drawing up the list of players to fly south for the summer, which was changed several times by the succession of committees that had to pass it before the manager first caught sight of it just six weeks before the departure date. He explains: 'I had no say in selection and I did object to that at the time. There were one or two players I wouldn't have taken because I didn't think they would give everything and I think I was probably right.

'I thought that, of the squad, there were talented and dedicated players who were going and would be magnificent, then there were dedicated players who would give everything and might make one Test, and then there were talented players who just got on the Lions team and said "I've made it" and relaxed. And it turned out like that.'

The presence of the latter group ate away at discipline and morale on tour, and O'Brien was criticised for not cracking the whip enough, a charge he accepts to a point, although he pleads guilty only to assuming that all players shared his own values. He says: 'I'm told I was a laid-back manager but I felt that because I would have given my right arm to have gone in 1950 – I still am disappointed really – they would give everything too. They didn't.'

O'Brien was as popular as a manager as he had been as a player and as a fun-lover off the field. When Cliff Morgan was picked for his Wales début against Ireland in 1951 he recalls his then Cardiff club-mate O'Brien sending him a telegram: 'Congratulations, Cliff. I hope your life is insured.' Ireland comrade Jimmy Nelson remembers the Guinness representative as being 'very fond of drinking his product himself but still as slim as a rake'. He adds: 'I asked him once how many bottles of Guinness he would drink in a week. He said, "About one hundred. I make ten calls a day selling Guinness and I always have a bottle for each call. Then at weekends I drink it for pleasure."'

O'Brien was determined to do the best for his charges on tour but had to battle against the penny-pinching culture of the unions. He says: 'My big achievement was I got them trousers. They were given two blazers and two ties, and all the playing kit, of course, but that was about it. I said to the tours committee, how about trousers because the previous manager, Brian Vaughan, told me to try and get the boys properly equipped. He said it happened a lot that they would be lined up on stage one by one, and he looked at his team and their smart blazers and below the blazers at one end of the row would be baggy Oxford pants and the other end would be blue jeans. Bill Ramsay, the RFU treasurer, rang me up and said, "Well, we've got the trousers for you, two pairs," and he added, I might tell you, that the Scottish Rugby Union had said that the trousers had to be returned to the union after the tour.'

Whether or not they had to be laundered first was not made clear, but the tourists spent much of the trip removing bloodstains from their playing kit. Many matches descended into violence and at one point there was talk of calling the whole thing off. Seemingly as ever for the Lions, it was the meeting with Canterbury that brought matters to a head for the management. O'Brien recalls: 'The New Zealanders were pretty rough in the beginning, there was a lot of off the ball stuff. The game against Canterbury was particularly rough, the boys were raked up and down and when I went in the dressing-room I was rather appalled by what I saw and said so at the dinner that evening. Jim Telfer was captain because we didn't have a vice-captain so when Campbell-Lamerton wasn't playing one handed out the captaincy match by match. I said to Jim, "I'm going to be pretty rude tonight about New Zealand rugby, you just be nice to them." Of course, Telfer being Telfer, he got up after me and said, "I don't know what the manager has been talking about regarding dirty play today. Every game I have played here has been absolutely filthy." That set the cat amongst the pigeons but things improved greatly after it.'

O'Brien's fortunes did not follow a similar course, however. Having been remorselessly sandbagged by the Australian and Kiwi press for not being sufficiently hard-line with his men, he was also criticised for his policy of rotating the vice-captaincy and when he went off the tour for a few days he was accused of not being able to handle the pressure. He says of that moment: 'I went off to Fiji for three days and got really slagged for it. What happened there was the tours committee wanted a game against Fiji because they were emerging then as quite a colourful community of rugby players. At the time, they were represented on the International Board by New Zealand and New Zealand refused to give up one of their 25 games so we could go to Fiji. Before we left it was suggested I should go to Fiji and say hello to them, so I did. I spent a whole day with them watching rugby, and it was an incredible sight. We looked down from this hill on about eight pitches and they were going all day. As one team came off, another came on; it was tremendous to see. I got slagged off for leaving the tour but in fact I think it did quite a bit of diplomatic good. The pressure never got as bad as that!'

Yet for all the press criticism, the Lions opponents warmed to O'Brien and clubbed together to help make up for the disappointment of never making it to the Land of the Long White Cloud as a player. 'I actually played a game in New Zealand,' he says. 'There was a charity match for the family of a guy who had been killed and they wanted some of the Lions to play. But they weren't allowed to play in anything other than the Lions matches, so I said I would play and the New Zealand coach said he would play too. I was captain of one side, he was captain of the other. I just said to the guys, "This is a fun game, let's go out and enjoy it," but we had a coach and he grabbed the ball and, "Bloody hell," he said, "this is a serious game," and he gave them a real roasting about how they had to win at all costs. And then he handed me back the ball and said, "You're on."'

There was more to come, however. 'I was playing number eight and at one stage we had a scrum on the opposition line. Brian Lochore, who was on my right, said we're going to heel this and go right. But the scrum slewed and I went left and I was saved by Colin Meads shouting, "Go back you silly bugger, go the other way." So I sort of scuttled back round the scrum and a whole row opened up and I scored a try and the cameras flashed. It was a set-up to give the manager a try.' It was 16 years too late but at last O'Brien's name could be added to those of McCarthy and McKay on the scoresheets of New Zealand.

# 5

# THE GOLDEN CHILD

IF THE LIFE STORY of Tony O'Reilly went missing from the biography shelves of any municipal library the first place to look for it would be mistakenly filed in the section marked 'fiction'. To anyone unfamiliar with the great man and his works, this Boy's Own adventure would simply be too good to be true. In sport and in business O'Reilly is a phenomenon. Aged just 18 it took him only five senior appearances to play his way into the Irish national team; another four matches and he was named in the Lions squad to tour South Africa, where he immediately broke the tourists' all-time try-scoring record. That mark did not last long; he shattered it on the very next Lions expedition as he posted tour, Test and overall totals that are unlikely ever to be surpassed, becoming the team's most-capped wing along the way. His international career spanned 16 years — another world record — he scored more tries for the Barbarians than any other man and was also a good enough footballer to play for the League of Ireland side Home Farm. Off the field, he was lined up for the part in *Ben Hur* eventually awarded to Charlton Heston, but failed to turn up to meet the casting director, and has become one of the world's richest men in a professional career as spectacular as his sporting one. His law examination results were the best in all Ireland; he almost single-handedly revived the country's dairy industry while rising to head its marketing board before the age of 30; went on to become president of US food giant H.J. Heinz; and currently heads his Independent Newspapers group and the famous Waterford crystal brand. He is a close friend of Nelson Mandela, a renowned public speaker and has enough honorary doctorates to set up his own one-man university. He can also play the piano and, depressingly for the rest of us, his great friend the former Ireland flanker Jim McCarthy confirms: 'You know, I don't think there's anything Tony isn't good at; he's a natural at everything.'

O'Reilly was the original schoolboy sensation as he rose to become an Ireland and Lions star at 18, having learned his skills at Dublin's Belvedere College and then under the telling eye of another great Irish Lion, the 1950 captain Karl Mullen. As leader of his country's only Grand Slam side, Mullen knows a good 'un when he sees one and the youngster stepping into his three-quarter line immediately stood out. He says: 'I was captain of Old Belvedere and he joined us straight out of school so I saw quite a lot of him as a young man. Even as a schoolboy, he was phenomenal: a big fellow with great skills. He would practise his side-stepping and his jinking and his acceleration for hours. He hasn't changed a bit, he was always a great raconteur, speech-maker and funny man. But he was never arrogant or thought a lot of himself. He never demanded more attention than the average fellow would get. He was a very, very easy man to captain, very easy to direct, he would do anything.'

He could do almost anything on a rugby field, too, which made him a captain's dream as any ball reaching O'Reilly had a better than even chance of being deposited beyond the try-line in the immediate future. But with Ireland a lack of such service was where his problems lay and was also why he showed his finest form on tour with the Lions in first South Africa and then New Zealand. He played much of his early international rugby in the centre as Irish wings in those days were only likely to get a touch of the ball by smother-tackling their opposite number. Nevertheless, he showed enough in his first international season to earn a place on the 1955 Lions tour to South Africa, where the tourists' back division was strong enough for him to play out wide and still receive a regular supply of possession, although in the four-Test series he twice reverted to centre. But regardless of the role, a star was instantly born as he ran in a then record 16 tries on the tour including two in the internationals as the side became the first Lions to share a series with the Springboks. Power and pace were his principal weapons, although he employed them with far more style and subtlety than his modern-day equivalents. Cliff Morgan, his out-half on the 1955 tour, says of his comrade: 'Probably the most glorious sight in rugby was to see him in full flight. He would run at his opposite number and then run away from him. Today they will knock you over or run through you like Jonah Lomu; O'Reilly would sway away from you because he had such balance in his running.

'He scored vital tries in Test matches and you got to expect that he would score whenever you gave him the ball. There was always a chance he was going to beat a man or do something. Like the rest of Tony's life, not one of the tries he scored was ordinary, everything was slightly spectacular. I would place Tony with Gerald Davies as the two finest wings I had the pleasure of playing with or watching. The most curious try I saw him score was on a Barbarians tour to South Africa. We had a movement from our own 25 and O'Reilly was finishing it off by going for the corner. He beat everybody, swung round and ran for the posts, but as he did so he fell over a chap who had jumped forward to take a photograph. He carried on but the referee gave the try where he had fallen, by the corner flag. We missed the kick and lost by a point.' And he adds: 'What made Tony a terrific player was that he understood the game. He said to me once that he never revealed himself to a game before it revealed itself to him. He would wait and watch what was going on before he made his move. That is knowledge and patience, and to be a great wing you have got to have patience.

'In '55 he was only 19 – he had his nineteenth birthday on tour – but he had the wit and wisdom of someone 20 years older than he was. I always felt that at 19 he was 39 in his knowledge not of rugby but of the world and everything around him. He gave the tour a touch of class. It made you feel slightly inadequate that you weren't in the same mental bracket as Tony. Hard work and his brilliance at grasping situations in sport and in business set him apart. His very presence suggested indestructability. He towered over you in every sense.'

O'Reilly made an instant impact in the Tests in 1955, particularly in the nail-biting opener that the Lions shaded 23–22. He says of the epic: 'That game in Johannesburg was the most striking Test of its time. It was the biggest attendance ever seen at a rugby match, South Africa led 11–3 and we lost our flanker Reg Higgins with a broken leg. There were no replacements, of course, so we had to play with 14 men, three scores down at 6,000 feet up in front of more than 100,000 Afrikaners baying for our blood. Then Morgan scored one of the great tries of his life, [Jeff] Butterfield made a beautiful break and put [Cecil] Pedlow away to score and then I scored and we had got to 23–11 from 11–3 down. But suddenly we ran out of puff and they came back at us. And in the very last minute Chris Koch crashed over and they had a very easy kick to win. Tom Reid, the big second row from Limerick, said: "Jesus, if he kicks this I'm turning Protestant." So that was the magnitude of what he felt about the kick. There was audible silence, van der Schyff came up and just pushed it to the left of the post. It was amazing but we had won. I went on that tour with no real name, I was second choice really, but I ended up scoring more tries than any other touring player to South Africa. So it was a singular experience for a young man.'

The Lions lost the last Test and with it the chance of a first-ever series victory, although they led at half-time and, as O'Reilly puts it, 'were perched on the edge of history'. Fittingly he scored their final try of the contest himself, but paid the price of a dislocated shoulder in the process, an injury that would dog him for the remainder of his career. The acclaim he received on the tour made it quite clear who the South Africans rated its most popular performer and personality, although the teenager kept a remarkably level head amidst the clamour. He says: 'It's very much a matter of your own particular temperament and I think I came with a well-balanced outlook. My father always said to me it's easy to win but it's hard to lose; whatever happens be gracious in defeat. So I came from that sort of background and I went to South Africa full of wonderment. I received a lot of attention but if you realise that triumph and disaster are the twin companions of any sportsman and that football mimics life you should not get too excited about it.' O'Reilly describes the fuss that surrounded him as 'ridiculous really', and his team-mates found it all as amusing as he did bemusing. Morgan recalls: 'All the girls used to come up and say, "Oh, I touched Tony O'Reilly" because they adored him. Tom Reid used to joke and say, "It's all immoral. It's like Our Lord, oh, I touched his feet!".'

Reid, the Garryowen and Munster lock who played in both the second and back rows in 1955, and Cecil Pedlow, O'Reilly's opposite wing, were two of the few tourists who could run him close as an off-field character. Pedlow, a dental student from Belfast, formed the trip's comedy duo with O'Reilly, their stock in trade being their relentless skitting of the Lions' disciplinarian Northern Irish manager Jack Siggins over the stern nature of his team-talks. The Ulster wing had very poor eyesight but that did not prevent him from being international class in every sport he played, with his tennis skills being of a particularly high order. Morgan says of him: 'He couldn't see a thing but he was a hell of a good wing, a good runner with the ball and he scored the first try of the Test match in Ellis Park when we won 23–22 and the only people who touched the ball were Lions.' And he adds: 'Cecil was an old-fashioned rugby player; he had this generosity of spirit, always smiled at everyone and had a laugh with everyone. He fitted in beautifully to that tour. He was my sort of bloke, all the Irish were because I found their sense of humour stimulating. Their generosity of spirit was terrific.'

Tom Reid was in a similar class: long of laughter, short of eyesight. Morgan recalls: 'When Tom died in 1996, a big chunk of your life left you. He was without question the perfect tourist. First of all, he was a hell of a good forward and made the perfect combination with R.H.Williams in the second row. But if he hadn't played rugby he could have made his living in musicals, singing and on the stage, because he had the most beautiful voice. I would play three chords and he would sing "September Song".The whole room would go quiet and listen. He had the most glorious voice.'

Diplomacy, too, might have been another alternative career for the heavyweight Munsterman. Morgan reflects on his initial contribution to the public profile of the tour: 'At the first cocktail party we went to – a lunch held by the prime minister – Tom was in a group with me, O'Reilly, Rhys Williams and Dickie Jeeps, and we were with some South African farmers. A little man, bronzed from the farm, came up and said, "What do you people think of the South African political situation?" Silence fell over the crowd. Tom was clutching a pint, calmly took a swig and said, "Well, sir, I think nothing of it. I come from Limerick in southern Ireland and I have my own political problems."' And he adds: 'Tom came on tour with a little school bag when the rest of us had big trunks. He'd just enough to see him through to the next day, a shaving kit and a couple of other bits and pieces. He loved going on tour because he got a new pair of trousers. Maybe he wouldn't play today because they don't need stage singers these days, they concentrate on the rugby. Tom thought rugby was "a little refreshment of my spirit", that was his phrase. He loved a jar of ale and like Pedlow he had bad eyesight. He went to live in Canada – stayed there after a Barbarians tour – and the Lions stopped off there to play a Test on the way back from New Zealand in '59.They were all lined up on the field before the start and this Limerick accent came out over the ground. And it said: "Hello Reilly, I know you're there. I can't see you but I can hear you all right!"'

In 1959 sound still preceded sight when O'Reilly made an entrance as he again attracted excited, buzzing crowds wherever he went with the Lions, putting on the same shows in New Zealand as he had in South Africa four years earlier. This time he teamed up off-field with Andy Mulligan, the London Irish scrum-half who arrived as a replacement but played his way into the fourth Test team ahead of the great Dickie Jeeps, to form an even more uproarious double act than he had created with Pedlow in '55, going so far as to broadcast a ficticious interview with Lord Wavell Wakefield on New Zealand radio. O'Reilly says: 'Andy Mulligan and I used to grab the microphone wherever we were and try to run a little sketch on the peccadilloes of the various players and particularly the officials. Someone once wrote that "O'Reilly lived in a state of armed truce with the management."' That ceasefire came closest to breaking when the press discovered the duo moonlighting as the house band in an Auckland restaurant. O'Reilly says of the furore: 'Luckily I now own the paper so I can supress the facts! But in truth I played the piano and Mulligan was the guitarist in a restaurant called the Hi-Diddle-Griddle and on the Thursday night before the Test we were discovered by the *New Zealand Herald* in a photograph that was blown all over the cover. We had great dialogue with the management of the tour over whether this was the right way to prepare yourself for a Test match.'

The All Blacks had the last laugh in the series itself, but O'Reilly was again the star of the tourists' show as he eclipsed his own scoring record for the team. He played 24 times on tour – more than anyone else in the squad – and scored 22 tries in those matches, including four in Tests, two against New Zealand and two against Australia on the opening leg of the tour. The O'Reilly–Mulligan pairing also proved its worth on the pitch in New Zealand, where the last Test victory owed much to the duo, with Mulligan's blindside breaks creating two tries, the latter for O'Reilly and which allowed him to break Ken Jones's record set in the same country nine years earlier and give him another Lions memory to treasure. He says of the tour: 'In '59 I was qualified as a solicitor and it was the interim year before I started on life's journey so it had a more reflective quality about it than '55 did, when I was a wide-eyed 18-year-old coming straight from school.

'It was a very exciting experience in '59 trying to equal Ken Jones's record, which I did four matches from the end and then had to try to find a way to beat him. I finally got the try to do it in about the last minute of the final Test, which was the great game of the tour for me. First of all we beat them fair and square and we beat them in Auckland, which was really their home ground, and I got that vital eighteenth try that I had been trying to get for the previous four matches. I can still feel the heavy ball and the mud on my face as I went through the last tackle of Don Clarke. I was a lucky Lion. I didn't get injured very much, I scored record numbers of tries in New Zealand, Australia and South Africa, and overall I played in ten Tests and scored in six of them.'

And he adds: 'I'm by nature a Lions-type footballer and the two records I'm most proud of are the most tries ever scored by a Lion and the most tries ever scored by a Barbarian. Both of those teams play the running style of rugby and I believe running rugby is the way to go. The game today is very exciting but not quite as flowing as you would like it to be. You've got to ask yourself if we are becoming a rugby-league-type game, in which case we will have to change the rules to make sure the great glorious game – the running and the probing – is allowed a less populous field to flourish on. It was an enormously rapid game under the old rules, terrific running and great speed by both sides.'

Ronnie Dawson, his captain with both Ireland and the Lions at the end of the '50s, says of O'Reilly's exploits: 'Records make heroes and Tony had been in South Africa in '55 and had a wonderful tour then and had another wonderful tour in '59. I would like to think there were a lot of stars in that side but because of his record Tony shone a little brighter than the rest. He had great size and pace even from being a schoolboy of 17 years of age, he was well over six feet in height and heavy and fast. He had a good change of pace, he could also beat a man right or left but usually relied on his pace and a pretty devastating hand-off. He probably scored most of his tries on the outside. He scored two magnificent ones in the Tests against Australia. He was a wing three-quarter in the classic mould.'

Despite all his remarkable playing feats, at home he rarely received the rapturous acclaim afforded him in the southern hemisphere, possibly because he did not get the same opportunities to shine in some variable Irish sides during the period, an assessment that O'Reilly will not disagree with. He says: 'It was an altogether better period playing for the Lions than for Ireland. Pedlow used to remark: "You know, the only time you ever see the ball on the wing for Ireland is at the dinner afterwards, and then only to sign it." The Lions play running rugby and I was a runner. I loved the freedom that I didn't get with Ireland, the thrill of receiving the ball ten or fifteen times in a game.'

Others agree that O'Reilly was rarely the prophet in his own land, with Ray McLoughlin, whose early career overlapped with the rising tycoon's later days, saying: 'Tony O'Reilly and Mike Gibson were streets ahead of all other Irish backs I played with, but there was a tendency to knock O'Reilly because he was a bit of a glamour boy in his early years. He didn't spend enough time at it because he was doing too many other things and he didn't play enough with enough good teams at Ireland level to show how good he was.'

Cliff Morgan, rated by O'Reilly as the most influential player the Lions have ever seen, is equally quick to his friend's defence, saying: 'I heard him say once that the Irish are quite like the Welsh, they dislike two things in life: success and failure. That sums up both nations. I remember going across to Ireland to do some talks after the 1955 tour and people would say O'Reilly can run, he's fast all right, but he can't tackle. I said to them, I don't know what you've watched but I've seen him at close quarters in the wicked heat of a Test match and I saw him fall in front of the big South African forwards and I saw him tackle and I saw him carry two Springboks on his back over the line to score a try. That is courage, that is guts.'

To those qualities O'Reilly was also unexpectedly able to add longevity when an eleventh-hour injury crisis gave him a shock recall to the Ireland side that faced England at Twickenham in 1970, fully seven years after his last cap. Having devoted more time to his business than his training at the time he was probably grateful that little action came his way that afternoon, but his penchant for turning up to practice sessions in a chauffeur-driven Rolls Royce gave the wags in the crowd plenty to work with. He was already established as one of the world's most able executives by then and although he had shown his acumen from an early age he missed a money-making opportunity in South Africa in 1955 that had not escaped an earlier sporting personality making his way there. Robin Thompson, the captain of that tour, explains: 'All the Irish players were invited to speak at a school and as we were being led along the corridor the headmaster said to us, "I hope you're not going to do a Len Hutton on me." I asked what he meant and he said, "Well, when we got to this point with him he turned to me and said, 'You do know my fee for this is ten guineas?'".'

Of course, rugby has now become a business in itself, much to the dismay of O'Reilly, who believes much of the game's spirit has been neglected in the dash for cash that has followed the arrival of professionalism. All the same, he insists there must always be a place in its heart and its calendar for the Lions. He says: 'The Lions are the bond between the four Home Unions. Do away with the Lions and rugby will dissolve into pockets of self-interest. There is no greater honour for a football player than to represent the British and Irish

Lions; they are emblematic of rugby in these islands and, provided they can serve up the rugby they have, the crowds that will want to watch them will be greater than the home nations could draw individually. With players who are able to challenge the authority of southern rugby it remains a wonderful concept.'

The Lions' principles may be unaltered but the nature of the on-field action and the preparation that goes into it have changed beyond recognition and Morgan for one is certain his old friend would not be leaping forward if given the opportunity to have his time again. 'Tony wouldn't have been a player today,' he says. 'Not because he wasn't good enough but because he wouldn't have given the time that rugby now demands, in watching videotapes of yourself and of your mistakes. He would rather be talking about something else.' And excelling at it too, no doubt.

# 6

# IN LEAGUE ON THEIR OWN

WHEN THE MONEY MEN of rugby league packed their suitcases – one for clothes, one for cash – and set off in search of union recruits in the 1950s, their destination of choice was more likely to be the valleys of Wales than the playing fields of Ireland. They would pile up their bank notes on kitchen tables in the Rhondda and the Ebbw Valley. Sometimes their quarry showed them the door, sometimes it swallowed hard and signed. Irish players rarely had to make the choice, often through lack of opportunity but also through lack of necessity. In an age where many Welsh internationals were still whistled up from the dangerous depths of the coal mines, the body of Irish rugby was drawn from less precarious professions, such as banking, medicine and education. The price of 'going north' was much the same in both countries – effective excommunication from the union faith – but the relative rewards differed wildly. The sums on offer were less attractive to Dublin doctors already climbing secure career ladders than to miners from Maesteg risking their lives daily in backbreaking work on breadline pay.

John C. Daly and Paddy Reid, two of the Grand Slam heroes of 1948, had joined Huddersfield the following season, but for Irish internationals in general switching codes was not the done thing. And it was certainly not the done thing for Irish internationals who were captains of the Lions, which is why the defection of Robin Thompson came as such a shock when he signed for Warrington in 1956. Not only was he the most recent leader of the Lions, but at that stage was also the most successful skipper they had seen as his 1955 tourists became the first to share a series in South Africa. Ironically, Thompson's league career did not leave him massively enriched, yet it still cost him the friendship of a rugby establishment that had previously fêted him. By all rights it should also have cost him his life.

Astonishingly, his capture was remarkably low key; no trunks full of tenners, no cloak and dagger meetings, no star-spangled signing ceremony. Essentially, a work-mate of his brother asked if he fancied giving it a go and Thompson said something along the lines of, 'Oh, all right then.' The former Instonians lock, a chemist by training, explains: 'I had a brother who was a doctor in Warrington and his senior partner was Tom McClelland, who had been an Irish rugby international from Ballymena in the early '20s. He had become chairman of the Warrington rugby league club. I was working for Fisons in England at the time, in Nottingham, and I used to go up there from time to time. One week Dr McClelland asked if I would come up and see the directors with him. I had no thought in my mind at all, but they asked me to sign and I did.'

If the then 25-year-old Thompson had not thought through the implications of his spur-of-the-moment signature, it was only a matter of hours before their full weight began to crush him. He says: 'After I signed I spent the night in torment, crying, people ringing me up asking what had I done. It was as if you had done a murder. At that time there were professional golfers and if you had had a talent for playing the trombone or the violin you could get paid for it. But the old school-tie attitude in rugby really detested professionalism. I remember the old Irish international and Ireland selector Ernie Crawford phoning me up and saying, "Oh, what have you done?" Paddy Reid from Munster had gone as a centre, but for a captain of the British Lions to go was absolutely taboo. I certainly was very much aware of the antipathy of some of the establishment.'

Thompson felt their cold fury even after he returned to Ireland, sooner than he anticipated and in circumstances that should have elicited the concern of even the most cold-hearted committee man. Illness and injury had already disrupted his union career, but nothing could prepare him for the shock that ended his playing days altogether. 'A quarter of the way through the season we had a cup match against Leeds. I was tackled and dislocated a shoulder. During the following week I started to have tremendous temperatures and "eggs" – the tremors – so they sent me to Manchester Royal Infirmary. They diagnosed a bone marrow disease, took a biopsy from my hip bone and I was given between three and five years to live. So I've proved them wrong – I've survived to become old and decrepit! But I had an enlarged spleen which meant there was a real danger of rupturing it, so I never played after that. That was my lot at the ripe old age of 25.

'When I came back to Ireland a local club, Bangor, rang me and asked if I fancied coming down to help them out with a bit of training. I asked if they were sure they wanted me, with what had happened and they still said, sure, come on down. So the first session, I saw three gentlemen in suits arrive and wave for the captain to come over. I knew what it was, and he jogged over and chatted to them. When he had finished chatting he walked very slowly back to me. I went over to him and said, "You don't need to say what happened. I'll just leave you now and I'm sorry if I've caused you any embarrassment." I just got in the car and drove away.'

Worse was still to come. Thompson continues: 'The hardest thing was when I was later doing television work. I went over to London for a match and went into the hotel to check the teams. A member of the Barbarians committee who I had known very well was standing in the foyer and I went over to say, "Hello there, I haven't seen you in a long time," and he just turned his back and walked away. That really did hurt me. One could never imagine rugby would change the way it has.'

Just a few months before Thompson signed himself into the union's black books, the same administrators who instantly cold-shouldered him had been bending over backwards to accommodate him as he struggled against illness to make the Irish side for a crucial international. He says: 'The season after the Lions tour I had appendicitis before the Barbarians game on Boxing Day and I just got home before the appendix burst and I was taken to hospital. I missed most of the games that season and when I came back I played for my club's thirds to get some games. Wales were going for a Triple Crown in '56 and were coming to play off for it in Dublin. The Irish selectors came to a game I was playing for Instonians against Trinity at Ravenhill and asked how did I feel. They also asked the referee to play an extra 20 minutes to see if I was fit.

'They were satisfied and I was in the team. And I remember Sammy Walker, the 1938 Lions captain, who was broadcasting that day, coming into the Irish pavilion just before the kick-off and he said to me, "Robin, I think you're foolish to play today in the championship but I wish you every luck." I went out determined to play the shirt off my back and I know I had one of my best games ever. We beat Wales 11–3 to deprive them of the Triple Crown.'

That was not the first time Walker's words had inspired

Thompson's deeds, as the younger man, who was still only 23 and had captained Ireland just three times when invited to lead the Lions, consulted regularly with his predecessor in planning his strategies for the 1955 tour. He says: 'I had a good number of sessions with Sammy Walker. The big things he warned me about were avoiding cliques, keeping the boys happy and no gambling. He also said that if you win half your games you will be lucky, and if you think Wales is a hot spot for rugby wait until you get to South Africa. You will never believe their fanaticism for the game.'

Walker may have been happily off the mark with that first prediction – they drew the Tests two apiece and just lost three of their 21 other contests – but he was spot on with the second. Thompson, who was first capped by Ireland against the Springboks at the age of 19, smiles: 'The hospitality we received was unbelievable. If I was ever lending a car to somebody it would certainly not be a touring rugby player. But I had so many put at my disposal it was unbelievable.'

But he adds: 'The intensity was amazing. You just couldn't get away from it. You might take a girl out for a meal and find that your bill had been paid but people would be round you constantly, you just couldn't get away from rugby. I felt that was the tiring part, the mental thing of not being able to escape from it.'

Thompson's team got their first taste of the continuous clamour that lay ahead on their arrival at Johannesburg airport, when they also played the captain's trump card that ensured them instant and lasting popularity. Thompson had written to each tourist individually soon after the squad was announced, and mindful of the fact that he would have no coach, invited PE teacher Jeff Butterfield to devise some training routines they could use on the tour. He also recalled touring Canada and America with Queen's University some years earlier (a trip he had quit his job to join), and the particular memory of the organised singing that kept morale high throughout the trip inspired him to put pen to paper once more. He says: 'I wrote to Cliff [Morgan] and asked him to be choir master. We also arranged for someone to come down from South Africa House and teach us some songs in Afrikaans. They did that and taught us "Sarie Marais" and we learned them so we could sing them with Cliff conducting. When we arrived at Jan Smuts airport in the early hours of the morning there must have been three or four thousand people there to meet us. It was unbelievable. I said to Cliff, let's get the boys down on the tarmac, and we sang "Sarie Marais" in Afrikaans. And from that day on we could do no wrong.'

That tour saw the first occasion that Thompson was offered money in connection with his rugby playing – a desperate South African phoned his hotel room to offer £400 for a pair of tickets to the first Test. The next time money was mentioned he took Warrington's payment for playing and was no longer his union's blue-eyed boy.

Thompson was made to suffer for his decision for decades after he had hung up his boots. Fourteen years later, he recounted his experiences to another young Ulsterman who was making the same journey across the Irish Sea to begin a new career in a new code of rugby. What he heard from Robin Thompson did not convince another Lion of Ireland, Ken Goodall, that he had made the wrong decision in joining Workington in the summer of 1970. Like Thompson, his career was cut short, but happily he never suffered the same level of discrimination as his predecessor. Goodall says: 'After I had signed I talked to Robin and he told me he had had a tough enough time when he came back. He felt that he wasn't welcome.

'I couldn't say what the immediate reaction to my decision was like in Ireland because when people found out I had signed I had already departed. But I didn't feel there was any adverse reaction. I never got a letter from the IRFU saying I was now banned or anything like that. But when I came back and things eventually resolved themselves as far as rugby union becoming a professional game was concerned I did get a letter from the IRFU saying I was now reinstated, welcome back into the fold and that they were happy to greet me and all this stuff, which I thought was a nice touch.

'I had only four years at league because I had a disc removed from my spine and I was told that if I played on and got my back hurt again I could end up in a wheelchair, and I didn't fancy that. That was the end of it in 1974 and I came back to Ireland. When I came back I was involved as a teacher locally, but after a few months I had a phone call from a lady called Joy Williams, who was the BBC producer for sport in Northern Ireland, and she asked me if I would be interested in doing reports on rugby matches at the weekends. I said certainly and that probably broke the ice as far as all the clubs were concerned because I was then able to go into them on another pretext and there was never any hassle. Anyone who was a genuine friend never wished you any ill because you signed for rugby league. I felt maybe a bit self-conscious going back into some of the clubs but nobody said anything. Or if they did they never said it to me.'

In 1970 Goodall's departure was considered a major loss to Irish rugby. Still only 23, he was rapidly maturing into the most exciting number eight of his generation and was being touted as a shoe-in for the following year's Lions tour to New Zealand. Ireland won 12 of the 19 internationals in which he played, and even today, Noel Murphy still insists: 'Ken Goodall was potentially one of the greatest. He should never have gone to league.'

The City of Derry loose forward had been selected for the 1968 tour but declined as he was sitting university exams at the time. He later joined the trip as a replacement but broke a thumb in his only appearance. Yet he had no second thoughts about giving up the chance of a second, more successful tour when word began to circulate that a league scout was approaching players at an invitation match he had organised at his club in April 1970.

Goodall says: 'I had just been married the previous December and I thought to myself that this was an opportunity to give myself some financial security. So I made it my business to talk to this person, a man called Alan Sandwith, who worked for a paper in Workington and was a friend of Tom Mitchell, the chairman of the rugby league club. I talked terms with him that night and eventually agreed a sum of money. He said he would come and see me in the morning having given me a bit of time to think things over. I met him in my mother-in-law's house in Londonderry and I had decided I was happy enough with the figures we were talking about. He asked me to sign a wee bit of paper, and as far as I was concerned that was me signed.

'My wife and I went over to Workington in the summer of 1970 and I was taken to sign officially. But then John Reason of the *Daily Telegraph* phoned me up. I don't know how he found out where I was staying but he phoned me up and said, "Don't sign. Tony O'Reilly is flying in to Cumberland and is going to offer you a job." Whether Tony O'Reilly knew I was in Cumberland or not, he certainly didn't call to offer me a job. Workington took me up to Border Television for the publicity and I signed the official forms there.'

And he adds: 'I've always said that if I was in the same position again I would do exactly the same. In any major decision you make there are always pros and cons, and you have to weigh them up. The major pro was it gave some financial stability to me and my family. That was the only reason for me to sign. I had nothing against the IRFU, nothing whatsoever. When Ireland played Wales in '69 in Cardiff, if they had beaten them they would have won the Triple Crown and I had been injured in the Scotland game prior to the Welsh game. I was in Newcastle at the time and the IRFU paid for me to go down to Cardiff, gave me a ticket and put me up in a hotel for that weekend. I believed I had a lot of friends in Irish rugby and I still do.'

At times it may have felt otherwise, but Robin Thompson, too, still has many admirers in the game, not least those who played with him as Lions in South Africa. Cliff Morgan, the recipient of more than one offer to go north himself, felt Thompson's honest grinder's style was more suited to union than league and was sad to see him leave the game whose stars he had led with real distinction. He says: 'Maybe Robin wasn't the greatest second-row forward the world has ever seen but his inspiration and enthusiasm were terrific. The captain's job is not an easy one but he did his duties religiously and carefully and always gave a very good speech at functions. What he said always made you feel proud to be a Lion.'

# 7

## THE MAN WITH THE PLAN

ATTENTION TO DETAIL HAS been the hallmark of Ronnie Dawson's life in rugby, as a player and coach with Ireland and the Lions, and as an administrator with both his country and the International Rugby Board. A meticulous analyst and assiduous reader of the small print, his reputation is that of a man who reads everything twice. Which in 1959 was just as well, as he would otherwise not have realised he was captain of the Lions. The Wanderers front rower had spent the mid-'50s behind fellow Dubliner Robin Roe in the queue for both the Irish and Leinster hooker's jerseys, and had made his international bow only in 1958. He made an immediate impact, scoring the try on his début that made Australia the first tourists to lose to Ireland, and being handed the captaincy in his second season. But by his own admission he was still 'basically a greenhorn' and had given no thought to the possibility of leading the Lions. So when a letter from the Tours Sub-Committee of the Committee of the Four Home Unions dropped onto his doormat, that was not the phrase he was fumbling for. 'When I first read the letter,' he recalls, 'and I saw, "Dear Dawson, I am pleased to advise you that you have been selected for the British Isles rugby tour to New Zealand, blah, blah, blah," I just threw my hands in the air and said, "Wow, brilliant, marvellous." But the last four words of the last brief sentence were "and to be captain". I had actually missed that on first reading.'

That was just about the first and last trick Dawson missed in a Lions career that saw him captain the side more times in Tests than any other leader and go on to pioneer the role of coach that would change the fortunes of the touring side in the early '70s. In fact, Dawson was effectively acting as coach from the moment of his playing selection in 1959. He remembers: 'The management comprised Alf Wilson the manager, a secretary, as he was called, Ossie Glasgow, and then there was the captain, me. We were also the selectors and although we consulted with some of the senior players, Alf Wilson was very much a man of his own mind and exercised his rights as manager very specifically. But the team preparation we did ourselves, through myself from an organisational point of view with a lot of the senior players like Jeff Butterfield helping in our training. We worked it out and kept a lot of competition in our training routines, always working with the ball. We spent a week at Eastbourne training and getting kitted out, and it became clear then that we had a very talented side with a lot of pace running right through the team but particularly in the three-quarters.'

Tactics were also the captain's preserve and now Dawson knew the strengths of his own team; as well as putting his men through their physical paces and trying to generate fluid teamwork among players who barely knew each other, he was also focusing on the opposition and their strengths and weaknesses. He says: 'Reading the New Zealanders and their team was relatively predictable – they had a well-established side and we had already seen most of them when they had toured over here – and we decided that our whole aim would be to obtain and retain enough possession in the pack for our three-quarters to use successfully. All sorts of phrases were coming into the game then about good ball and bad ball but we reckoned that any ball was a ball we had to use, and we usually managed to use a greater percentage than not through a brilliant set of backs.'

The Lions tour started off with what was then seen as a gentle warm-up in Australia, where Dawson joined Tony O'Reilly among the try-scorers in two Test victories over the Wallabies but was still swotting up on the infinitely tougher challenge that awaited across the Tasman. He recalls: 'Bill McKay, who had played for Ireland in the Triple Crown years of 1948 and '49, was a good friend of mine and was living in New Zealand at the time. He came across to Australia and I had long conversations with both him and the New Zealand correspondent T.P. McLean about the style of play we would encounter over there. They both issued thinly veiled warnings that our forward play was too loose. I took this very much to heart but I didn't fully appreciate what we were up against until we arrived in New Zealand and played our first match, against Hawke's Bay up in Napier.

'The Hawke's Bay side kicked off with us lined up in normal scrum formation to receive the kick. The three of us in the front row turned round as the ball flew over our heads to go and get into the ensuing maul, and as we did so I remember being hit flat on my face by the following-up New Zealand forwards. I looked round and there was [prop] Hughie McLeod flat on his face as well. Neither of us was anywhere near the ball but that didn't matter, they just stormed through, took the ball on up from a mistake by whichever of our side caught the kick-off and within a relatively quick succession of maul, ruck, move, had gone up and scored a try within the first two minutes. I remember thinking, "Bloody hell, what's all this about?" We went on and won the match well, 52–12, but clearly we had a lot of work to do.'

Dawson had just one minor match in which to get his men up to speed before the first of the big provincial games, against the Auckland side of All Blacks skipper Wilson Whineray. They survived that test – just – but like Karl Mullen's Lions before them they came unstuck against the rucking masters of Otago. Their victim remembers: 'That was the first game we lost, to a side with a great forward tradition and coached by the great Vic Cavanagh, who used to say you should always be able to throw a blanket over the forwards as they move around the field. They executed everything very well through very fast forwards with great body positions and I remember picking up for the first time the three words that apply to mauls and rucks: bend, bind, drive. They really were terrifically effective at this sort of thing and we had just never experienced this type of forward play at home, where everything was more sedate, a scrum was a scrum, a lineout was a lineout and whatever followed followed.'

A 3–1 series defeat in the Test series that followed suggests the Lions did not learn enough quickly enough, yet the bare facts conceal the many achievements of Ronnie Dawson's side. Had they not run into Don Clarke, the Waikato full-back whose All Blacks points-scoring records stood for more than a quarter of a century, in the prime of his rugby life, the tables would likely have been completely reversed as he kicked the Lions to death in the first Test, where under the old scoring system his six penalties eclipsed the visitors' four tries by a single point, and stole the second with a converted try at the death. The Lions had to make do with the consolation of scoring more points than any of their predecessors or successors, and the Irish among them could point to O'Reilly's record 22 tries and the form with hand and boot of David Hewitt, the tour's top scorer.

The Lions had not been expected to win against an All Blacks side that had not lost a series in the southern hemisphere in a decade, but they headed for home with Dawson ruing what might have been. He says: 'A couple of Clarke's penalties in the first Test were very dubious and we surprised ourselves by doing well against that New Zealand team. They thought they were going to win it fairly readily, largely because they had a very good forward pack, all of whom had long and illustrious careers. There was Wilson Whineray, Ron Hemi was the hooker, Ian Clarke the other prop, then Tiny Hill and Colin Meads. Dick Conway, a shortish guy with red hair, was eighth man, shortish for New Zealand anyway, but bloody hell he was all over the place. He was like Jock Hobbs much later, one of those guys who won the ball on the ground all the time, and he was with Kelvin Tremain, who was a brilliant flank-forward. They were a really powerful side and that was our challenge against them: to win ball, retain ball and use it immediately. We placed our emphasis on making the best of primary possession, then creating overlaps and bringing in strong support play. We had the players to do that but if it went into what they now call second or third phases New Zealand were totally on top. Their rucking and mauling was four times better than ours.'

Dawson had plenty of opportunity to polish his motivational skills in the aftermath of the first Test defeat, the manner of which left his players, '. . . very sore. We took quite a bit of picking up because we really had done enough to win it.' Another body blow to morale was just around the corner. The Lions had reached New Zealand with a rising injury list caused by the bone-hard grounds of Australia and by the time of the second Test they had been further decimated by the belated effects of widespread blood poisoning, apparently caused by the fertilisers used on the cricket squares that lay in the middle of most of the Australian pitches. Again they were given no chance, yet once more they had victory within their grasp. 'Again we did quite well up front,' says Dawson, 'and were leading with only a couple of minutes left to play. We had a penalty on the left-hand side of the ground and were playing into quite a big wind, as always in Wellington. I called up Terry Davies from full-back and asked him to kick to touch because really all we wanted was a few more lineouts and bits of messy play, keep hold of the ball and we would be fine. Terry wanted to kick at goal but I was afraid that kicking into the wind the ball wouldn't carry to the posts and Don Clarke, who was the menace, would be there to run it back at us.

Well, one way or another the kick to touch was sliced and the very thing we didn't want to happen, happened. Don Clarke was right underneath it and stormed off down the left-hand side of the field and broke a couple of tackles. Within a move or two the New Zealanders were rucking inside our 25, with a big blindside. They went blind, scored the try and it was goaled and that was the game gone. So a bit of bad luck in the first Test and a bit of stupidity in the second and we were 2–0 down in the series.'

The Lions also led in the third Test but ended up losing 22–8 – 'We were hammered, really hammered,' admits Dawson – and kissing goodbye to their hopes of drawing the series. The captain says: 'We were leading and had a breakaway back movement with a three to two situation which then left David Hewitt and Tony O'Reilly out on the left wing with only Clarke to beat. David possibly held the ball for a little too long and he was caught. The ball went loose and that should have been another score behind the posts. At that moment you could feel our bubble being burst and the New Zealanders, recognising the let-off, suddenly began to thrive.

'We won the rest of the provincial matches and went on to win the last Test 9–6, which was the first time the Lions had beaten a New Zealand side since 1930. That was a consolation and we could also point to the brilliance of our back line, where the speed of Hewitt and O'Reilly was extraordinary. The forwards grew into their role and we ended up securing equal possession in the set scrums and lineouts, which was equally extraordinary. We weren't badly beaten for possession in any match except possibly Canterbury and the third Test, but the real lessons lay in their back-row play and their rucking and mauling. I took that home and never forgot it, throughout the rest of my playing career and on after it.'

As well as having his eyes opened to new possibilities of play, Dawson had also learned a lot about preparing a Test team and about the perils of selection. Much debate had accompanied the tour over whether the captain was actually worth his place in the Test side on playing terms alone, with much of the press claiming that Bryn Meredith was the better hooker for his abilities in the loose. Dawson was a strong enough character to have coped with leaving himself out if he felt it was the right thing to do, but he was also strong enough to back himself against his critics. With Wilson's blessing he played all six Tests in the two countries, appearing in 19 of the 31 matches in total, and says now of the situation: 'It was probably bound to happen. Bryn was a great player, a member of a great Welsh front row and had been to South Africa with the Lions in '55. We are great friends and were great adversaries on the field back then. But I never gave the issue a second thought. Bryn was a superb player and it could be argued that he was a better all-round forward. That is for others to judge but as a ball winner in set scrums, which was a very important facet because we had to win primary possession, I had no doubt that I was at least as good as Bryn as a hooker plain and simple.' Dawson's record of strikes against the head on that tour backed his judgement to the hilt, as does the testimony of his team-mates. Noel Murphy, flanker in four of the six Tests, says: 'They were both exceptionally talented hookers; both of them could win four, five or six balls against the head with ease. There was a debate, and maybe I was biased because I was Irish, but it never occurred to me that Ronnie shouldn't have been in the Test side.'

And he adds of his captain: 'It was an incredible amount of responsibility for a young player to take on. Alf Wilson would have had a good knowledge of rugby football but he would be the first to admit that on any matter of rugby football Ronnie carried them. He was a meticulous player and meticulous in his approach no matter what job he took on, right through his career as a rugby administrator.'

His duties on that tour pushed the future IRFU president towards coaching at the end of his playing career in the mid-1960s, a time when the concept of the coach was slowly becoming accepted in the northern hemisphere. Wales were the first of the Home Unions to take the plunge by appointing David Nash to take charge of the national team in 1967, and the Lions followed suit the next year. John Robins had been in charge of coaching as assistant to Des O'Brien in 1966 but Dawson was the first to be given the official title. Ironically, Ireland would not appoint a supremo of their own until the autumn of 1969, so Dawson was in the unusual position of being coach of the Lions before he was coach of his country. A spell as a national coach has since come to be seen as a trial for the Lions job, not the other way round.

The 26-year-old architect was under no illusions about the scale of the task he faced, although at least there was a clearer division of responsibilities than in the hierarchy O'Brien, Robins and captain Mike Campbell-Lamerton had struggled unsuccessfully to work with two years earlier. The 1968 tourists to South Africa returned with just one draw to their name from the four Tests they played but again they endured the luck of Dawson's 1959 party and were a better unit than their record suggests. The real value of the tour was in the coaching framework the diligent Dawson established for his successors. The two tours that followed, 1971 and 1974, saw the first series victories of Lions history and the architect of the latter triumph is in no doubt as to where the foundations were laid. Syd Millar, Lions coach in 1974 and a player under Dawson in both 1959 and '68, says: 'Ronnie was starting at the top as a coach rather than having the benefit, as I did in '74, of having come through a coaching system. His job was much harder than mine or Carwyn James's in '71 because there was no coaching structure for him to draw on. He concentrated on fitness and the game plan and he did a very good job. Without what he did in '68 we would have had nothing to build on in '71 and '74.'

One of the few luxuries Dawson enjoyed as Lions coach was the extra preparation time allowed by the tours committee's decision to name the management team nine months earlier than usual in response to the failure of the 1966 hierarchy. The Wanderers and Leinster coach used every minute wisely, spending a year compiling dossiers on the top South African players in what proved a successful attempt to predict the patterns of play the Lions would come up against and which was instrumental in securing the tourists' best-ever record against provincial sides. Dawson says of his planning: 'I had done a lot of reading, spoken to a lot of people in South Africa whose opinions I respected and produced an overall concept of what South African rugby was. I knew all their players from '55 and although the players had changed there was still a hell of a lot of background information there. So we then knew how to prepare the side, how to deal with hard grounds, the difficulties of playing at altitude, the differences between going up to altitude and down to sea level, the right type of training for both locations, the strengths of South African play. We had a pretty good rundown on it.'

With the planning done, Dawson got down to work with his players when they met up once more in Eastbourne to complete their pre-tour preparations. His methods were heavily influenced by what he had seen in New Zealand in '59 – highly organised sessions working on fitness in the morning and unit skills in the afternoon – and he decided to work primarily on physical conditioning at the expense of contact work, partly to avoid exacerbating injuries picked up over a long season but mainly to cope with the unique nature of the South African game. He says: 'We tried to use the time in Eastbourne for familiarisation because at that stage there were great differences in style between some unions and others. I felt it much more important to concentrate on the understanding between the players and on the transfer and movement of the ball. We were also aware of where we were going, that our first match was up in the Western Transvaal, and from there we went down to Western Province, so we were starting straight away on that up-down thing. I wanted to get people in good physical condition to deal with this and then work on the contact side when we got there.'

Hours of fitness work rarely endear a coach to his players, but Dawson was popular with his men on a tour that has become as well known for its off-field exploits as for those on it, particularly in the division between 'The Wreckers' and 'The Kippers', the latter being those who liked to get an early night and the former those who favoured getting as late a night as possible. 'He kept us out of jail at times,' says Mick Doyle of Dawson's tolerance of The Wreckers. In fact, the coach almost found himself back among the players when he was suddenly in line for a game against North West Cape before hooker John Pullin and prop Jeff Young recovered from injury to make the kick-off. Stepping into the breach would not have been a problem for the coach, who had already proved he was one of the fittest men on tour by beating both Rodger Arneil and 20-year-old Welsh flyer Keith Jarrett in interval sprints in training.

But fitness and a renewed team spirit were not enough to subdue a Springbok side in desperate need of a win after being knocked off their perch in the previous couple of seasons. Unlike in '59, Dawson did not have brilliant backs playing at the peak of their powers; the likes of Gareth Davies (who suffered with injuries in '68), Barry John (invalided out of the tour with a broken collar bone) and Mike Gibson would all reach their peak in 1971. The forwards broke even in terms of securing possession but they were too inflexible in their tactics – particularly in the lineout – and were beaten in the loose by the Springbok back row. Dawson says: 'There were some undistinguished performances and some competent performances, but if I were to pick one factor in our Test defeats it would be the quickness of their back row. They really did create far more opportunities from broken field for their backs than we did. It was a very happy tour but what mattered didn't happen – the Test matches.'

All the same, crewing a happy ship was an achievement in itself after the bad atmosphere that had soured the previous expedition.

Tom Kiernan, the Cork Constitution full-back who captained the side in 1968, recalls: 'The 1966 tour to New Zealand was apparently a divisive tour; it never settled down and there were some controversies over who should be captain. The general feeling after was that it should be one of the prime objectives of our tour to re-establish that Lions team spirit. We didn't do anything magnificent on the football pitch because our forwards weren't good enough and our backs were injured, but we did rekindle that Lions spirit.' The winning coaches of 1971 and '74 owe thanks to Ronnie Dawson for more than just that.

# 8

## THE SCRUM LAID BARE

AFTER WINNING THE FIRST Test against the Springboks, thanks to the famous conversion miss that Tony O'Reilly could not bear to watch but over which he later claimed to have been in direct communication with the Vatican, the 1955 Lions received their first taste of the South Africans' rugby fervour and considered opinion of their own place in the sport's greater scheme of things.

The Lions captain, Ulsterman Robin Thompson, was introduced to the South African prime minister, Johannes Strijdom, after the match and, having been congratulated on his team's victory, was all set to exchange compliments over a game that is still rated as just about the finest ever seen at Ellis Park. Instead, Thompson recounts, 'I remember him shaking his head, stony-faced, going, "Terrible day for the Springboks. I don't know what's going to happen now." I actually thought he was joking so I started to laugh. But the next day a cartoonist in the paper drew the prime minister and the Springbok selectors heading onto a rickety old boat, with a little sign saying "abroad" on it. People couldn't believe that we could have won.'

From then until 1974 the best the Lions could manage in South Africa was two draws from eight Test matches as the Springboks won both the intervening series 3–0. Those results, together with victories in their previous three series against Australia and New Zealand, ensured that the Afrikaners' superiority complex was once again the unquestioned article of faith it had been before Thompson's men stripped it bare in '55. So if drawing a series against the Lions had brought calls for the prime minister and selectors to be sent into exile, imagine the chaos wrought by Willie John McBride's tourists in 1974, 3–0 winners of the Tests, victors in all 18 of their provincial matches and scorers of more tries and points than any other visitors to the republic. 'They were rocked by it,' chuckles McBride today. 'And they are still rocked by it 25 years on.' Had the South Africans looked beyond their laager and seen the man plotting their dramatic downfall, they might have been less surprised at their fate. Syd Millar, the coach of that peerless party, has a Lions pedigree against which only that of McBride himself stands comparison. He had also already demonstrated that he could succeed against the odds, and had done so on South African soil to boot.

In the mid–1960s, Millar's Lions career was considered to have ended with his second tour in 1962. Two years after that trip he had been dropped from the Irish team and was even discarded by Ulster, both sets of selectors considering him too old to continue propping their scrums. The versatile Ballymena tight-head was having none of it, however. He dieted strictly, trained like a man possessed and by 1968, at the age of 33, he was back in the Ireland side, this time in the loose-head role he had filled with the Lions in both '59 and '62. His performances in the International Championship that year were so commanding that he was considered the only loose-head in the competition to look capable of standing up to South African scrummaging. His place on the Lions tour was assured and he went on to play in the first two Tests of the 1968 series there as well as captaining the side in the match against South West Districts. His comeback was complete and continued until 1970 when he played his last international for Ireland.

Millar then quickly turned his hand to coaching, first with Ballymena and then up and up the ladder to the appointment to the 1974 Lions that crowned his career but which also came as little surprise to his mentor Ronnie Dawson. His former front-row colleague had coached the '68 Lions and seen enough of the mature Millar's thinking then to recognise a sporting strategist in the making. Among a squad that contained four future coaches of Ireland, Dawson says of its elder statesman: 'Syd was obviously one who had a fine rugby brain, was a good communicator and tactician. He was a man who always had his priorities very clearly set, was able to transfer his opinions to others and, most importantly, get things done.'

With three Lions tours and a 37-cap Ireland career stretching across 12 years, Millar had plenty of experience to draw on, starting with his first Lions trek, to New Zealand in 1959. He rates that team as the best he ever played in, even if it did lose the series 3–1, and believes only the 1971 party had a back division in anything like a similar class. But one throwaway line from that early experience stayed with him longer than any other, 'Something the New Zealanders told us at the end of the tour,' he says. 'They said, "If you guys were organised we would never have got near you." They were right. We were the better team in three of the four Tests but they were more worldly wise and had Don Clarke as a kicker. That was the difference.'

Ronnie Dawson, captain of that side, felt the same and tried to bridge the gap when he became the Lions' first official coach in 1968. Millar's similar efforts in '74, particularly his local knowledge, clear vision and attention to detail, were key to the tourists' success but he now views many of those efforts as laughably primitive in comparison to what he saw as a committee member on the Lions tour of 1997. 'If you relate '59 to '97, that last tour had 35 players and 20 other individuals to deal with all other aspects of the trip. Every angle was covered by some sort of expertise: fitness, nutrition, video analysis, the whole gamut.

'They were very different days in '59. I think we played 33 games; the next tour to Australia will be ten. Australia couldn't take a full Lions tour in its old form because they didn't have enough fixtures, so we played six matches there including two Tests on the way to New Zealand. Now they can have their own tour because they are now of much shorter duration. One of the problems of the shorter tour is that the first Test comes much earlier, so gelling players from four countries before then is a real task for the coach. On the last tour [manager] Fran Cotton did very well to bring in outside consultant types to get them bonding. They had them building bridges and so on to develop team spirit, and it worked by fast-tracking the concept of a team from the four countries.'

Team-bonding sessions in the mid-1970s would have been more likely to comprise a couple of gallons of ale and setting fire to a hotel dining room than a cross between *The Krypton Factor* and a scout camp, but some aspects of preparing international rugby teams remain unchanged across the years. Millar reflects: 'The way we play the game hasn't changed much; things like the importance of quality possession, the importance of space and pace, and particularly the importance of identifying the game plan. All the game plan is is deciding on the opposition's weaknesses and how you might capitalise on them, and what their strengths are and how you might try to neutralise them. The difference is in how you identify that. In 1974 I had information from ex-pats, people I knew out there. Now guys have video analysis for defensive and attacking patterns. Their opportunities for devising counters and putting pressure on can be much greater. All I tried to do was say, "There's a few areas we might put pressure on them in." For example, asking how can I expose a slow back row becomes the basis of the game plan and you devise ploys to exploit that weakness. That hasn't changed.

'You also ask where they are going to pressure us and try to organise your defence to relieve the pressure. One thing that has impressed me immensely in the modern game in that regard is the defensive expertise of rugby-league coaches, which has been very important to teams like Australia, who don't give tries away. The Lions in '97 benefited considerably from the few rugby-league players who were there in their professionalism and their defence, Alan Tait particularly. Those guys brought something different to the party, a professionalism they had known for a long time.'

As a player himself, Millar built his reputation as a big, powerful prop, his six-foot, sixteen-stone frame equally effective in either defensive or destructive duties on both sides of the scrum. Tight-head was his favoured berth but he was good enough to appear on the left on each of his three Lions tours. Millar was more than just a hard man in the tight, though, and used his weight shrewdly in broken play where he was a safe handler of the ball and difficult to halt when on the charge. He also savoured the opportunity 'to be professional with a small "p"' that Lions tours provided in terms of their daily training routine. He says: 'It was marvellous for someone like me from a relatively small club to have the opportunity not just of playing against the best in the world but also with the best of these islands. A lot of experience rubbed off from playing with very good players.'

The bulk of that accumulated expertise was picked up in South Africa, the destination of two of Millar's three tours as a player, which made him the ideal man both to coach the 1974 Lions there and to manage their successors six years later. Playing against the All Blacks was no less of an education, but back then the two southern-hemisphere schools offered very different curricula. Millar says: 'New Zealand rugby, in broad terms, is about the lineout and the ruck. South African rugby is more about the scrum and maul. South African forward play was physically bruising and hard, much more so than New Zealand's in a way because in New Zealand the pitch and climate is much the same as at home. In South Africa, you were playing on hard grounds and in thin air and playing a type of game where the ball wasn't on the ground much, a real mauling game.'

Some things were the same in both countries, principally the fact that the tourists could never rely on getting the benefit of the doubt from most of the home referees they came up against. Millar recalls: 'Every series had its controversies. In '59 Don Clarke was given penalties we thought were unfair to us, and we had a try disallowed. Then in '62 we had a pushover try disallowed. The referee said he was unsighted but everyone else in the ground saw it was a try; '68 also was controversial at times.'

Millar could be referring to any number of incidents, but the nadir came in the second Test in Port Elizabeth, which the Lions remarkably managed to draw 6–6 despite one of the most bizarre pieces of refereeing they had come across. Two Tom Kiernan penalties and some heroic defending earned them the draw but they played most of the game with virtually no possession from the scrum after Millar gave the order for John Pullin, a scrupulously legitimate hooker, to stop striking for the ball as the referee, J.P.J. Schoeman, was penalising him for foot up every time his studs left the pitch. Under the tour agreement, if the Lions asked for a referee who was not on the South African international panel and the hosts did not agree with their choice, they were allowed to appoint one of their own reserves, none of whose identities were known to the Lions. Or, as Mick Doyle, another of the Irish tourists, puts it: 'You could put up four or five referees you wanted and they would ignore them and pick the other guy, the one you didn't want.' Mr Schoeman was unlikely to figure on any future Lions wish list because when Pullin stopped striking he then turned his attentions to Gareth Edwards and began warning him for not putting the ball in straight, his definition of which appeared to the Lions to be a direct trajectory into the Springbok second row.

Millar says of the Port Elizabeth controversy: 'Scrums were harder than they are today. Rugby should be about a fair competition for the ball and now that it's put in crooked, it's not. In those days you could strike for the ball at every scrum, but in the second Test we were being penalised so often for foot up that we just tried to hold and push. We lost a few as a result but we were being penalised so often that we just couldn't afford to strike.' And he adds: 'In those days, Test referees were from the countries we visited. I'm not saying they favoured the home team but they certainly seemed to referee the Lions more than the home team. At least today with neutral referees there is no inference that he is favouring the home side, although in 1980 we had French referees and in the first Test some of the decisions were not pleasing to us. But at least you had the benefit of saying he's not refereeing just one side. I'm not suggesting referees were cheating but it was inevitable that the touring side got more attention than the home side. I think maybe in '74 we got the refereeing sorted out to a better degree, although, of course, there was still the controversy of Slattery's "try" at the end. The referee had a difficult job and he didn't have the benefit of touch judges' talking flags and all the other things they have now. It was very much a personal decision.'

Max Baise's decision not to give Slattery his score late in the final Test handed South Africa the draw and saved them from a 4–0 series capitulation. Their humiliation was no less for that let-off though, as the Lions had beaten them at their own game by destroying the traditional Springbok power base of the scrum. It was a brave move by Millar to attack the opposition at what was perceived to be their strongest point, but he knew it was a gamble worth taking and that he had the personnel at his disposal to pull it off. He says: 'In '74 everyone identified South African rugby as being built on the scrum and saw what they were doing off that with their back row and half-backs. We said if we can destabilise that base, all the other things that follow from it we can change. We spent an enormous amount of time on the scrum so they couldn't use it as a platform. We also played Roger Uttley, who had been playing in the second row for England, on the flank to give us a fourth lineout forward, so we had an advantage over them there. That left Slattery, who was quicker than most backs and able to play a very loose role, free to do his running with Mervyn Davies tying things up.

'The aim also was to keep it very simple. People criticised us for not running more ball despite the fact that we scored more tries and points than any other Lions. We had to create a pattern of the game and then change it when the opposition got used to it. That's how you expose weaknesses. When we ran tries in late in the game, it was because of that. Our pattern helped wear them down physically, a lot of which we did through scrummaging.'

When the Lions did decide the time was right to strike, speed was then of the essence. 'We wanted quick ball,' says Millar. 'It's often hard for forwards to give up the ball, which is why I spent most time with the forwards, as do most coaches, and just tried to get the backs to identify for themselves what options they had and might use. To determine the path of the ball was important, to understand straightening the line was important so they didn't drift. Dick Milliken was very good at straightening the line to leave space for J.P.R. to come into the line and create more space again for J.J. on the wing.'

He may have been happy to give free rein to the backs but overall Millar left no stone unturned, no eventuality unconsidered. Manager Alun Thomas reported that 'no team has ever gone on the field better prepared' than those his coach sent out in 1974. The men who played in them agreed. McBride recalls: 'Some of the training sessions were tougher than some of the games. We knew that because there were no neutral referees we would have to be that much better than the opposition to win, so we knew we had to put it in.'

That meant the entire 32-man party, not just those who were playing in the next match. For Millar, the Lions would stand or fall collectively and that meant every player had to work as hard as the next regardless of his place in the queue for a spot in the starting line-up. He says of his thinking: 'When it was all over I said to the players that whether you made the Test side or not, your contribution was part of the success of that tour and you can wear your blazer with pride. Of course, everyone wanted to play in the Test side, but the performance of the midweek team was absolutely vital.

'The dirt-trackers have disappeared as the games have become fewer but in the past it was very important that the midweek team pushed the other guys. I think a good example of that was Donal Lenihan and his team in 1989. There was a respect from the Test side for the guys who were pushing them and respect for the midweek team as a whole as supporting the main team. You have to respect each other.'

The heroes of 1974 had that regard for their fellows, and also for the man who was guiding them. Mike Burton, the England prop, did not appear in a Test on that tour but remembers that Millar never made any of the dirt-trackers feel like second-class citizens. If anything, he worked them harder than the Test side. Burton remembers: 'On a big match day, with the crowd all arriving and all the fuss, he would say to those who weren't playing – and the subs – "Right men, into the minibus," and take us to a quiet field somewhere miles out of town, and f\*\*\*ing hell he used to hurt us. You knew that morning that you were playing next week and there would be no messing about. He made sure you were in some condition.'

But he adds: 'He had the utmost respect for all the players; I think his care of the players and his attention to detail endeared him to everyone. Syd always made time for people. He didn't just look at the blokes he had on the field or those who were playing that day. I was injured in Stillfontein and every day he came up to see if I was OK.'

Millar knew how to handle his players, but he also knew how to operate around his masters at home to ensure he got exactly what he wanted. He made a stand in 1974 to ensure that Ken Kennedy, a controversial omission in '71, was included in the squad and demanded McBride as his captain. He got both, and says of his reasoning over the latter appointment: 'I wanted Willie John to captain the Lions because I wanted to work with someone who knew what I wanted. We were from the same club and we had a good working relationship. I had been coach of Ireland and he was captain. He knew my philosophy: I prepared the team and decided strategy, he did the motivational bit.'

He adds: 'There were others who had a role to play. As a coach or manager you must remember it is a players' tour. Yes, I was there to coach but the more you can involve the players in things other than playing, the more they feel part of it. We had a good players' committee that I would listen to. I wouldn't comment but I would listen to their opinions on how things were going training and selection-wise, how they saw us in the Tests, who they would prefer and why. They said things that we would react to and change if we thought it was necessary. I listened to what they had to say and then made my own selection with the captain and the manager. Being allowed to get on with my own selection helped.'

There was plenty to distract Millar from his team-picking tasks, both as coach in 1974 and as manager in 1980. In the former case, he had to find ways of dealing with a hostile press out to sensationalise the Lions' antics off the field, while in the latter it was politics as much as rugby that occupied most of the discussion surrounding the tour. Being pursued by the South African press pack was not a new experience for the Lions. Before the 1938 tour Ronnie Cove-Smith, captain of the 1924 party, warned the tourists of his own experiences. He wrote: 'Sometimes, it is true, we were saddled by gossip writers with crimes during matches and pranks after them which we never committed . . .'

Half a century later, little had changed. Millar reports: 'Young men are training hard every day and after a Saturday game they are always allowed a little bit of licence to have a few pints and enjoy themselves. What we classed as boisterous behaviour was written up in the press as hooliganism. There were one or two incidents people would rather forget but nothing really serious. The press in South Africa were looking for something to write about and guys were less on their guard on tour. The best behaved tour I was ever on was 1974, and 1980 was very good as well. The players were very responsible. They let off steam but no more than other young men. But if they were seen having a couple of pints they were drinking, if someone broke something it was always deliberate. East London was the worst; every tour we had a problem there. We eventually discovered there was one guy there who just followed the tour around to see what he could find. In '74 and '80 we had no problems anywhere except in East London. In '74 it was "Lions involved in naked scrummaging". What had happened was that one of the players had come out of his room with a towel on and the door had closed behind him. Somebody, as a joke, of course, pulled his towel off and a bit of wrestling ensued as he tried to get it back. But by the time the press were finished with it . . .'

Six years later Millar was invited to manage the next Lions team to tour South Africa, coached by his old friend Noel Murphy. He initially declined and could have been forgiven for ruing his decision to reconsider when he found on arrival that his main task was to field the political flak flying around the controversial trip to the pariah state. Rugby tours involving South African teams had always attracted mass protests from the anti-apartheid movement. There was the infamous 'flour bomb' Test in New Zealand in 1981 and the sight of coils of barbed wire surrounding British and Irish pitches for the visits of the Springboks in 1969 and '70. The Lions of '74 had been besieged by demonstrators before they set off, while the '86 tour, to have been coached by Mick Doyle, was called off just two months before its departure date after the initially intransigent four Home Unions bowed to mounting international pressure. In 1980 both the government and the Sports Council, then headed by former Lion Dickie Jeeps, had called on the unions to abandon the tour. The committeemen refused to cancel and the Lions flew to Johannesburg with Millar first in the political firing line. Even the press problems of 1974 were no preparation for what he was about to face.

Millar says: 'The political situation made my job difficult. We had 60 or 70 reporters following the tour and a good part of them were purely there for the politics. We had gone from the days of having nominal contact with the press to having press conferences where a lot of the questions were about politics. People were saying we shouldn't have been there and I had to try to field those sort of questions and leave the players out of it. That was a very difficult part of it. The rest of it was as in 1974 really but that was a very different type of experience.'

The players, though, were glad to have the benefit of Millar's wisdom to guide them through the minefield. Ollie Campbell, who appeared in three Tests on that tour, describes him as 'a bit of a poacher turned gamekeeper from his previous history as a player' but adds: 'Syd was an extraordinary manager and a good man. I have the utmost time and regard for Syd Millar. He had such a presence about him, just absolutely unflappable no matter what the pressure or what the situation. You just felt in safe hands with Syd. He was like a big bear and you just felt safe with him. It was great to go to South Africa with him as manager because he had been there and done that and he was just so solid and spoke such sense all the time.'

The Lions lost the series 3–1 but Millar was on hand again to see them return to winning ways on his happiest hunting ground as a tours committee member with the 1997 team. The success of that tour, he is delighted to say, was built on many of the pillars still standing from his own playing days and secured the future of a unique rugby institution. He says: 'Every Lions side I was with had a very good team spirit despite being drawn from four countries, maybe because it had to be worked at; '97 had the same thing.' And he adds: 'The Lions are a peculiar thing. People have said they are an anachronism. They certainly are not. They are the biggest crowd pullers in New Zealand, South Africa and Australia. It's also something to do with touring every four years – as well as their reputation for playing a particular type of rugby – so they are not seen that often. It's important to avoid over exposure with the Lions. Nothing is better than your first cap but to be a Lion is very, very special and I don't think that will ever change.'

# 9

# SPREAD OUT IN A BUNCH

IN 1958, AUSTRALIA WERE rated a soft enough touch for Ireland to risk fielding four débutants against them and still come away with a 9–6 win. That was less of gamble than it sounds, as the four new boys were Noel Murphy, Ronnie Dawson, Bill Mulcahy and David Hewitt. A little over a year later the entire quartet were proud Lions, too, with Dawson captaining the tourists and the other three playing varying roles in one of the most exciting of all Test series seen in New Zealand. They went on to enjoy differing fortunes in the remainder of their rugby careers, too. Dawson led the Lions in more Tests than any other captain, while Murphy remains the touring team's most-capped flanker, and both men went on to coach the Lions in South Africa. Mulcahy, too, advanced to become at one point Ireland's most-capped lock, to captain his country and also to lead the Lions' midweek side in their 1962 campaign.

That left David Hewitt as something of the odd man out. The Belfast-born centre was the most talented footballer of the four, and if that sounds an unfair comparison with the grafters of the pack, any of those who lined up alongside him would back his ability in any company. A majority of those heroes of the 1950s and '60s featured in this book named Hewitt without hesitation as among the two or three most gifted players Ireland has ever seen. More than a few rated him as potentially the finest of all, ahead even of the great Jack Kyle and Mike Gibson. However, 'potentially' remains the key word. Hewitt had all the attributes needed to become a world-class rugby player but never quite got the rewards his talents deserved. A quiet man with a wry sense of humour who has always shunned the limelight, he won 18 Irish caps between 1959 and '65 and starred on the first of his two tours with the Lions before seeing his career interrupted by injury and his profile lowered by his modest, diffident nature. That latter trait manifested itself in occasional hesitation and uncertainty in his play, although Ray McLoughlin, perhaps the finest of all Irish rugby thinkers, believes his team-mates rarely got the best out him, lamenting: 'David Hewitt was a tremendous talent, but tended not to be properly used.'

Hewitt certainly had the pedigree to play international rugby. His father, Tom, his uncles, Frank − the youngest ever Irish international when selected as a 17-year-old − and Victor, and his cousins, John Hewitt and Gerry Gilpin, all played for Ireland. David himself made his full Ulster début while still a schoolboy out-half at the Royal Belfast Academical Institution, Alma Mater of former Lions captains Sammy Walker and Robin Thompson. He moved to centre while studying law at Queen's University and made a near perfect international début while still just 18, creating a vital try for fellow new boy Dawson as Ireland recorded their first victory over a touring side. At 19 he was a Lion, thanks to his pace and midfield vision as well as the accurate goal-kicking he had shown under pressure in that year's International Championship, particularly in helping defeat eventual winners France at Lansdowne Road.

Hewitt appeared to have it all ahead of him, but that 1959 odyssey would be the pinnacle of his career, the three months in which he produced the best rugby of a playing lifespan ultimately curtailed partly by a succession of hamstring problems that began around the time of his second tour as a Lion. He says of the problem: 'I think it was a consequence of my type of play. My strength, if I had any, was my speed off the mark in an explosive burst. That puts quite a strain on the hamstrings. Nowadays they would give you particular training to strengthen them but once your hamstring tears a couple of times it becomes stretched and more likely to tear again. I tore a hamstring in Paris before the '62 tour and I only just passed the fitness test to go to South Africa. Then I tore it again within half an hour of my first match. That didn't necessarily mean I didn't enjoy it as much as '59; those were the days when they didn't send you home if you were injured, so you were there as a tourist rather than going through the hard grind every day.'

Tony O'Reilly's record try-scoring exploits grabbed all the headlines on Hewitt's first trip, but inside him in the centres the youngest member of the party was coolly handing the winger his bullets and quietly kicking his goals to end up the overall top points-scorer with 112, including 13 tries of his own, from the 18 matches he played. He missed the second New Zealand Test through injury but played in the other three – as well as the two internationals on the Australian leg of the tour – and enjoyed his finest moment in the third rubber against the All Blacks. The Lions lost 22–8 but Hewitt scored the try of the match just before half-time, taking a pass from Phil Horrocks-Taylor just inside the home 25 and stunning the midfield defence with a blurring outside break before side-stepping his way through the cover to score near the posts.

In that one movement he demonstrated his main strengths, his perceptive eye for an opening and the devastating acceleration with which to exploit it. Hewitt was not the only member of the party to be clocked at under ten seconds for the 100 yards, but over half that distance or less – the yardage that really counts on the pitch – there was no one who could get close to him. Fellow tourist Syd Millar, who has the benefit of five Lions tours as player, coach and manager to measure against, says simply: 'David Hewitt was the quickest thing I have ever seen over 20 yards on a rugby field.' His team-mates all knew it, too, and that fact once counted against him when his wrong decision cost O'Reilly another try in that third Test when the series was still in the balance. He recalls: 'We had an overlap and I didn't pass to him. I told him I thought he was in front of me so it would have been a forward pass. He replied, "Hewitt, there's no way I could be in front of you over 20 yards." I should have passed to him but I went myself and was tackled. I got a clip round the ear from Ronnie Dawson in the middle of the game for it, too. That would be child abuse now!'

Hewitt may have been one of the most gifted of all players but he admits he never had the single-mindedness and commitment needed to sustain a career at the top for as long a time as, say, a Mike Gibson, who followed him into the Ireland and Lions centres in the 1960s. That he faded out of the international scene was as much due to his waning interest as to his straining muscles. He says today: 'It was a combination of hamstrings plus career plus other interests that were important in my life. When I came back from South Africa in '62 I had operations on both legs but by that time I was beginning to lose interest in the game. Your target is to play for the province and your country and then there are two Lions tours, to New Zealand and South Africa, that come around. By the mid-1960s I had been on them both and I was getting to the stage of qualifying as a solicitor and having to pass a few exams. I was never totally committed to rugby. It was a pastime but never a priority and I was very much involved in Christian youth work as well.

'Tours are very glamorous but they are only maybe five per cent of rugby. The rest was playing in the Northern Irish winter in four inches of mud against local teams who were quite happy to prove that this Lion wasn't up to all that much. That isn't quite as glamorous when you are also getting to an age where you have to train harder to keep up. Jack Kyle's last match for Ireland was my first and he told me you don't need to train until you are 24, the natural fitness of your youth will see you through until then. I was 22 or 23 on my second tour and was getting to the serious stage of having to train. When you're on a Lions tour you tend to be fitter than normal, but in '59 being the baby of the team also meant I was more naturally fit than any of them.

'Also, I was never a student of the game. I'm often amazed when I'm with other players watching rugby matches how they are able to see things happen and appraise a player's contribution to the game. Probably some of the best players I played with were forwards but I had no idea what they were doing in there. In '59 I can recall playing with senior players who could read a game, and that was something I had never come across before. People like Malcolm Thomas and Jeff Butterfield would size up the opposition in the first ten minutes and then decide how they would play the game. That was completely new to me and when you're playing with people like that, who can tell you where and when to run, it's a lot easier.

'I don't think I would have liked to have played in an age where your income depended on it, especially with large bonuses riding on results. I was one of the place-kickers in the team and if you missed a kick and lost a game because of it, it was just a case of, oh, too bad. Now it's a lot more serious than that. The only answer is to get out and practise your place-kicking and I can't think of anything more tedious. I don't think many of our era would be able to cope with the tedium of playing professionally. I suppose if I were 19 or 20 years old today I would just fit in but I still think I might need a mind transplant first.'

Back in the '50s and '60s, Hewitt's mind was often somewhere else during the course of even the tightest games. As well as his incredible pace and the perfect balance of his running, Noel Murphy also recalls him as one of the game's most laid-back customers. He says: 'We were playing Taranaki and the ground was set in a kind of bowl with a mountain range behind. It was a lovely day and the colour of the sky was incredible. David had a camera which he used quite a lot and halfway through the match he just said, "Oh I wish I had my camera with me to take a picture of that sky.'"

Murphy was also one of the 1959 tour's keener cameramen, although his work did not always share the artistic sensibilities of Hewitt as he got to grips with the then modern technology. He says: 'I was christened Cecil B. DeMurphy because I had an 8mm cinecamera. We would get the films developed and show them to ourselves and I would have to spend an hour explaining why I had managed to take nearly three minutes of an oil tanker sitting in a harbour.'

On the field, Murphy's vigorous, all-action style at flank forward rarely left him with any explaining to do, other than to opposing out-halfs wondering what exactly had hit them. His fellow forward Millar depicts him as 'very quick and an immensely hard competitor. He never flinched and he never drew back. He was very strong mentally, a huge tackler and a good footballer too.'

Murphy is a teetotaller with sufficient natural high spirits to be known universally as 'Noisy'. Ray McLoughlin, who played alongside him in the Lions pack of 1966, says: 'It didn't matter whether he was captain or not, he wouldn't shut up. But he was a good guy to have on your team. He was a natural leader, read what had to be done very quickly and was good at organising things on the spot. Having him around gave you a lot of confidence.'

Like Hewitt, Murphy was following in the family footsteps onto the international stage as his father, Noel Snr, also a wing-forward, had played for Ireland between the wars. At 20, he was two years older than his fellow débutant against the Wallabies and he wasted little time in revealing his durability when riding a second-half haymaker to see out a famous finish. His strong tackling, ability to run with the ball and the combination of his intelligent positional play and speed around the park made him equally effective playing open or blind, and although he initially preferred the open side with Ireland, it was as a blind-side that he made his Lions début in New Zealand and as which he later went on to specialise.

The Cork Constitution stalwart says of that trip: 'It was a wonderful education both on and off the pitch, particularly in what rugby meant to the New Zealanders. I remember the prime minister of New Zealand saying at a function that he would rather have been an All Black than prime minister of his country. I certainly came back with my character not changed but enlightened to the ways of life.' There were, though, some things Murphy would rather not have become acquainted with, most of them coming in the tour preparation week in Eastbourne. He explains: 'That was the first time I had come under PE instructors like Jeff Butterfield and Malcolm Thomas. They introduced us to new exercises and we were using some muscles for the first time ever. Some of us were going up the stairs backwards or sideways because we were so stiff.'

Murphy, whose muscular charges through broken play brought him five tries in the Antipodes, including one in the 31–0 Test hammering of Australia, as well as an unstoppable hat trick on the way home against the Canadians, believes that groundwork and the quality of the Lions play that year were not adequately rewarded, insisting a series lost 3–1 should have been drawn at the very least. 'We were the better team,' he says. 'We had some of the most wonderful backs ever to play for the Lions – and I say that humbly knowing what the '71 side had – and although their forwards were their strength we had a pack that could equal them.'

The last of the quartet of Ireland débutants against Australia was one of the more unsung heroes of that unit, the tireless second row Bill Mulcahy. The medical student from County Limerick was a master of the tight phases, solid in the scrum and lineout and a reliable touchstone in the heart of the pack when the going got tough. He played in two Tests on the 1959 tour and 13 games in total, and that he managed that many was in itself a tribute to his commitment to the common cause. In 1997, Mulcahy had an operation to fit a steel ball in his shoulder joint and a rod down the middle of his humerus, a direct legacy of the injury he suffered falling on a bone-hard pitch in the midweek match that followed his first Lions Test against the Wallabies. He says: 'I found myself in the middle of a back movement and I gave the classic swing of the ball across the body and a guy threw himself beneath my knees American-football style. I was thrown up in the air and couldn't break my fall because I had my hands across me finishing the pass. I landed on my shoulder and we were playing on a cricket wicket, which is why it did me so much damage.

'In New Zealand two weeks later I was training on the morning of a match, because we were expected to train if we were not playing and if you didn't you were made to feel distinctly uncomfortable. I went out for a light jog holding my lapel to keep my shoulder from hurting, the grass was wet and my feet went from under me. Once again I landed bang on that shoulder. I'm sure that didn't help and I had tremendous pain for three or four weeks, to the point that I had terrible insomnia because of it. Even in the last Test I couldn't pull my prop in – the flanker had to push him in for me – and I had to do my jumping on the left touchline because I could only get my right arm above my shoulder. Years later my left arm would still stick on the way up in the lineout and let me down.'

The same could never be said of Mulcahy himself as he became a fixture in the Irish pack and crowned his career with a second Lions tour in 1962, playing in 17 of the 25 matches – a total bettered only by Mike Campbell-Lamerton – captaining the side on several occasions, leading in all four Tests a pack that became known as 'Mulcahy's Boyos' and acting as Ireland's representative on the selection panel. Lions great Dickie Jeeps rated him as good a lock as South African legend Johan Claassen, captain of the Springboks and their most capped international. Mulcahy backed his judgement when the two first locked horns as the Lions met Claassen's big scrummaging Western Transvaal side, enhancing his reputation as an excellent lineout supporter as his team won a titanic forward battle to triumph 11–6.

The UCD, Bohemians and Bective Rangers lock was also at the centre of two of the flashpoints of the tour. Captain Mulcahy stood out amid the mayhem of a 20–6 victory as Combined Services produced what one local newspaper declared 'one of the most disgraceful spectacles in South African sport' and which the headline writers of London's *Daily Express* summed up as 'Lions Slay Punch-mad Services'. Hours afterwards one battered Lion did not even know how the game finished, while Mulcahy said: 'I am sorry that this match was played and have no hesitation in recommending that it be erased from future itineraries, for it cannot do any good for the game or South Africa. I do not want to see another exhibition like this or the whole point of the tour will be lost, for rugby football is a game and not organised warfare.'

The second incident came at the death of the second Test and prevented the Lions from taking a series lead – the first Test had been drawn – and put an entirely different complexion on the remaining rubbers. With a minute remaining the tourists were 3–0 down but had a scrum on the Springboks' line. The strike was won, Mulcahy called the wheel and as the Lions eight pivoted across the goal-line in textbook fashion his second-row partner Keith Rowlands dropped on the ball. However, South African referee Ken Carlson disallowed the try on the grounds that he was unsighted and immediately blew the final whistle before the Lions could have another go from the resulting five-yard scrum. Mulcahy says: 'There was little doubt that we got the try and it would probably have been a five-pointer because it was eminently convertable. The back five were lying across the line and the ball was clearly to be seen. There were a lot of home decisions on these tours.'

The Springboks won the last two Tests to take the series as injuries began to take their toll on the tour party, to such an extent that Mulcahy, known to his team-mates as 'Wigs', a nickname apparently dating back to his schoolboy habit of doodling wigwams on his exercise books, was pressed into emergency action in the back row. He recalls with a smile: 'I had played a little bit of back row in college and it was too late to send home for another player. I played blindside, Budge Rogers played openside and we agreed a back-row defence off the lineouts. At the first lineout the Springboks got the ball straight out to Keith Oxlee at number ten and I came straight at him under a full head of steam. He knew there was a rookie at number six and he waited and waited and then stepped inside me. I can still hear to this day this plummy English accent of Budge Rogers despairing of me: "Oh no, Wigs!" I can still hear that ringing in my ears now.'

Hewitt was also a member of that party but his tour was disrupted by hamstring injuries which initially looked like ruling him out of the entire trip before he had even appeared in a match. The South Africans would have been happy to see him go as, despite rating him and fellow centre Mike Weston 'the poorest tacklers in international rugby today', the Rand *Daily Mail* admitted that, along with English stand-off Richard Sharp, he also posed the Lions' most dangerous attacking threat. He proved the latter point with a try on his belated début against Boland but aggravated his injury in the same game and was effectively ruled out of the first two Tests. He came in for the last Test, where the supposed worst tackler in the international game was the only one of a succession of Lions defenders to bring down the mighty Frik du Preez in full flight to end a 50-yard run.

His best years may have already been behind him, but for Tom Kiernan, the Ireland full-back and another member of that tour, he had already proved himself on his day 'probably the best of them all', although Kiernan clarifies: 'He was a different talent completely to Mike Gibson; he was an incredibly individualistic player but he would be admiring the cloud formation in the middle of a Test match. Mike Gibson was a great player in all circumstances, 100 per cent of the time. David had more skills in the context of his acceleration and side-step but he treated rugby as a leisure pastime.'

Neither Hewitt nor Mulcahy played for the Lions again, although Murphy made his second tour in 1966, having been ruled out in '62 after breaking his collarbone against England. The expedition was not a success, either on the field, where the team suffered a whitewash, or off it, where morale hit rock bottom soon after arriving in New Zealand and went downhill from there. Murphy says: 'We went through Australia too easily and were being classed as potentially one of the best of all Lions sides. That never materialised. We were sent down into Southland and Otago early on and we were nearly a month into the New Zealand leg before we won a Saturday game.

'We just weren't good enough and some of the players weren't ready for what they would experience in New Zealand, particularly the power of their play, the attitude of the New Zealanders to what it meant to be an All Black and the responsibility that went with it. The intensity of feeling about rugby football in New Zealand was very high. I can remember Ray McLoughlin and myself – I wouldn't like to use the word lectured – but being told, in no uncertain terms, by the chambermaid on our floor how the Lions could improve.

'The '59 tour had been full of excitement playing-wise. Now I experienced another side to touring with the Lions. I would be lying if I said there weren't times when you wished you were back in Cork. I would hope that many of the Irish players on that tour would have tried to give the team great spirit, but our performances hurt us. Some of our performances were embarrassing and the pressure that put on [manager] Des O'Brien and [captain] Mike Campbell-Lamerton on that tour would have to be experienced to be understood. I know that as an ordinary player it had an effect on me. Our attitudes changed.'

Murphy played his last international in 1969 and moved into coaching in the following decade, steering Ireland to a series victory in Australia in 1979 to earn himself the tracksuit duties with the Lions side of 1980 in South Africa. Again he found himself up against it as the squad suffered the worst run of injuries any Lions have known. He says: 'All our injuries were in key positions, we had eight replacements and we never had the same back line from Saturday to Saturday. When you look at the players we lost, at full strength we would have won the Test series quite easily. Fran Cotton was diagnosed with a suspected heart attack and we had fellows like Rodney O'Donnell breaking necks. Players like O'Donnell and Colin Patterson had their careers ended on that tour.'

Despite their fitness problems, the Lions were unbeaten in the provincial matches, were not far off the pace in the Tests and enjoyed a fine team spirit engendered by Noisy's unique style. Ollie Campbell, who was plucked from the wilderness by Murphy to star in Ireland's Australian adventure the previous year, says of the coach: 'Noel had a good record with Munster and Ireland, and was considered the most outstanding coach in the Five Nations at the time. You're never really a prophet in your own land, so Noel was familiar to us, but the other guys were very excited about the idea of being coached by Noel Murphy because he had quite a track record.

'With the Irish team he had this little warm-up drill where he would divide the team or squad into threes and fours along the try-line and go along doing little interpassing routines and that sort of thing. When we arrived in Johannesburg, Noel decided there would be a light training session just to shake out the legs before things started in earnest the following day. So as usual guys would just go out and kick around and do their own thing. Noel came out, blew his whistle and everyone came in. And you could feel everybody waiting for the first words of wisdom from this new coach. And his very first words, and I kid you not, were: "Right lads, I want you all to spread out in a bunch." The Irish guys knew exactly what he meant but you can understand the bewilderment on the faces of the English, the Scots and the Welsh. The Irish knew exactly what he meant, the others only knew exactly what he said.'

And he adds: 'Legend has it that in the team meeting before the first game against Eastern Province, Noel was saying a few words and he could get quite excitable at the end of his various words of encouragement. The ring finger on one of his hands is bent backwards from an old rugby injury and it was always very disconcerting, waving it around. So Noel's there with that hand and he's finishing on a crescendo and he's banging the table. And he's demanding "80 per cent effort, 80 per cent effort, for 100 minutes". That was Noel's introduction to the Lions team of 1980.

'But he was respected and I think to this day he would have been up there with some of the renowned coaches, but unfortunately coaches are judged on results. We went through that tour unbeaten in provincial matches, we won one Test and were narrowly beaten, very narrowly beaten, in the other three. That could have been a follow-on from '74 but we lost the series and no one ever talks about it. It's amazing. I do meet Noel quite regularly and the successful Irish tour of '79 will come up much more often. At that level it is just results. The bottom line is the winning and losing.'

The Lions records may not be able to bracket Murphy the coach alongside Carwyn James, Syd Millar and Ian McGeechan, but he will always be top of Campbell's list as 'the man I would really owe my career to' for selecting him ahead of the then golden boy Tony Ward for the Tests in Australia in 1979. He says: 'I don't know finally who made the big decision in '79 – it would have been down to the triumvirate of [captain] Fergus Slattery, [manager] Jack Coffey and Noel himself – but I feel with him as coach and being such a strong personality that it was probably his call. It was a monumentally brave decision to make, to pick someone who had no track record really, just one international cap three and a half years previously, someone who was hardly known even in Ireland, over the European player of the year.'

The new man responded with an Irish record points haul to justify Murphy's decision, although the long-running controversy that ensued is still a source of laughter to the three men involved. Campbell says: 'We had a reunion of that Test squad in 1998 on the eve of Ireland's game in Brisbane. Noel was still vice-president of the Irish union so he couldn't join us because he was with the current squad in Australia, but we had a meal out on the Friday and were then meeting in a pub here in Dublin the following morning to have a champagne breakfast and watch the game on the big screen. And there was a fax there waiting for us from Noel Murphy, wishing us all the best of luck and that. And it ended with the line "I still think Jack and Fergus got it wrong." And it was actually signed Noel and Wardie, who was out there as a journalist with *The Independent*. It was just perfect.'

# 10

## A New Water Hazard

### at the Wanderers

TOM KIERNAN IS AN ACCOUNTANT by profession. Firefighter or conjuror might have been more appropriate trades in light of the number of rescue missions he mounted and rugby rabbits he pulled out of hats in his long and distinguished career as a player and a coach. He first stepped into the breach in 1960 when he moved from centre to solve the Irish selectors' long-standing full-back problem, going on to break almost every record in the role, including Jack Kyle's appearance total, over the next 13 years. As a coach he masterminded one of the biggest upsets in sporting history when his 1978 Munster team bushwhacked the All Blacks at Thomond Park and he then turned water into wine with Ireland, whom he transformed from wooden-spoonists in 1981 to Triple Crown champions in 1982. As captain of the Lions in South Africa in 1968 he could not lead the tourists to a first-series win, but he did play a major role in re-establishing them as a credible footballing force and close-knit community after the on and off-field disaster of 1966.

The 1968 expedition was Kiernan's second Lions tour, and despite losing the Tests 3–0 with one match drawn, he enjoyed the experience far more than on his début in 1962, despite having to deal with the added burden of captaincy. The cheerful Corkman was in his prime in the final years of the '60s and proved it when representing the best of both Ireland and the four Home Unions. He played a then record 54 times for his country, broke new ground with his goalkicking in the number of total points, penalties and conversions he scored – the last mark beaten only by his nephew Michael – and captained the side on 24 occasions, a figure that remains unmatched today. With the Lions of '68 he finished up second-highest scorer with 84 points from 13 games, but in the Test matches, where it mattered most, he kicked a record 35 points in the series and 17 of the Lions' 20 points in the first international in Pretoria. That one-off mark has only been bettered twice – first by Tony Ward in Cape Town 12 years later – and his series figures stood for a quarter of a century.

With that remarkable roll of honour to look back on, it seems incredible that Kiernan might never have taken a single shot at goal for the Lions Test team had the fates not conspired in his favour. In fact, at one point, he actually considered leaving himself out of the side completely. The 60-year-old, now Ireland's representative on the International Rugby Board, explains: 'The conditions for kicking were nearly always perfect; the ball was nearly always dry, the ground was firm and on the high veld it flies through the air. In the provincial games before the Tests my kicks were all right but were just going the wrong side of the posts. Bob Hiller [the other full-back in the squad] was kicking every single one of his goals and there was a real question mark over who would play in the Test team.'

Coach Ronnie Dawson gave his compatriot the nod, but more for his certainty under the high ball and his sound judgement of when and where to make an appearance in the attacking line. Barry John, the 23-year-old Welsh out-half, would take the place kicks. Sadly for John, it never worked out like that, but the Lions were fortunate in having Kiernan on hand to take charge of the situation. He says: 'Barry John was taken off in the first Test after breaking his collarbone and didn't play again on the tour. If that hadn't happened I might not have kicked at all. I would never have considered myself a great kicker, it just went well for me over there. I played all right but there were times in '62 when I felt I played better. But in the Test matches I seemed to kick the goals and in the provincial matches I missed. I felt sorry for Bob, who played very well and kicked well, too, but never got his chance. He went on tour with me and then with J.P.R., but he was always a great supporter and a great tourist.'

Indeed, Kiernan credits Hiller with perpetuating the legend of The Wreckers and The Kippers which made the 1968 tour one of the best remembered off-field parties. In the words of Mick Doyle, a confirmed Wrecker and the Blackrock College number eight, 'The kippers slept a lot and generally alone.'

The dynamic Doyle, who played in the first Test but was felt too slight to take on the giant Springboks at the back of the lineout in the remainder of the series, remembers his captain as trying to keep a foot in each camp – but revealing his true colours on one of the squad's social activities in Johannesburg. He says: 'Tom Kiernan wanted to be a Wrecker and a Kipper. Which one was he really? Well, one day we had a golf tournament at the Wanderers and only the keen golfers took it seriously. The rest of us were quite glad we didn't sink many putts because Kiernan had gone round ahead of everybody piddling in all the holes.'

The captain and future president of the IRFU will himself admit to being in at the very beginning of the Wreckers' life. He says: 'We had a four-day holiday in the Kruger Park in the middle of the tour and we had a game of cricket. Bob Hiller captained one side and I captained the other. They called my team the Wreckers and his team the Kippers. Bob was a great wit and he really created the myth of the two sides. It was a very happy tour. The fellows got on very well and there was a fair amount of rugby activity off the field, not at the expense of fitness or anything but purely as a reflection of team spirit and mostly in in-house parties. One or two of them were reported in the South African press and similar activities now would create problems. They were typical of rugby touring at the time but wouldn't be accepted now when players are professional and people think they aren't allowed to enjoy themselves.

'It was tremendous to be with a bunch of fellows with the same interests for four months. If you were injured you were pissed off, but if you were fit there's nothing like it, training every day and playing a couple of times a week with great players. Now it's a bit of a business trip, all the games are geared towards the Test matches and there aren't many of them. I would have thought they had less time to enjoy it now. I'm just glad I was there when I was.'

The Lions' international-class party-throwing and shirt-burning actually landed Willie John McBride in hospital, where he received eight stitches in a leg and two in a finger after slipping over as the team drowned their sorrows following the narrow first Test defeat. Perhaps it was just as well they didn't win. Most of the stories that appeared in the South African press about Lions running wild had little substance to them, although on one occasion, after a match against the Griquas in Kimberley, the party that raged through the night, onto the plane to Cape Town and then onwards through the team hotel there was widely considered to have been firmly on the Roman side of excessive. John Reason, of London's *Daily Telegraph*, wrote in his book *The 1968 Lions*, on a page headed 'Boorishness', that the Lions behaviour 'only becomes public property if it affects their performance as rugby players or if it affects other people. The trouble which started in Kimberley did both these things . . . What mattered was the way a few Lions conducted themselves in front of other guests at the hotel. Only three or four Lions were involved but they brought disrepute upon the whole party.'

It was also suggested that the incident distracted the Lions from their task of winning the imminent third Test, victory in which they needed to get back in the series after losing the first rubber 20–25, and salvaging a draw from the controversial second match, in which they were whistled almost to death, with two high-pressure penalties from the Kiernan boot. The third Test had been targeted for the introduction of Ken Goodall, the outstanding City of Derry back rower, who it was hoped could change the fortunes of the side as a replacement for the injured Barry John. Goodall was not an out-half but with Mike Gibson in the party Dawson and Kiernan felt they could gamble and reinforce the back of their pack instead, where the home team had a decisive edge. They knew Goodall well and knew what he could do. His brilliant performance that helped Ireland beat Wales earlier in the year had also effectively clinched Kiernan the Lions captaincy ahead of his beaten opposite number that day, John Dawes, and he had been selected for the initial tour squad only for exams at Newcastle University to rule him out of the early weeks of the trip, and the tours committee to refuse to allow him to join up afterwards.

The then student remembers: 'If you don't go at first your chance is more or less gone because you are waiting for someone to get injured and you don't really want to wish that on anyone. I definitely was not an out-half and I really could not understand why they would send for me when Barry John got injured. All I knew was that this was my opportunity and that come hell or high water there was no way that when they asked me to attend a fitness test I was going to pack in and say I wasn't fit. But I had been training and knew I was in good enough shape. The test was in Belfast at North of Ireland rugby club. I went up there and was told to run round and round the field. There was a schoolboys' cricket match going on and I ran round and round it for about an hour and did sprinting up and down and all sorts. After I had done the fitness test I asked Des O'Brien, who was conducting the test, if I was fit enough to go and he said, "I can't tell you. I have to report back and someone will get in touch."'

The summons of Goodall had been delayed by the red tape that surrounded the tour agreement's provision for the use of replacements and there were to be further delays when he finally touched down on South African soil. He could actually see and wave to his Lions team-mates on the tarmac at Windhoek airport but was not allowed to join them, as South African officials insisted he fly on to Johannesburg to clear customs there before coming all the way back to meet up with the tour party. In all, Goodall probably spent more time travelling than he did playing rugby. He considers many of his achievements to be down to his good fortune of playing in one of the best of all Irish teams – he was only on the losing side in five of his nineteen Ireland appearances – but with the Lions, Lady Luck failed to accompany him beyond customs at Jan Smuts. He says: 'I was there a couple of weeks before I played my first game in Springs. I injured my thumb about ten minutes into the game but I played on until the end. My hand had swollen up but it was the Monday before I got it seen to and X-rays revealed I had a broken bone in my finger and a broken bone in my thumb and they eventually had to operate and put a pin in my thumb. That was the end of the tour, obviously, for me. They sent for Brian West as a replacement for the replacement and I flew back a week early. So I travelled out on my own and I travelled back on my own, having played one match. That was the sum total of my tour.'

The Lions could have done with Goodall's all-round excellence in the third Test, which they lost 11–6, with Kiernan again scoring all the points and leading by example with his never-say-die attitude, still chasing hardest after Gibson's desperate garryowen as the Lions sought an equalising converted try in the dying minutes of the match. This was the true Kiernan in action, a sight South Africans had been largely deprived of on his first visit with the Lions back in 1962. He says: 'I had one ankle injury after another, sprained them both several times on the hard grounds. One would get right then the other one would go. Once you've sprained an ankle it's always a weakness and you didn't have the medical facilities you have now, so they were all three-week injuries and when you have a 15-week tour a couple of those mess you up. I only played in seven out of the 25 matches so it wasn't a great tour from a rugby point of view. But to be part of a collective group for three and a half months was something you could only dream of when you were 21.

'My most abiding memory of that tour was Frik du Preez scoring a great try against us at Potchefstroom. There was a lineout on the

22, he came round the front, I was standing on the right upright, and he took the ball on the tap and went along the touchline. I came across and he just blew me away. I think that was the only time I participated in a great try!' But he adds: 'He was a bit unique: a second-row forward who could run like a stag. He must have had a ten-year career with South Africa. Most of their locks are big, strong, dour forwards but he was quite an athlete.'

In '68 it was the Springboks back row that provided the platform for their victory but despite the Lions' defeats Kiernan still impressed the locals as both an ambassador and a player. Although criticised for his sometimes variable tackling, the South Africans rated his defensive positional play and athletic catching ability as the best their country had seen, and admired the ease with which he could kick with either foot. He also had a classic, textbook place-kicking action – head down, good follow-through – and was a clever cover defender with a flawless big- match temperament. Ray McLoughlin, who preceded him as captain of Ireland, says he cannot recall ever seeing him drop a ball, while Ronnie Dawson remembers him as 'a very good player and a very fine captain of Ireland and the Lions. He was an excellent player right from his schooldays. He was a very astute judge of a game and how it was going and also a good communicator.'

Kiernan, who made his international début while a student at University College, Cork, before playing the bulk of his career across the city with Constitution, had initially made himself unavailable for the 1968 Lions selection due to pressure of work, but eventually changed his mind to lead the party into Africa. He says of the differences he found from his earlier visit: 'You've more responsibility and you're always busy, from attending every breakfast meeting through playing and training to selecting teams, fulfilling social functions, making speeches and visiting lord mayors. But we had a terrific management in David Brooks and Ronnie Dawson, plus you are much more mature at 27 or 28 than you were at 21 or 22.'

The captain was also showing signs of the man-management skills that would come to the fore in his later coaching career, when his wiles and cunning earned him the nickname of 'The Grey Fox', particularly in his handling of Keith Jarrett, the 20-year-old Welsh wunderkind who had spent the first half of the tour struggling with injury and coming to terms with the pop-star adulation that followed him round the country. When he finally got into the tour,

Kiernan went out of his way to get him off the mark by handing him an easy kick at goal early in the game against Rhodesia. Jarrett said afterwards: 'Not many captains would have done that. If they are goal-kickers, they like to take the easy ones themselves. Points are points and people never remember the ones that are given away.'

Jarrett never played in a Lions Test but the 1968 tour proved a testing ground for many of those who would go on to star in the series wins of the following two tours: the likes of McBride, John, Gibson and Gareth Edwards. Had injuries not deprived Kiernan of some of their services at crucial moments, he might now be looking back on a famous victory. Instead, he at least helped lay the foundations for the successes of the '70s.

# 11

## ON THE SLAB WITH
## THE CANTERBURY BUTCHERS

A THEN RECORD 40 caps as an Ireland prop, plus two seasons as captain of his country, provide a reasonable reflection of Ray McLoughlin's contribution to the Irish game. But a mere three Tests for the Lions do scant justice to his influence on two tours and the key role he played in masterminding their first-ever series win. Happily, those at the heart of the Lions machine are ever ready to put the record straight. Willie John McBride, who should know a player when he sees one, rates him as the finest Ireland has produced, not just for the standard of his scrummaging and general forward play but for the innovation of his thinking and the continued impact of his ideas long after he had left the scene himself. Ken Kennedy, whose hooking he supported in the Ireland and Lions front row, believes simply that had McLoughlin been appointed captain of the 1966 tour party, so inspirational was he that not only would they have avoided the first 4–0 whitewash but might even have won the series in New Zealand itself.

That McLoughlin was not honoured with the leadership of that Lions team was part of a career-long pattern that saw him exert his influence as often from the wings as from centre stage. The vision he brought to the Irish team when appointed captain in 1965, and the determined manner in which he implemented it, was little short of revolutionary and proved too much for some committee men – and even for one or two of his team-mates – so that they dropped him from the role at the first opportunity. Then in 1971, as the strategies McLoughlin had been instrumental in drawing up with the Lions achieved their goal of defeating the All Blacks on their own soil, he was excluded from the celebrations, as regulations had demanded his departure from the tour after a broken thumb ended his participation as a player before the first Test.

Lions coach Carwyn James, captain John Dawes and McBride, the man who succeeded him as pack leader, all remembered his contribution, although McLoughlin insists that his role was slightly over-egged by at least one newspaper of the time. He says: 'On the '71 tour there was a great feeling of confidence from the start — which quickly disappeared after the first match, which we lost to Queensland, completely to everyone's amazement. We recovered to beat New South Wales and going to New Zealand there was restored confidence and great belief again. The All Blacks were weaker then than they had been before and would be after. Between 1970 and '76 they were in not too much of a valley but enough of one to create an opportunity that might not have been there at other times.

'I remember after we lost the first match in Australia. I hadn't played and on the way down to Sydney I sat with John Dawes and Carwyn James, who were having a post mortem and deciding what we should do. I had a pad with me and was writing things about this, that and the other, and when I had finished I just tore them up and put them in the bin. Some years before I was asked to coach Athlone but didn't have the time. I did, though, write 26 pages on how to coach a rugby team, which one guy later sent on to his brother who was a priest in Sydney. Come 1971 a journalist got hold of it, got the wrong end of the stick and a story came out that after the Queensland defeat John Dawes and I had sat down on the plane together and devised a plan to win the series and had had it typed up on 26 pages.'

If nothing was actually committed to print, Dawes and James certainly drew heavily on the thinking of McLoughlin, who had been one of the outstanding students of his era at University College, Dublin, and went on to be involved in the early development of computers in both Britain and Ireland. Along with fellow countrymen McBride and Mike Gibson, he was part of the senior players 'brains trust' that James, another rugby intellectual, used as a sounding board to draw up tactics and plans. His technical expertise and leader's authority made him the *de facto* forwards coach, allowing James and Dawes to focus on the backs secure in the knowledge that the pack would be working on the elements they needed to thrive. McLoughlin was also the tour's senior forward and captained the side on several occasions, including the notorious 'slug-fest' against the 'Canterbury Butchers' that ended his tour the week before the opening Test. Ironically, had he followed his initial reaction to the violence he might have avoided the injury entirely.

He says: 'Canterbury certainly had a reputation of being harder, as they call it in New Zealand, than everyone else. I knew from my earlier Lions trip, as did others on it, that New Zealanders are great ones for intimidating guys on the grounds that once you've done that they are a walkover. This was going to be a very difficult match and I had been urging everyone to show their teeth immediately in the face of the intimidation that was bound to happen. That was essential to avoid being psychologically beaten. A real intimidation effort did take place and a couple of guys were injured. I was the leader of the pack, there was a mêlée going on and as part of this philosophy I charged in and proceeded to hit Alex Wylie. I was pulled by my jersey as I did so and ended up hitting the side of his head with my thumb and chipped a bit of bone. I could have played on but I would have risked developing arthritis in the thumb. To my later amazement I declined to play on with it.'

But he adds: 'In that game there was a degree of intimidation that to my mind was unacceptable. I was captain that day and I was tempted to take the team off the pitch on the basis that it was the best way of making a protest and, properly handled, could be presented as not being afraid but as requiring more courage than not doing it. Maybe I chickened out but I felt that with the macho approach New Zealanders had it would be seen as weakness. While I'm not squeamish, I felt strongly enough to think seriously about it. Even so, I still don't consider New Zealand rugby as a whole to be dirty.'

That Canterbury carve-up, dubbed 'The Game of Shame' by the local press, threw the Lions' Test plans into chaos as it cost them both first-choice props, McLoughlin with his broken thumb and Sandy Carmichael with a multiple fracture of a cheekbone. Other victims were Fergus Slattery, who had a handful of teeth loosened for his troubles, Mick Hipwell, John Pullin and Gareth Edwards. Sean Lynch, who would perform superbly in replacing Carmichael in the Test team, was a spectator that day and recalls: 'Put it this way, I was injured for the Canterbury match and even from the stands it was one of the most vicious matches I have ever seen. They were the heavy mob and you had to go for them because they were going for you. My idea on the field is to take your own man out and if everyone does likewise you'll be all right.'

The Dublin publican, who was one of the characters of the tour and became famed for his consistent failure to escape the notice of

Carwyn James when trying to sneak an extra pint or so above his rationed limit, more than held his own in the internationals that followed, and thanked McLoughlin for the education he had passed on in Lynch's lone international season prior to the tour. Despite facing some of the world's top props in his 17-cap Ireland career, the St Mary's tight-head always rated the Ray McLoughlin he faced in domestic club matches as the toughest opponent he met, and says of his influence on the Lions forwards of '71: 'He drilled that pack and did a lot of the preparation with Willie John McBride. These guys had been there before and knew what it was all about. Ray had great ideas on the game, particularly about the formation of the pack and he did a lot of the power training. He had us carrying three players on our shoulders over 25 yards. That sharpened you up. His vision of the game was light years ahead of other people's.'

McLoughlin saw his Ireland team-mate shine in the first Test at Carisbrook, but when it became clear that he would play no further part in the series the tour agreement insisted that he left the camp. The then Gosforth player, who turned out for the club while a postgraduate at Newcastle University, remained close to the series, however, and still feels part of the squad that made history. He says: 'I stayed on for a month doing my own tour after I left the party, which I enjoyed almost as much. There was a tremendous camaraderie and *esprit de corps* which has survived the years. It's amazing how you slip into comfortable and relaxed dialogue with guys you haven't seen for years.'

McLoughlin already knew his way around New Zealand, having toured there in very different circumstances with the Lions of 1966 under the management of former Ireland number eight Des O'Brien. The tour was holed beneath the water line before it even set off, thanks to the fudges and compromises that had been made in drawing up the management structure, which for the first time included a coach, John Robins of Wales. Looking back, McLoughlin, who scored a try in the first Test against Australia with a clever break round the front of a lineout, takes a rosy view of the experience but can still pinpoint the main failings of the trip. He says: 'You forget the bad times and there's a far greater sense of remembrance about your first trip. Going on a five-month tour was a far bigger deal than touring today. Now it's just an overnight trip; then it was a big adventure. We went to all the big cities in Australia and all the places in New Zealand. We had a week in Hawaii and in Canada and a day in New York on the way back. I had a lot of respect for New Zealanders and learned a lot as well. The simple things I remember most, like arriving in Perth after a 39-hour flight and having steak and eggs for breakfast for the first time, and being one of only five guys who weren't too travel-sick to come down for breakfast. Also arriving in Christchurch at midnight and finding a load of Maori girls singing songs for us.

'One thing that captured the spirit of the tour was before the second Test in Wellington. The first team had been practising with the Wednesday team and the Wednesday team were then sent to the back pitch without any direction as to what they should do. They were basically abandoned. I was in the Test team and we were practising away and eventually John Robins called for the others to come back. No answer and no one could find them. Then, after about 10 minutes, we heard the noise of a tractor and turned round to see the entire B team driving onto the pitch on the back of this tractor. That reasonably reflected the discipline and disorder that was a Lions tour. They were chastised for that but it didn't have any effect.'

And he says of the tour as a whole: 'Although we lost eight matches, including four Tests, we had beaten Australia twice and in my view we were good enough to have won two Tests in New Zealand. We were basically a bunch of good players who never got it together. A lot of guys didn't worry about that. To them a match was just a match.'

O'Brien and his captain Mike Campbell-Lamerton were widely blamed for the Lions' generally slack attitude, but McLoughlin insists that the buck should stop much further up the line. He says: 'Des O'Brien is a lovely man who had a philosophical approach to management and in my view did the job well. One of the difficulties about that tour was that it was the first occasion that there was a coach. Previously the captain was everything – captain and coach. But on this occasion there was a complete vagueness over what the coach's role was and who was the boss. In the eyes of some officials back in England the coach would have been seen as just a trainer, a physical-fitness man. John Robins saw himself as more than that. He was a good rugby technician and thought he should run the show. Mike Campbell-Lamerton thought differently because no one had told him otherwise.

'On the tour there were no rows or politics but there was a lack of focus as far as leadership was concerned with each man not wanting to step on the other's toes. It would have been better if any one of them had had total control and run it with an iron fist. But there was nothing the manager could do about it because he didn't have the mandate from home. His terms of reference wouldn't have allowed him to tell the coach or the captain "do this". Maybe a different kind of guy might have assumed a mandate and attempted to do things but I don't think you could judge Des badly on that. I loved the tour. Despite the defeats it was a happy occasion and I think he did a good job. Undoubtedly the team had a lot of potential, undoubtedly we could have done better in New Zealand if we'd been more focused. And undoubtedly the lack of focus and clarity at the top had a lot to do with that, but I would regard that as a fault of the system and organisation rather than of any of the individuals involved.'

McLoughlin might just have been the man to assume that mandate had he been named captain instead of Campbell-Lamerton. He knew he was favourite to lead the side but the decision of the less enlightened Irish selectors to relieve him of his country's captaincy had a knock-on effect for the Lions job. The fact that in his first season he had taken the team from the bottom of the table to within one game of the Triple Crown and touching distance of the championship counted for naught as Ireland faltered in his second.

Of his efforts to add a measure of direction and control to the side's rumbustious give-it-a-lash approach, Ken Kennedy says: 'He was a thoughtful tactician who brought a radical change into the way Irish teams prepared for games, and this discipline produced very tangible rewards. Until then preparation had been a little haphazard. In the dressing-room, tactics were not too well thought out and the training was nothing too serious either before he came along. He made unit work important and knowledge of the tactics in all the players essential. It sounds straightforward now it's what they do all the time, but 30 years ago it wasn't. He was quite radical and this produced a discipline that enabled us to compete well with all the countries. Unfortunately, he put a few noses out of joint at committee level and because of this they fired him from the captaincy of the team in a match before the Lions were picked and that effectively ruled him out of being captain of the 1966 Lions. I feel that if he had been captain on that tour it would have been more successful.'

Tour manager Des O'Brien is even more certain and says with regret: 'Ray should have been captain of that side. He would have made a hell of a difference; he has a tremendous brain, very mathematical in working things out, but he just decided to be a foot soldier and that was it. The captaincy was a problem. Mike Campbell-Lamerton was a delightful character and a really good man but his playing days were nearly over – in fact, I don't think he captained Scotland that year – and the one thing I said to the selection committee was they were electing a captain who wouldn't play in the Tests, and they said they accepted that.'

The cracks were painted over on the opening leg of the tour as the Lions breezed through Australia with McLoughlin to the fore, scoring crucial tries on consecutive weekends in Sydney against first New South Wales and then Australia, the first earning a 6–6 draw and the second an 11–8 win. They finished off by walloping the Wallabies 31–0 – still a record victory – but found the All Blacks and their kin a very different proposition indeed. McLoughlin explains: 'It was different between Australia and New Zealand. Australia weren't as strong then and the type of game we played in Australia was a case of trying to play fast and with continuity, like today, but continuity was developed at the expense of ensuring that quality ball was delivered to the outside part of the field.

'In Australia you had the ball with a little bit of time to spare. But when we hit New Zealand we hit the South Island first at a time when they were the rucking champions of the world. No matter what the style of play, they always figured out how to do it. That continues to be at the heart of their success and a lot of that is bred into them. They played the basics well and the laziness of the Lions was exposed: we lost the first match 14–8. The average weight of our pack would have been more than 16 stone. We had strong guys, stronger than the All Blacks physically, but in terms of playing the game the All Blacks were more efficient through their method because they played to a pattern more than we did. We were physically far superior, in size, strength and speed, but in terms of how to play rugby we were boys against men.

'Against Southland we had a lineout with six or seven in the line with a three-yard gap between them. These were the days when it was par for the course to hit a guy as he got the ball, and how you were expected to deliver ball with an All Black up your arse is hard to imagine. So we never had a chance of catching it, we had to tap it back. But then if you've got three-yard gaps these guys just come pouring through them. The same thing happened against Otago. The players knew where the problem was but the management had the concept of making for a flowing game, which was built on a false premise.'

McLoughlin was restricted on the longer leg of the tour by a hamstring injury suffered while kicking a football about and also had to pull out of the second Test team when he developed a raging temperature on the morning of the match. He played in the fourth Test alongside the recalled Kennedy but Noel Murphy missed out as he joined an increasingly long injury list in the tour's closing stages. Several of the wounded had suffered at the feet of the locals and their take-no-prisoners rucking style, which was a completely new experience for the visitors. Dirty play was a major talking point of the tour, with even the governor general stepping into the debate at one point, but McLoughlin reflects that the rough stuff was never in the same league as what he experienced five years later in Canterbury. He says: 'They played with great drive and determination, and had the philosophy that a guy who lies on the ball and prevents good second-phase ball is a criminal of the worst kind and if the referee can't get him out of there then the thing to do is walk on him, and there's a fine line between walking and kicking. In those days when rucking was key to the game, and to the New Zealanders in particular, a couple of guys locked on to each other to hit a ruck at the same time, and if there was a guy there they just walked on him. As they saw it, it wasn't dirty, but there are different ways of walking and there was the odd kick.

'There are dirty players in every country but I never regarded them generally as dirty. I regarded them as hard and uncompromising and the sort who you didn't want to get in their way if you could avoid it, but never dirty. In fact, I think they were a joy to watch. Even in 1960 when people said they had a very forward-dominated game they were still terrific to watch. It was a myth that they played a tight, unattractive game; the rules didn't promote the game to be as attractive as it was in the '70s or now. As far as the rules allowed, I thought they were terrific to watch. Fred Allen's team played some very attractive stuff, and they did in the Tests of '66 against the Lions, too.'

Only two Irishmen appeared in all four Tests, the great Mike Gibson and the Instonians number eight turned flanker Ronnie Lamont, whom his contemporaries rate as potentially among the finest of all back rowers, before his career was effectively curtailed by the injuries he picked up on that Lions tour. Lamont, a teacher from Belfast, had made his Ireland début in McLoughlin's first season as captain, scoring the winning try against England in only his second match and earning his Lions spot with his form the following term after he added an extra half stone of bulk to his fast-moving frame. His country's captain recalls: 'In the back row the best player we had was Ronnie Lamont. I remember several times saying he was twice as good as the next best player. Maybe that was exaggerating a bit, but not greatly. He had speed, absolute fearlessness and a savage tackle, plus the ability to retain top pace right through every match. He was a bit like Fergus Slattery in that respect; he would be going as fast in the eightieth minute as in the first.'

Lamont's willingness to put his body on the line exacted a high price for the seven tries he scored in his new role on the side of the scrum, a tally that included the Lions' first try of the Test series, earned by his speed to the breakdown when Welsh winger Stuart Watkins was stopped on the goal-line by Ron Rangi in the third rubber at Christchurch. Badly damaged muscles and tendons left him with one arm paralysed for a week after the Otago game and subsequently put his whole rugby-playing future in doubt. The problem meant that he did not play for Ireland again until 1970, when he appeared for a final full season on the flank. McLoughlin, too, was restricted by injuries on returning home, in his case to back and knee, and endured an even longer international exile, having to wait until 1971 for his next cap. He made his fortieth and final appearance in 1975 and but for that four-year absence might have won half that number again and added a third Lions tour to his honours board. McBride for one considers it 'a great shame' that his team-mate was unavailable in 1968 and insists: 'Of all the Irish Lions I believe Ray McLoughlin was the best, which seems peculiar because he never played in many Tests. But he had a tremendous influence on the game in Ireland. He changed people's thinking in '65 and '66 when he was in the running for the Lions captaincy – he brought in a new culture. He made players aware of their responsibilities, made them think about their job on the field and within the team.'

# 12

# THE LION KING

WILLIE JOHN MCBRIDE'S MOST treasured rugby possession is not one of the 63 caps he won for Ireland, nor a marker of the world records he set for consecutive international appearances and as the game's most capped lock-forward. Pride of place in the McBride trophy cabinet goes to a simple silver water jug presented to him by the players on the 1974 Lions tour to South Africa, engraved with the words: 'To Willie John. It was great to travel with you.' In its motto and its provenance it sums up the values that made McBride the greatest of all the Lions: loyalty and success.

As a player, the strapping second row from Ballymena offered the unswerving dedication and faithfulness he demanded as a captain, and which in turn rewarded him with the leadership of the greatest Lions of all. McBride needed every ounce of that dogged perseverance and belief; he went through the tunnel of three Lions tours and nine Tests before emerging from an international victorious at the tenth attempt. Being Irish at a time when his country was in the midst of a 23-year International Championship drought, he was at least used to that sort of sequence, although in fairness he did not have the ultimate preparation of being from Connacht, where a new coach once asked Mick Molloy if there was anything particular he felt they should work on in training and reputedly received the reply: 'How about running back to the halfway line from beneath our own posts?'

Not that defeat ever sat easily with McBride. His enormous will to win was a key factor in dragging both Ireland and the Lions out of the darkness of regular defeat. A true sportsman in everything that word demands, his honesty and respect for his fellow men never caused him to lose sight of the fact that winning was not the main thing; it was the only thing, a philosophy it took a while for the men at the top to cotton on to. 'The administrators, they didn't have a clue,' he says of the lean years for the Lions. 'It was this old thing of it's not the winning or the losing, it's the taking part that counts. That was a load of bullshit. You went out to South Africa to beat the Springboks in a series.'

It was not until 1974 that the tourists reached that goal, in a sensational series that joined McBride's 1971 success as payback time for the disappointments he had suffered over the previous years of his Lions life. Captaining the side was 'the peak of my career,' he says, but his appointment by coach Syd Millar was one of the most inspired choices the master tactician ever made. Millar knew McBride better than almost anyone in the game, hailing as they did from the same club, Ballymena, and having already proved they could work well in tandem as Ireland lifted their first outright championship since 1951 that Lions year. Millar also knew how valuable McBride's charismatic, forthright leadership would be in welding together a real team from the components of four wildly differing nations. The coach could concentrate on the tactics, the captain would motivate the troops.

And motivate them he did. His status as the most experienced player in Lions history – his final tally of 17 Tests is a record that will never be broken – commanded the respect of his men. The fearless, dignified example he set on and off the pitch, and the way he never asked any man to perform a task he was not prepared to carry out himself, fired them to go with him the extra yard, tackle the extra man and hit the extra ruck. In his *History of the British Lions*, Clem Thomas quoted the manager Alun Thomas's end-of-tour report on the captain's work, which spoke of the 'natural leader': 'He was literally worshipped by the players, not only because of his own courage and strength of commitment, but because they saw in him all the things they would like to be. He shielded them, nurtured them and, above all, inspired them.'

McBride is a man who played for his team-mates and for his jersey, and had seen enough on his previous four Lions tours to know that all 30 tourists – not just the 15 in the Test team – would have to stand as one if they were to have any hope of emulating the success of their immediate predecessors of 1971. Time was not on his side and he made the most of the short period they had together in England before leaving for South Africa, using the feeling of siege created by the massive anti-apartheid protests against their visit to bind the squad together. The spirit he created is still envied by many of those who felt that the same magic tantalisingly eluded them in their own experiences as Lions. Ollie Campbell, a tourist to South Africa in 1980 and to New Zealand under McBride's managership in 1983, says: 'I'm not sure we ever managed to get the feeling Willie John managed in South Africa in '74. He tells the story of the Welsh supporters coming to him on the night before they flew out to South Africa and saying they had nine Welsh jerseys they wanted to present to the Welsh players. Willie John said, "I'm sorry, there are no Welsh players on this tour." They said, "What do you mean, no Welsh players?"

'"No, no," Willie John said, "there are no Welsh players, there are no Irish players, there are no Scottish players, there are no English players. There are only Lions. If you've 30 of them, one for everybody, you're welcome, we will take them. But there's no division." That was a superb thing to have done, but I'm not sure we quite managed to blend to that extent on the tours I was on.'

McBride knew exactly what he was doing in making his point so clearly so early in the tour. He says of the importance of getting the players on each other's side: 'When you are away for three and a half months there are going to be trials and tribulations so you have to be tolerant of people. We're all different – it was an amateur game so there were people from all walks of life. I think what I did as captain was shared responsibility, but not on the field. I was very aware that being away for three months and speaking with the players as a captain on the training field every day, they could get fed up pretty quickly with my voice. So what I would do is if we were asked for lunch or dinner somewhere I would say to someone, look, I want you to say thank you before we leave. So I shared responsibility. I think that was good for building a team and it also developed guys. Most of those players could then get up anywhere and face a public, give their views and say what they thought. I think that was good.

'We also formed little committees. We had a social committee; the guys got all sorts of invitations to things, but you can't do them all so we said have a look at that and see what you want to do. Syd and I would have a committee that would sit and talk to us from a playing point of view, from a training point of view, from a travel point of view, things like that. So we shared it a lot; it was very much a team thing. We had players who believed in themselves but apart from that there was tremendous camaraderie, tremendous loyalty to each other. We had a job to do and we knew how to do it. They were a great team, they had remarkable balance. We had a few piss-ups but we knew when we were at work and when we could relax. That's the secret in life. But not only that, they were a team who got on well together.'

That was half the battle, but McBride knew that the other half was having the players and the organisational nous to compete with the kings of the southern hemisphere on level terms. Prior to 1971, the teams he had played in had some of those qualities but never the requisite full set. In 1962, McBride believes, the players were good enough to have at least shared the series with South Africa but were brought down by a lack of preparation and planning; in the same country in '68 the Lions' organisation was beginning to improve with the appointment of Ronnie Dawson as the first official coach, only for the players he was working with to fall just short of the highest class; and in between times, in New Zealand in 1966, a good team fell apart through poor morale and the failings of a management system in transition. He says of the bad old days:'There wasn't a hope we were going to win. We didn't even have a team identity. We had jerseys to play the games but we didn't have tracksuits or anything like that. I remember we had to go ourselves and make an effort to buy some sweaters with some sort of team identity. It was farcical, absolutely farcical. We had no coach, either, the captain did everything, we just talked it through ourselves.

'We had good players in those days but we just weren't organised. After '62 the same thing happened in '66 when we went to New Zealand. Des [O'Brien, Lions manager that year] is a super guy and was a super international for Ireland but he had lost touch with the game and was being patted on the back because he was a good lad. We had John Robins who came as assistant manager and he tried to coach but then he snapped his Achilles tendon and was ruled out of it. We had a lot of good players and tried to sort things out among ourselves but New Zealand is a tough place and we got another hiding.'

While McBride looks back on the introduction of an official coach as the point from which the Lions' organisation began to improve, the advances made were all relative. When he travelled to New Zealand as manager in 1983 he found that some things hadn't changed: 'No research was ever done by the rugby administration about the itinerary and that was probably more evident to me as a manager in '83. We were dragged from one end of the country to the other and back again. I remember I queried it twice and was more or less told, "Oh, we've agreed to this." But nobody had sat down and said this makes sense, that makes sense, this is acceptable, this isn't; they just agreed and that was it. So there was some sharp practice, which I don't blame the New Zealanders for if they could get away with it, but it was crazy. We would have easy games and then tough games just before the Tests. It was absolutely crazy, nobody did any homework back here.'

McBride had made his first Lions tour more than two decades previously, at the age of 21, having not even picked up a rugby ball until well into his teens. He had lost his father at the age of four and was brought up by his mother through some hard times on the family farm, coming to the game only in his last few years at Ballymena Academy. Tall, powerful and both physically and mentally hard, he rose rapidly through the ranks on the back of his commitment, courage and ever-sharpening technical skills, particularly in the lineout where he could win ball in pretty well every position. That versatility, alongside the ballast he added to the scrum, took him swiftly into the Ulster team, on to his first Ireland cap, against England in 1962, and finally into the Lions party that year as understudy to his Irish partner Bill Mulcahy and the massive Welshman Keith Rowlands. Tom Kiernan, one of the full-backs in the squad, says: 'Willie John really emerged on that tour. He wasn't expected to get a Test place but he ended up in the team for the last two Tests. He was a relative newcomer to rugby, he wasn't playing at five or six years of age, so he was still immature but his value in securing possession was pretty high even then.'

McBride improved his skills as an aggressive, muscular mauler against the big men of the veld and would develop in that respect with each tour that came round. Kiernan explains: 'He had two halves to his career: the first he was getting the ball out of touch, the second he was stealing the ball off people.'

The bank official's value was, of course, heightened by the free-for-all nature of the lineout jungle, where his strength and size stood out against even the masters of New Zealand, where he first toured with the Lions in 1966. Team-mate Ray McLoughlin says of his contribution there: 'Delme Thomas and Brian Price were terrific jumpers but Willie John was probably the best all-round second-row forward. He wasn't an outstanding jumper relative to the others but when contact was a key part of lineout play he was very strong and well set. His physical presence made him very effective in ball-getting. He was probably physically the strongest and a match for anyone he came across. He was also an All Black-type runner with the ball and quite quick too. He slowed down in the '70s but in the '60s he was very quick. He could also be relied upon to put in the effort right through every minute of every game.'

McBride learned a lot on that trip and two years later travelled as one of the senior forwards to South Africa, his favourite rugby destination, of which he says: 'It was a marvellous place to tour, tremendous hospitality, wonderful country and twice a week they kick hell out of you. That sort of spoilt it a bit!' McBride enjoyed himself off the field as a prominent member of the late night fun-lovers, The Wreckers, and played in all four Tests of a series lost 3–0, with one match drawn, also scoring the tourists' only try of the first international despite being hampered by a knee wound that turned septic. He also showed an unknown versatility in the third rubber when he played almost 15 minutes at tight-head prop while the Lions raced to get a replacement on for the injured Mike Coulman. Tour regulations insisted that substitutes had to sit in the stand in their blazers and flannels until required, so McBride had to fill in in the front row while Delme Thomas charged down umpteen flights of stairs and scrambled around the dressing-room getting stripped.

The tour also became notorious for the refereeing of the home officials, whose decisions were at best idiosyncratic and at worst offered the Lions no protection from local hard-nuts – sometimes off the field as well as on it. The latter point sometimes cut both ways, though, as one spectator found to his cost when being on the receiving end of a McBride right-hander at the infamous 'Battle of Springs', where against Eastern Transvaal the Wales prop John O'Shea became the first Lion to be sent off for foul play when he threw a punch after the referee had already warned both teams about the con-sequences of the next act of aggression. McBride, an increasingly irate spectator that day, takes up the story: 'The referee sent John off on the opposite side of the field and he had to walk all the way round to reach the dressing-rooms. It was most humiliating. They were throwing cans of beer, oranges and all sorts of things at him. Then this guy ran out and hit him as he came round towards us. I was in the stand and I was boiling at this because no one went to his assistance, nobody. He didn't know where the hell to come off the ground so I went to his rescue. It was a sad point because there hadn't been a Lion sent off. But in those days they were all local referees, there were no neutral referees, and sometimes it could become a bit physical with guys who wanted to be the tough guy and games could get out of hand.'

The spectator against whom McBride got his retaliation in first escaped lightly in still being conscious when the police read him his rights, for Colin Meads, the legendary iron man of New Zealand rugby, credits his long-time rival with delivering the hardest punch he ever took. Note the use of the word 'took' as no doubt 'Pinetree' declined to be felled by the blow. The two great locks of their age first tangled in New Zealand in 1966 and on their next meeting in '71 the All Black finally surrendered his crown as the world's finest second row to his Northern Irish foe. The end of the Lions series marked the end of Meads's international career, albeit not in the manner he might have expected. McBride outshone him in both tight and loose as the Lions took the honours 2–1 with the crucial last Test drawn.

McBride says of that triumph: 'For the first time we had a proper coach and people who had sat down and really selected a team, not just patted guys on the back for being good guys. What a difference it was to be properly organised. On the previous tours you did get a bit fed up when you knew you could do better if you were more organised. But we didn't have that winning culture and in some ways we still don't have it when we play southern-hemisphere sides.'

Coach Carwyn James handed McBride more responsibility as he took another step towards becoming the greatest of all Lions leaders, bringing in the uncompromising lock alongside Ray McLoughlin to lead the forward pack both on the field and in training. McBride says: 'Carwyn was one of those people who made players think. He wasn't a guy who dictated but he got players to think the way he wanted them to. He picked out a number of players, I suppose you might call it an advisory committee, and we would talk things through. At the end of the day he got what he was wanting but he got it from us rather than by telling us. He and [captain] John Dawes maybe didn't know a lot about forward play but they knew the ball they wanted and they knew they had players who could influence things up front. I was leading the forwards in that series and he made us think absolutely about where we were on the field, exactly what we had to do, what our job was.'

The task facing McBride and his men in 1974 was fairly straightforward: match the heroes of '71 by beating a South African nation now already on their guard and determined not to go the way of their old rivals New Zealand. It was a daunting prospect but the captain and his coach knew exactly where the series would be won and lost. The stoker of their engine-room recounts: 'South African rugby at that time was largely based on strong forward play, strong scrummaging, and we worked like never before on scrummaging. To me it was remarkable. I had been there twice already and this time to go out in a Lions team and push the Springboks,' he says with a shake of the head, 'what a difference.

'It was a pretty simple approach, which I believe rugby football should be. It was strong forward play and then when we had domination we stretched the ball, we used the space. It's a different game now but back then we made space, we found space and we looked for space. The basis was a strong pack and then we would use the back line, which was tremendous, maybe not as great in names as in '71 but just as great in terms of completing the job. We had Gareth [Edwards], Phil Bennett, [Ian] McGeechan and [Dick] Milliken in the centres, J.J. [Williams] and Andy Irvine on the wings and J.P.R. at fullback. That's not a bad back line and of course we broke all the records in '74. We scored more points, more tries, more everything.'

The full story was that the Lions won all 18 of their provincial matches and three of the four Tests, with the other drawn only because the referee disallowed Fergus Slattery's match-winning try. They scored a best-ever 729 points in the Republic and effectively reduced South African rugby to rubble. Before they could do that, however, they had to win the right to play. The past experiences of Millar and McBride told them that for the war to be won there was a physical battle that had to be fought first. In the captain's most famous phrases, the Lions would 'take no prisoners' and 'get our retaliation in first'. Of the psychological importance of not taking backward steps when the fists sooner or later, and probably sooner, began to fly, he says: 'South African rugby was always physical and we had always been dominated, played second fiddle, in years gone by and they just couldn't believe that we could stand up to this. There were one or two ugly incidents in that tour but I think you will always get that, and they were always in provincial games, not the Tests, because you will always get one or two guys who think they'll sort you out.'

Some observers accused the Lions of being a violent outfit, largely as a result of the image created by their take-no-prisoners philosophy and the notorious '99' call used by McBride as an emergency measure when things looked like getting out of hand. On the signal, all 15 Lions would pile into the nearest opponent, not only to show the Springboks that they were more than ready to mix it with them but also to reduce the risks of a sending-off as the referee was highly unlikely to dismiss an entire team. The call was used twice in the ultra-physical third Test but McBride insists it was only then a last resort and did not characterise the style of play of a team that scored more tries in South Africa than any other Lions. He says: 'We were physical, yes, but certainly not dirty. In fact, it was one of the things we particularly did not want to get involved in because we knew we were the better players and the better team when we played rugby football. You can't be a good team and a dirty team at the same time.

'That thing [the 99 call] has been overplayed. I would say there were possibly four incidents in all the games and that was about it. It was a good thing because it showed South Africa that the Lions at last were going to stand up and weren't going to take this nonsense. On previous tours there is no doubt about it, they were bullied and we weren't prepared to accept it on this tour.'

The collective nature of the 99 call, as well as the fact that all 15 Lions responded automatically, says much about the spirit McBride engendered in his side through the way he handled both himself and his players on and off the field. England prop Mike Burton, one of the understudies of the squad, remembers: 'Probably the leadership of Willie was the thing that stands out. He was a poacher turned gamekeeper really because he had been a bit of a handful himself on his previous tours, so he allowed us a certain latitude but not to any extreme. Celebrations were always OK as long as Willie was in command. He said the one thing that happens on these tours is that if men are seen in states less than sober or with a cigarette in the hand, this would not be good for the public image. It's very difficult on tours like these to get out of the public glare, so he arranged that we would have a team room wherever we went, where we could go in all day and play table tennis, have something to eat and so on. That is fairly commonplace now but it wasn't then. And in the evenings it was fairly easy to turn this into a private bar. Of course, that's what he did.

'One of the best moments was after we had won the first Test, and of course the seven matches in the run-up to it, in Cape Town in very wet conditions. The South Africans were all saying afterwards, 'Wait till you get to the high veld, we'll kill you,' and so on. Willie never got involved in that, he always gave the magnanimous speech, thank you for your hospitality, hands across the sea and all that, but after it was over we went into the team room and all took our blazers off so we were all casual and locked the door. Willie then ripped the chandelier out of the ceiling and said, "Men, I take no responsibility until next Wednesday." That's when the next game was, of course, but it was typical of Willie's style.'

McBride managed the Lions in 1983 but is less enthusiastic about getting involved in the professional business his beloved sport has now become. Of his watchwords, success is still as highly prized as ever, even if the motivation for seeking it may well have changed, but loyalty, he fears, is sadly on the wane. He is no soured, better-in-my-day nostalgist, but admits: 'When I look at the game today and when I played, I wouldn't change my era. I played with some of the best players who ever played rugby football, especially when I think of the backline of '71. It was just a privilege to be on the field with them.

'I don't think I would make a good professional. I did my own motivation, my own preparation and in some ways played the game my own way. I didn't like to be told what to do, which professional players do today. I think I would be bored to tears living with the game all day, every day. I think I lived with the balance of career and rugby football very nicely and hopefully very successfully. It was a marvellous era to live in and play rugby in, to see the game develop from no-hopers to winners. It was just great to be a part of that.'

# 13

# A LONG DAY AT THE OFFICE

MIKE GIBSON MAY ONCE have described the business of playing rugby on tour as 'like going to the office at home', but he was never one of the game's pen-pushers or clock-watchers. The Belfast solicitor earned his rating as probably the best centre of all time through his extravagant range of skills, his tactical appreciation and the remarkable period of time over which he performed consistently at his peak. When he compared touring to work Gibson did not mean that his five long Lions expeditions ever became a chore – 'if you found it a grind there would be something wrong with your character', he says – but rather that they provided an opportunity to devote to his game the sort of time and attention normally monopolised by the demands of his job. 'It is all a matter of self discipline,' he concluded back in 1977.

In that succinct analysis of the tourist's art, Gibson summed up the philosophy that was at the heart of his greatness. His natural ability and feel for the play whirling around him in midfield would alone have been sufficient to earn him his place at the game's top table, but what made him stand out even among the élite was the sheer dedication and commitment with which he applied his gifts. He knew he had talent in abundance but was determined it should never be undersold by a lack of preparation or by neglect of the basics. Teetotal, single-minded, ultra-competitive and as strong in character as in physique and stamina, he earned a reputation as the game's first professional, not in the financial sense but in the work ethic he applied to his sport. Inherent class made him the finest three-quarter of his age, but that meticulous approach ensured his era stretched across 15 golden years, an unprecedented 69 appearances for Ireland and five Lions tours which took his tally of international caps to a world-record 81. During that extraordinary career Gibson's form truthfully never dipped and when he retired at 36 he was as phenomenal a force as ever. His Test début saw Ireland record their first win at Twickenham in 16 years, while his farewell was made in helping his country to a superb 2–0 series win in Australia, a feat that none of the other Home Unions has ever matched and at which number 8 Willie Duggan still marvels when he remembers Gibson's final contribution. He says: 'I wouldn't be a great one for congratulating people on their performances – I've never done that in my life – but the second Test Mike Gibson played for Ireland in Australia in 1979 was absolutely unbelievable. You would not believe an individual could do so much. It was the first time I ever crossed the dressing-room to shake someone's hand.'

Duggan might have found a queue, for there has never been any shortage of admirers wanting to press the flesh or willing to testify to his genius. England prop Mike Burton roomed with Gibson on the 1974 Lions tour and maintains, 'That was as close as I ever got to tackling him.' Three years earlier in New Zealand, Sean Lynch was always delighted to emerge from the front row of the scrum and see the ball reaching his countryman in midfield. He says of his colleague: 'Mike Gibson was the jewel in the Lions' crown, he was just magic. He had everything you could ask for: speed, ability and he knew how to handle a ball. He could dummy-run, scissors, beat a man on the outside or inside and he could read a game very well, too.'

Gibson was a beautiful, fluent runner with the ball, as he showed when in perhaps the best form of his life on that '71 Lions tour to New Zealand. One example was the perfect arc his footsteps described against Bay of Plenty as he took Chris Rea's pass in centre field, swept outside the opposing defence and swung round to score behind the posts in a smooth single movement. But his passing, or, more specifically, his hand speed and the timing of his delivery, was even more impressive and most appreciated by the team-mates he invariably put into acres of space outside him. The try with which the Lions levelled the second Test in Christchurch is generally remembered for the jinking, weaving improvisation of J.P.R. Williams that started the movement with a breakout from his 22, and for the 50-yard, ears-pinned-back dash with which Gerald Davies finished it off. But the brief involvement of the third man in the middle was arguably its most crucial component. As J.P.R. entered All Black territory with the cover closing in, it was Gibson who ghosted onto his shoulder in support. He made no effort to emulate the shoulder-dipping style of his full-back but instead took and gave the perfect pass to suck in the converging defence and hit Davies at full tilt outside him with no need to break stride on his way to the line.

It was generally considered that the 1971 tour saw Gibson burst spectacularly into full bloom as he spent far less time on the back foot than he did with Ireland. The Cambridge University and North of Ireland playmaker agrees that those tourists were provided with the ideal environment in which to flourish, but also believes that Irishmen in general are the best equipped of all the Home Unions players to thrive as Lions. He says: 'The starting point is to look at the character of the Irish. Despite the talent that the Irish players have, they are laden with respect for every other person. Because of that the Irish in rugby tend to be unpretentious, they tend to be very grateful for what opportunities they are given. Their charcter means they blend very easily with their team-mates and also with their hosts. The Irishman on tour is likely to be happy and content and enjoys what I would call the integration with the host country and its people. Other members of the Lions party can regard the hosts as the enemy and are distant – they slip back into the siege mentality – but you never get that with the Irish. Because he is content in his mind and in the company of the people he is with, the Irishman is going to play to his potential, whereas often on a Lions tour not all players actually do that.

'The second stage is in the technique or basic ability. A very important aspect of the Irish player's make-up is the passion with which he plays. I know each country claims that they play passionately – which is a claim I have my reservations about – but I know from my own experience how Ireland play as a team. They realise that maybe because of a slight deficiency in the number of players who are of Lions standard they have to commit themselves totally to the game and produce that passion every time they go out on the field. That is a good start for a Lions tour. Also the Irishman has had to develop as a rugby player under greater pressure than others because of the lack of numbers we have and because of the fact that the Irish team would rarely get anything without having to work for it. There are some teams where players appear to be good because they are playing in a very good team and are surrounded by world-class players, but as an individual that person may not be a world-class player. Because the Irishman has developed his skills under pressure those skills are much more valuable, much more ingrained and much more likely to stand up under intense pressure than those of the person who has had an easier introduction to international rugby. Certainly as a back I was very appreciative of possession and opportunities, which didn't always present themselves playing for Ireland.'

The more of the ball Gibson saw in 1971, the better he looked, and he attributes the prime years that followed to the assurance he gained from his experiences in New Zealand. He says: 'The Lions who were successful in '71 developed an increased sense of self-belief. There was a confidence instilled by Carwyn James and his methods of training which were very different to what we had known before. There was nothing harsh about the man and yet such was the respect we felt for him that he didn't have to be harsh because if you did something wrong there was a sense of disappointment that he didn't deserve that and we should have played better for him. It didn't happen too many times but we played well because he encouraged us to be free to rid our minds of any fear. Having done that we were able to achieve things we hadn't thought about and so our self-belief developed too. I have no doubt that everybody who was on that '71 tour came back with an increased knowledge of rugby, increased confidence and the awareness that they could compete with the best in the world. That's where I think the '71 tour was so significant. I'm not sure the '74 tour would have been successful had it not come on the back of the previous success. People like Gordon Brown and Willie John could go out to South Africa knowing the Test series could be won.'

Work commitments meant that Gibson could not commit to the whole of that 1974 trip but he was able to join the tour in its second half as a replacement for the injured Alan Old. It says much for the quality of the Test centres Dick Milliken and Ian McGeechan that they retained their places ahead of the late arrival but it also says much for Gibson's loyalty and diligence that he was content with his role as an ever-ready understudy. He says: 'My contribution in '74 was reduced by not being available for selection initially and then going out after the second Test, at a stage when the side was winning and established. My role there was one of simply maintaining a high quality of play so that in the event of somebody getting injured I was at a standard that would allow me to go into the Test side. It would have been difficult if you had been out there from the beginning but I have always regarded people who come on tour as a replacement as being nothing more than that. The first team has been selected and is established and known to each other so there is a unit in place and it would only be if something had gone wrong, if there was a loss of form or a change of plan, that you would be required and it would be disappointing if something like that had happened. I didn't feel any disappointment because I knew what my role was. I went there with the ambition of making sure that I was playing at a high level and then just simply rejoiced in the success.'

That Gibson was in sufficiently good shape to play at a lung-burning altitude of more than 6,000 feet less than a week after his arrival came as no surprise to the rest of the party and gave great comfort to a management that could sleep easy in the knowledge that he was fully prepared to step in to the senior side at a moment's notice. Constant among the tributes his contemporaries pay him is a wonder at the vigour and zeal with which he approached his relentless training regime. He would invariably go in for extra sessions after running out with the Irish team, possessed the discipline to put in solitary hours of conditioning work and turned to the innovation of athletics techniques to sharpen his speed and sprinting style. It is no coincidence that he is the player most admired by Fergus Slattery, another glutton for the physical punishment of the practice pitch. Gibson says of his regime: 'I always enjoyed training and I always enjoyed practising because I became better at the various skills I practised. To me it was easy to go training, even by myself. I enjoyed that and my objective in training was to get myself as fit as possible so that at no stage of the game would I doubt that I could do something or chase something, so that I could make a full contribution without being worried my fitness level was up to the demands that would be placed on it. I have felt much more fatigued at the end of a training session than I ever did at the end of a rugby match.' And he adds: 'I also benefited a lot from training with athletes. It was something different; they had only a passing interest in rugby and they talked about athletics a lot. They were all good runners with good technique and we all had the common goal of getting faster.'

Doubt and worry are not emotions a player of Gibson's talent might be expected to experience in a rugby context, particularly over the importance of fitness. Superior conditioning has elevated many a moderate player into a good one but often those with the supreme natural skills have neglected the physical side of training knowing their gifts will more than compensate for any lack of puff in the game's later stages. Gibson's perfectionist streak, however, did not make that an option, particularly after he first identified the combination of skill and strength that made the All Blacks the world's very best. He says of his first Lions experience, as a 23-year-old in 1966: 'That was a very difficult tour. We were up against a New Zealand team which was in the middle of an outstanding era and we were well beaten, but the experience made me a better player. I could then appreciate what exactly was required of me as an international player in terms of mental strength and physical stamina. I was content that my technique was able to stand up to the pressure but I then knew that development had to come mentally and physically. In 1968 I had the next stage which was playing against a good South African side in different conditions and playing a different style to the New Zealanders. Those things all contributed to my development as a player.'

Gibson was a quick learner and had plenty of opportunity to gauge his progress on that first New Zealand trip, playing in 19 of the 25 matches, including all four Tests, and being rated by the locals as the most stylish performer in the Lions back division.

It was no coincidence that Gibson shone in the centre, able to play in his favoured position by the presence in the party of the dazzling little Welsh out-half David Watkins. Ireland, conversely, rarely had stand-off resources of a similar calibre so the former Campbell College pupil played much of his Test rugby in the '60s wearing the number ten jersey until the emergence of Barry McGann at the end of the decade. Neither role troubled Gibson unduly. Tom Kiernan, his captain with Ireland and the Lions during that period, rates him 'the best outside-half we ever had and also the best centre we ever had', while the man himself says: 'My view has always been that if there is a class fly-half I would prefer to play in the centre but if there isn't I would prefer to have first bite at the ball and control the game from fly-half.' But he adds: 'It is probably easier to play in the centre. There's greater freedom to stay close to the ball, to support play and just generally to be involved in the game.'

The Lions tour to South Africa in 1968 might have given Gibson a second opportunity to play centre at the highest level, as Barry John was ripe to emerge on the international scene. Sadly, injury ensured their Lions link-up would have to wait until the next tour as they never played in the same team in '68. Gibson badly sprained his right ankle in the opening match against Western Transvaal and did not re-emerge until the Rhodesia game five days before the first

Test. That left him too short of match fitness to start the international, allowing John briefly to step into the breach; briefly, as he lasted less than a half before his tour was ended by a broken collarbone, suffered when he was knocked to the ground by Jan Ellis's outstretched arm. Gibson came on as the first Home Unions player to appear as a replacement in a Test and went on to start in 11 of the last 13 matches as the management elected to use the loss of John to bring in Ken Goodall to strengthen their back-row resources rather than fly out another stand-off.

Again, Gibson's dedicaton to fitness and preparation allowed him to fulfil such a sapping schedule even though he was still troubled by his damaged ankle. Such ascetic devotion to self-improvement gave some observers the idea that he was somewhat aloof and austere, but the impression was a misleading one as Gibson prizes the friendship of his fellow Lions above all the honours heaped upon them. He explains: 'I often think about the individual sports, about people who win the men's singles at Wimbledon or the Open Championship at golf, and there is nobody at that winning moment who can understand how the person feels. He has no one with him to share the moment, except maybe his wife and family. That's a joy, but as Lions we had 30 people sharing the moment and all of them know how we felt. Because of that when we meet now we can still feel the excitement of what we achieved. When you see the reaction of the Ryder Cup teams, where you have real individuals drawn together as a team, and witness their excitement, that's the sort of feeling touring with the Lions or with Ireland gave us.'

His closest colleagues recall acts of generosity of spirit on and off the field. Dick Milliken, who played all his international rugby for Ireland alongside him in the centre, recalls the way the old hand settled the newcomer's nerves on his début at Twickenham in 1973. He says of the moment: 'About ten minutes into the match there had been a break down the blindside and we moved the ball very quickly into the backs. When Gibson got the ball there must have been ten or fifteen metres to the line and I think if Mike had pinned his ears back he would have made it, but he decided to flick the ball on to me. It seemed like the ball was floating through the air for about five minutes and all the while I could hear Wally McMaster on the left wing screaming at me to pass the ball. I didn't believe that there was anyone around me at all but he was screaming for the pass. I caught the ball and I think I dived the ten yards for the try. But that was typical Gibson because he knew what it would mean to score a try in your first international. He could have scored himself, I think, but he was having none of it and gave me a perfect pass.'

More important to Ken Goodall than any pass he ever received was the hand of friendship Gibson extended to him at a time when the number 8 feared widespread ostracism on his return to Ireland after a spell in rugby league. He says of the incident: 'When I came back in 1974 I went to watch my old club, City of Derry, playing North of Ireland, who Mike played for. He spotted me on the touch-line and came over to speak to me. I had just come back from league and I felt that it was nice of him to do that. But that was the sort of person he was. I always found him to be totally dedicated, very committed and a nice person as well, although I've also met people who wouldn't have such kind things to say about him. But I had a lot of respect for him as a person and a lot of respect for him as a rugby player.'

Gibson had reached his playing zenith – a Table Mountain of a peak whose high plateau would extend to the end of his international days – with the Lions in New Zealand in 1971, where Colin Meads among others singled him out as the finest figure in what is considered the most talented of all the tourists' back lines. Slattery for one agrees with the verdict of the great Pinetree, saying: 'Of the stars of '71, a lot of credit was given to Barry John. Personally I thought Mike Gibson was the best all-round performer, especially when you consider a big part of rugby in New Zealand is defending.'

Carwyn James, the cerebral coach of that tour, thought likewise and regularly sought Gibson's opinions on tactics and personnel during the trip. He prized Gibson's attacking abilities and the speed of thought that allowed him to sense precisely where he needed to be at any particular time, but also highlighted the power of his defence, commenting on the team's return: 'So often on tour Mike Gibson put us in contention with the quality of his tackling.' One moment that illustrated James's point came in the defeat of the second Test, where Gibson used his defensive skills to build an attacking platform deep in the All Blacks' danger zone. Under pressure in his own 22, he launched a massive clearance kick that pinned New Zealand wing Bruce Hunter to the touchline inside his 22. Gibson, flying up in pursuit of his own kick, showed remarkable pace and timing to arrive moments after the ball and hammer Hunter into touch to give the Lions an attacking lineout in a rare position of real danger.

Gibson naturally rates that tour alongside '74 as the highlights of his Lions experiences, saying: 'We settled quite quickly and we played a type of rugby which was as good as I have ever been involved with because we had hard-working and committed forwards who produced enough ball for us to play with and to attempt variations in our patterns of play. When you spend three months or so playing with names who will go down in history as being world-class players of their time you appreciate that you are playing at a very high level.'

But once more, success did not come as of right and nor did Gibson expect it to, his mind again returning to the level of dedication he believes it is essential to put in. He says: 'Approaching the tour you have to clear your mind. Yes, I would like to be home with my wife, be playing with my children, that sort of thing, but I have to say I'm off here for three months, I'm committed to it and I must not compromise. My view was that it was like the office: this was my job for three months. In fact, when I went on a Lions tour that was my life for three months. The attitude I took on tour was: I'm going to play as well and as hard as I can and I'm not going to do anything to compromise my ability to do that. In place of work I had substituted rugby and the opportunity to train and simply try to improve myself as a player.

'When I look at Lions tours even now I am looking for the Irish to benefit from the high quality of their colleagues and I want to see them return to Ireland as improved players because they have a duty to improve the standard of their Irish colleagues who didn't tour. If they have improved in training, technique and attitude that is going to have a beneficial effect on the other Irish players and even on their club sides.'

That commitment to being the best was partly born from the fierce will to win recalled by his long-time team-mate Ken Kennedy, who says: 'Gibson was one of the most competitive, talented rugby players that I've ever known, and I knew him from Under-11s, when he was my scrum-half. Mike would be competitive in everything he did, in cards before the game, in getting the best seat on the bus, and in the game itself he would be always thinking two moves ahead of what would be happening, rather than some people who might be trying to remember what they should have done a minute ago.'

The last of Gibson's five Lions tours, a total that only Willie John McBride can match, came in 1977 when he was back in New

Zealand again but, as in '74, failed to appear in a Test. Injury disrupted his tour, although Duggan believed he was worth taking a chance on even in less than perfect nick, saying today: 'If Mike had been on the Test sides we would have had a totally different back-line situation; we would have had experience and a world-class player in there and that could have changed things for us.'

Gibson was equally frustrated by a problem that would flare up just as he seemed to be hitting his familiar top form. 'Two things were disappointing about the 1977 tour,' he says today. 'The main one was that I injured my back in about the second training session in New Zealand and it affected my hamstring and thereafter I was rarely in a position to compete for a Test place. It was particularly disappointing because at times I was playing at a level that was good enough for the Test team, but in the main I spent more time on physiotherapists' couches than on training grounds. You often used to think that if you had an injury you could have a super time on tour, but you didn't. You just wanted to play rugby and I was disappointed I wasn't able to do that because that was what I had committed myself to doing.' And he adds: 'The second disappointment, of course, was losing the series because we had the forward domination which should have guaranteed us success, but we didn't make full use of it. That was sad because it could have been a wonderful '70s for the Lions and really it ought to have been.'

Only a perfectionist would consider a decade in which the Lions recorded their first-series wins in almost a century of trying anything less than wonderful. But perfectionist is perhaps the word that describes Cameron Michael Henderson Gibson better than any other. And for those who saw him, of all the players in his position he came closer than any of them to meeting its most exacting demands.

# 14

# EXPRESS DELIVERY

WHEN SYD MILLAR PLACED his demands for the 1974 Lions tour to South Africa in front of the Four Home Unions selection committee, his demands were relatively straightforward but entirely non-negotiable. His captain, Willie John McBride, he got without demure. But his insistence on taking Ken Kennedy as one of the two hookers raised eyebrows across the Twickenham table. The Ireland hooker, whose last Lions tour was eight years previously, had been overlooked for the last party and so was on few shortlists this time around. Although Kennedy will still say that missing out in '71 acted as a spur to carry on playing at the highest level, many of his contemporaries considered it a scandalous decision motivated more by rugby politics than playing considerations. And there was no reason to suspect that the same fate would not befall him in '74, until Millar stepped in.

The coach would not be moved on his old front-row colleague's inclusion and almost every member of the most successful Lions side of all would soon be grateful for that stance. Millar and McBride attribute the success of '74 to the fact that every man in the party, not just those involved in the Tests, made an equally valuable contribution to the tour. Kennedy, who was then playing for London Irish after moving to England to further his medical career, would have been at the forefront of their thinking as he genuinely did the work of two men. As well as giving his all on the fields of both training and play, he acted as an unofficial team doctor, ministering to the sick, treating injuries and playing a key role in preparing the squad for the unique demands posed by the topography of South Africa.

However, Millar's meticulous planning meant he would not risk his side's chances by taking along a virtual passenger in the key position of hooker simply for the sake of his skills in administering a few sticking plasters, and he insists that Kennedy's playing capabilities were the prime criteria for his selection. The coach could be counted among those who believed that despite now being in the twilight of his Test career at 33, the enthusiastic Ulsterman had been good enough to be a Lion in '71 and remained good enough to be one in '74. All the same, Kennedy's medical expertise added extra weight to his claim and in South Africa came to be as valuable to the side as his abilities as an understudy to the eventual Test selection Bobby Windsor.

Millar says: 'Ken was chosen because he had an ability to get the ball even in the most awkward positions. That was the big thing as far as he was concerned. We had other excellent contenders, like John Pullin, but in addition to performing his role on the field Ken performed another role as doctor. He had a great interest in sports medicine, which is his specialism now, and his work was invaluable. Some players might have said, "I'm here as a player, not a doctor," but he never had that attitude. He did his training and then spent hours with the injured. We had many players back quicker than would otherwise have been the case because of his expertise. The only player we lost from the Test team before the series was won was Billy Steel. In 1980 we lost nine of our team and our Test side was decimated. Part of our success in '74 was that we had a virtually unchanged team and a lot of that was due to the ministrations of Ken Kennedy.'

The Lions may have been grateful for Kennedy's medical expertise in South Africa, but on another occasion when an Ireland team-mate required his assistance they left his company convinced he should not abandon sports medicine for midwifery. In February 1975 Feidlim McLoughlin, brother of Ray and also a prop, had spent many matches as a replacement waiting for his brother or Sean Lynch to suffer an 'injury' so that he could come on and win his first cap. Usually they forgot the plan but this time, as Ireland travelled to play Scotland, Ray told his heavily pregnant sister-in-law Penny that this would be Feidlim's big day and brought her up for the game on the quiet as a surprise for her husband. She had a wasted journey as Ray and Sean again 'forgot' to limp off, but at least her presence meant Feidlim was able to attend the birth of his daughter Rachel. He says: 'At about three in the morning Penny had a ferocious pain. I went to get the team doctor but he wouldn't come out because I was always messing about with him, putting things in his bed and so on, and he thought it was another joke. So I went and knocked on Ken Kennedy and Mike Gibson, who were just about the most difficult people to get up at that time of the morning. Ken came along in his silk dressing gown, mumbling swear words in English and French – he always insisted on speaking French whenever possible – and took a look at her with all the lads peering in from the hallway. He said, "She's all right, all she needs is an aspirin," and turned to leave. With that her waters broke and the baby was nearly born in the lift.'

Kennedy received more thanks for his efforts in South Africa, where the Kent-born, Belfast-raised doctor was quite happy with his dual role. As well as working flat out to keep the Test side in one piece he saw the tour as an opportunity to road test many new ideas in the field, all of which helped give the Lions the edge. 'It was fun,' he says. 'In '74 I was at the end of my career and I was more interested in medicine than in two more caps, so it was nice to do the training and then look after any problems and to put into practice some of the theories I had on how to train at altitude. We did various things for replenishing salts lost when you exercise so you have the right electrolyte balance. We gave various salt additives to the players, which was the first time that had been done. We also did various exercises to increase respiratory capacity. Instead of doing press-ups some of our training was to improve puliminary function, which had a huge bearing on us being fitter than the South Africans. If you are playing at 5,000 feet you run into the wall very quickly. If you're scrumming, scrumming, scrumming, you don't want to be running too fast across the pitch. At high altitudes in the Transvaal, Northern Transvaal and Free State you've got a big problem unless you've prepared well. Then when you go down to the coast at Durban you've got the humidity to contend with. If you're not replenishing yourself with fluids – which again we started – you become dehydrated, and if you become dehydrated you become weak. The standard of the set scrummaging in the 1970s was high and if you think of the energy needed and the sweat that's pouring off you, you really need those fluids. It was nice to see it was their players going down with cramp and not ours because we had taken the right additives.'

That medical input had begun before the Lions even left home as Millar's military precision took the team's fitness tests into a new realm. Kennedy says: 'Syd virtually ran that tour. He had investigated properly all aspects before the tour went, including the political leanings of the referees, the hotels and the training facilities and the possible people we would be playing against. We were able to have improved pre-tour training and assessment, which was something he let me do. We were able to do blood tests and fitness tests to see the degrees of fitness and pick up people who had major problems. We picked up a couple of people who had quite marked anaemia and this could be treated before we got to places where they would have been greatly disadvantaged by not having enough red blood cells to get the oxygen flowing round.

'I was totally amazed that we didn't have any medical back-up until then. Not to take a doctor or a physio was quite incredible and it was subsequent to that tour that they started to bring them.' But he adds: 'It wasn't atypical of the four Home Unions' thinking, though. When we went to New Zealand with the Lions in '66 they hadn't even given us tracksuits or pullovers. We got laundry bags and towels with our numbers on but no tracksuits or pullovers. And New Zealand can be a pretty cold place.'

Harsh, too, as Kennedy discovered on his first Lions trip, in only his second season of international rugby. He remembers it as 'the trip of a lifetime' for a newly qualified medic, but also 'one of the big growing-up experiences of my life' as the tourists found themselves under the All Black cosh. The Lions suffered for their naïvety and Kennedy suffered, financially at least, for his hooker's art. 'I was a houseman in the Royal in Belfast,' he says today in his office in London's Harley Street, 'and I was earning £780 a year. My pay stopped on the day I walked out of the hospital and I had saved £50, which was all I had for the four and a half months of the tour, plus 50p a day – one Australian dollar – subsistence allowance, and we still thought we were kings.'

The Lions were fêted as such as they made their way unbeaten through Australia in a dream sequence before their rude awakening in the Land of the Long White Cloud. Kennedy thrived on the hard surfaces on which the first leg of the tour was played and earned acclaim as a relatively slight front rower who combined excellent technical skills with the speed and antennae of an open-side flanker. In the set scrum he had a rare ability to strike quickly and cleanly regardless of the angle at which his opposing prop forced him to operate, and could return the favour by packing so low that bigger opponents might have preferred his medical specialism to be that of an osteopath. Adopting the body position of an ostrich seemed to have no effect on the efficiency of his ball-winning, as some swore he could hook the ball back with the flick of an eyebrow as his fringe dangled in the dirt. He was an accurate thrower of lineout ball, too, picking out the Irish beacons of first Bill Mulcahy and then Willie John McBride, and outside the confines of the tight he loved to run wide and free with the three-quarter herd, racing his flankers to the breakdown and in support play. His exertions in all four corners of the field never left him too tired to speak, though, and he enjoyed a reputation as one of the game's talkers, to officials and opponents alike. Ray McLoughlin, his prop and sometime captain with Ireland, recalls him as 'always in the opposition's face', most memorably in the fourth Test of the rugged 1966 series in New Zealand when he screamed abuse up at Colin Meads after the giant lock had flattened little Dai Watkins with an almighty shake of his Pinetree branches.

But perhaps the try he scored to win the opening Test 11–8 in Sydney best typified his perceptive and energetic style. He threw in, the Lions took the ball and McLoughlin headed off round the front of the lineout to make instant ground and trigger a bout of interpassing among the forwards. The ball then moved into the backs and along the line, across the field to Mike Weston, whose long pass found Kennedy looping round from his initial starting point on the far touchline to catch and score in the corner. Kennedy recalls: 'It was a superb challenge playing against Australia because they were top of the pile then. They had just beaten South Africa in a series so they were effectively the world champions. My main memory is of scoring that try, which was written up as one of the best team tries ever seen. Although I finished it, about 11 people handled in the move before I got the final pass. I remember the celebrations were rather long after the game.'

When the Lions beat the Wallabies by a record 31–0 in the second Test in Brisbane they were being talked about as potentially the best of all Home Unions touring sides. The management seemed to believe the hype and felt the side was good enough to be tinkered with in the crucible of New Zealand. They soon found out that it wasn't. Kennedy says of the experience: 'The achievement we had in Australia was huge. We were unbeaten but when we then went to New Zealand I think our management probably tried to change things when they didn't need changing, and therefore we didn't play our Test team in the matches we should have at the beginning, so we got off to a losing start. At a time when New Zealand were very strong we couldn't afford to do that. Apparently, they decided to give everyone a game, which was the wrong decision, and then there were some tactical errors of putting second rows into the front row to see if we could get more lineout ball. Playing Campbell-Lamerton and Delme Thomas at prop wasn't the best tactic. It was only towards the end of the tour that they went back to picking the strongest side for the hardest matches.'

The All Blacks, on the other hand, would never field anything other than their strongest XVs and if anyone felt they could improve on the incumbent combinations they would have to fight for their chance to prove it. They were also hell-bent on putting the tourists in their place. Lions manager Des O'Brien, the former Ireland number eight, reveals the extent of his party's lack of readiness for the intensity they were about to face when he says: 'I remember being quite shocked when I went to their hotel to wish them good luck on the morning of the Test, and Brian Lochore, who is such a nice man, walked straight past me and ignored me. They had been working up the hype – we hate the Lions so much – since the previous evening.'

New Zealand played a different, tighter, meaner game to the Wallabies and the softer underfoot conditions meant Kennedy had to employ almost all his energies in holding the bigger All Black forwards in the scrum and the maul. He and his team-mates in the pack, including fellow Irishmen McBride, McLoughlin, Noel Murphy and Ronnie Lamont, did just that, but in concentrating their efforts up front the team neglected the backs, who had been rampant in Australia, and paid the ultimate price in a 4–0 series whitewash. Kennedy says of the restrictions he had faced: 'Being lighter and smaller your efficiency is that of an extra wing-forward. On the muckier, heavier grounds of New Zealand, having a lighter forward could be a disadvantage, although both hookers were much the same build. In New Zealand we all had to muck in a lot in the tight, but I don't remember not enjoying my rugby. I thought it was a great challenge taking on their top forwards because technically our scrummaging was miles ahead of theirs. And subsequent to this started the change of the laws relating to the scrum, instigated by New Zealand so we wouldn't get too far ahead of them. We had better technique in the props, in the angles of push we had in the scrum and in taking balls against the head. The scrum was one area of British rugby that was far superior to that of New Zealand rugby, as opposed to their loose play which was far superior to ours.'

And he adds: 'What certainly came out of the tour was that people like McBride, Jim Telfer, certainly Mike Gibson and myself would never let that sort of thing happen again. From that tour was born the successes of 1971 and '74. Even though we were whitewashed we gained exprerience that money cannot buy. I became aware of the need for a tighter type of play than I was used to and of the need to produce a more defined approach to what the team was going to do on the pitch, and this could only be effected by consistent coaching and training from junior up to senior level. You had to have the same style so that you produced the same red apple each time, not had a few green ones coming in. This was something I was able to incorporate into London Irish when I was in charge of them, with the juniors playing like the seniors so that when there was interchange they had no trouble fitting in. Each person in the New Zealand team knew what they were expected to do and had been coached well from an early age.

'There are reports written at the end of each tour but not a lot was ever done about them. I'm afraid that for many years it was more individuals and teams who were intelligent and visionary and brought these ideas into their clubs. A lot of the experience gained on tour was completely wasted by the rugby authorities until about 10 years down the track.'

Kennedy had emerged as the best all-round hooker in the northern hemisphere during the International Championship of 1966 and he was still the acknowledged leader of the European pack when the next Lions tour came round in '68. Ireland's most-capped hooker was again a certainty to make the trip until he injured a knee against France in Paris and had to undergo cartilage surgery. Although he made a quick recovery he did so too late to prove his fitness and had to make do with being a standby reserve for whom the call never came. That disappointment was followed by the far sorrier blow of his omission from the 1971 Lions tour, which came at a time when Ireland was beginning to emerge from the lean years of the 1960s. He says of the period leading up to his Lions recall of '74: 'In the early '70s we beat France twice and England once but Wales and Scotland wouldn't come over. It was a gross shame that we hadn't got a Triple Crown. We shared the championship once before we did finally win it in '74 on the last day, when we didn't play. Those were good times because we had achieved a tremendous spirit in an Irish team who weren't afraid to take on anybody and had a lot of class players. I suppose the regret is that we didn't win the championship in '72 and that the Irish rugby union didn't mark our championship in '74 with anything, not even a dinner.'

Making the Lions party of that championship year went some

way towards softening earlier disappointments, even though Kennedy knew he was going into an even tougher scrummaging environment than he had faced in New Zealand. And whereas in '66 giving the backs more scope to play might have given the Lions a better chance of success, this series would be won and lost up front.

Kennedy says: 'Whenever they played against British teams, New Zealand never put that much emphasis on the set scrum. The set scrum is to start play and then you get your big forwards into the loose. South Africa thought you crushed people in the scrum and when they had done that their backs would run through you. The first time I played South Africa, in Dublin in 1965, I came off the pitch with no skin on my shoulders because they put so much pressure on. But when they lost contact with the outside world they lost their superiority and in 1974 they were totally unprepared for the strength of our forwards. They had been in isolation for a while and had difficulty in assessing their strengths because they had only been playing against invitation sides and in their Currie Cup. They had had a lot of rugby but not against major touring sides. They had huge problems dealing with the packs of forwards we produced on that tour. In addition, we had backs who were superb.'

Outside of the Tests, Kennedy played in ten of the eighteen provincial matches, scoring two tries on the hard grounds that were still to his liking. His most important contribution was made behind the scenes but his front row colleagues could testify that he also still had more to offer on the pitch than merely keeping the man in the Test team honest. Mike Burton, his partner at prop in many of those provincial games, recalls: 'As well as being the team doctor and a real confidant, he was a great hooker and I had one of my greatest ever days with him. We played against the Leopards and in the whole of the game they only struck one of their own heads. [Sandy] Carmichael was the loose-head, I was the tight-head and Kennedy hooked all bar one against the head. They took one scrum right near the end and Ken said to me, 'Well, they've had their break for the day,' and then carried on taking their ball for the rest of the game.'

# 15

## Bouquets and Barbed Wire

THE FIRST TIME FERGUS Slattery faced the Springboks, he did so surrounded by barbed wire. The second time he played against them, with the Lions of 1974, the South Africans only wished that he did, as that was about the only way they could have stopped the firecracker flanker from laying waste to midfields and half-back pairings across the length and breadth of their country. Slattery had won his first Ireland cap four years earlier against the touring Springboks whose controversial visit to Dublin required a ring of steel encircling the Lansdowne Road pitch to deter anti-apartheid protestors from disrupting the match. Had the demonstrators breached the barbed-wire barricades they would have struggled to do as much damage to South African morale as that day's débutant would later manage on their own parched soil. The Dublin student, whose preparations for his big match included taking part in a University College debate on whether the match should take place, did well enough in an 8–8 draw, but his finest hours would come when unleashed on the hard grounds of the republic itself.

Slattery went on to become rugby's most-capped flanker, and arguably its most dangerous one. His main assets were his punishing pace, extraordinary endurance and physical commitment to securing possession and making his contribution in attack. His 65 international appearances for Ireland were stretched across 14 years, a period over which his speed never seemed to slacken and if anything was even sharpened further as a weapon by the ever keener anticipation that experience brought him. Incredibly, he went on both his Lions tours expected only to act as a back-row understudy, although in 1971 he also had arguably the most difficult assignment of all – acting as bodyguard to Sean Lynch, the tour's carouser in chief who Cliff Morgan, then covering the tour for the BBC, remembers having to dissuade from dismantling a telephone booth late one night. Slattery says of his fellow Dubliner: 'In 1971 Sean Lynch was probably the biggest character and the biggest rascal. Carwyn appointed me to keep an eye on Sean, which I did with some success. I was his minder on that tour – so my lips are sealed!'

The future captain of Ireland was only 22 on that New Zealand trip but he made an instant impact on his hosts, who quickly likened him to his great Irish predecessor with the Lions of 1950, Bill McKay. They identified similar traits of speed and bravery in the two men, the latter quality most evident in the brutal battle with Canterbury in which Slattery was the first victim of the notorious 'butchers' on what he condemns as 'a bad day for rugby football'. With his rattled teeth all safely accounted for, the young Lion's progress was rewarded with a place in the third Test team, only for him to be forced out by a sore throat and high temperature on the morning of the match. John Taylor, the man dropped to make way for the rising star, made the most of his reprieve and played well enough to hang on to the jersey for the final rubber.

There were to be no near misses in '74, though, as the fast-talking auctioneer outshone his rival, England great Tony Neary, from the off-on surfaces made for fliers like himself. He played in all four Tests, killing many a Springbok attack at its out-half source, pinballing about the loose and captaining the team against the Proteas, the Lions' first match against a non-white team in South Africa. When the sides were a few minutes late in emerging from the tunnel, more than one wag suggested the new skipper's team-talk must have been to blame.

In more serious matters on field, it remains no coincidence that the back row he formed with Roger Uttley and Mervyn Davies is considered the best the Lions have seen, and the one he graced with Willie Duggan and John O'Driscoll for his country is also rated by many as the finest to appear in the Irish green. Slattery was the common denominator in both. Duggan may have been grateful to find someone who enjoyed the running he so disliked, but says of his open-side flanker: 'With Fergus you had a combination of everything. He was quick around the park, put a lot of pressure on the opposition half-backs and then skipped out to the first or second centres with myself supporting. Then to have the follow-up support of O'Driscoll was unbelievable. There was no one going to get through there.'

'They shall not pass' might have been the motto of Slattery and the Lions in 1974 as they heaped indignity upon indignity on the hapless Springboks in taking the Test series 3–0. The Blackrock College fitness fanatic stood out for his work rate and foraging as well as his sandbagging tackle and ability to pop up as a link man in attack, the last a trait that made him more of a creator than a scorer of tries, even though his delivery of a pass was widely considered to be the least outstanding of his gifts. He managed only three touchdowns in his entire Test career, although in '74 he was denied what would have been by far the most valuable of the lot when South African referee Max Baise failed to award him what looked a clear and fair touchdown in the final seconds of the drawn last Test when victory would have given the tourists a 4–0 whitewash. The official later revealed he had not been able to see that the Lions number seven had grounded the ball properly.

Today Slattery is philosophical about the whole affair, pointing out that one wrong decision had gone the Lions' way earlier in the game and that a draw was the right result for a team that by then had one eye on the airport and the flight home. He says: 'Roger Uttley didn't touch down his try in the first half and in both that case and mine Max Baise was very badly positioned, he couldn't see what was going on. He made a call but was just in the wrong place. At the end of the day the result was probably fair because we didn't play well. I think you could sense it in the build-up; guys were packing their bags and preparing to go home, one or two guys played with injuries and we had lost a little focus. Most of all, we probably paid the price for the euphoria of having won the series and annihilated the Springboks in two of the three previous Tests.

'I don't think you could really say Baise cost us the win but in general on Lions tours, local referees were a big factor. While some would be extremely fair, because of the unfortunate structure of the appointment of Test referees clearly some referees tried to favour themselves to get a Test nomination. The appointments had to be agreed by the touring side as well as the host side, but sometimes there was the feeling that referees would be generous to you to get your vote and then stuff you in the Tests.

'In '71 we lost to Queensland and just sneaked past New South Wales and the penalty counts were something like 21–3 and 15–3 against the Lions, and the Lions were not a bad side. That shows the problems referees posed. Because of the approach of the management, I don't believe that referees had any negative impact in the Tests, but in some of the provincial games we were defied by them.'

Among the local referees' principal failings was their reluctance to offer the Lions any protection from the queue of hard-cases ready to soften them up on behalf of the Springboks. That left the tourists with little option but to defend themselves, which they did with the attitude of getting your retaliation in first and in the safety-in-numbers philosophy of the 99 call. But, looking back, Slattery is at best ambivalent about those tactics, or at least the way they have been portrayed since then. He says: 'The big physical game was the third Test and the infamous call of 99. Personally, I didn't think much of it. South Africa had picked nine forwards in their side – the scrum-half was a number 8 called Gerrie Sonnekus – and they brought in a few known gorillas, so clearly their intent was to physically take us apart. They were doing a good job but, as on both tours, the physical side never buckled.

'The 99 call has been glamorised and I think that's a mistake. I think there are times when you have to stand foursquare and cut out the messing – and in that sense I don't have a problem with it – but I don't think something like that should be glamorised because it's not a good reflection on the game. It shouldn't be necessary in the first place but in '74 it was. It worked because it probably got rid of the problem in an untidy two minutes rather than a drawn-out fracas.' But he adds: 'We had problems in Natal because of that. I remember J.P.R., who was very physical in 1974, having a go at Tommy Bedford and I think he was probably a little over the top. We stood in the middle of the pitch and the match was suspended as the crowd threw oranges on to the pitch because of it. It was quite a sight: the whole field looked like an orange grove.'

Any sore Lions heads that day might still have been throbbing, not so much from the impact of Natal fists but from the series victory party the previous weekend, a knees-up that went on way past dawn and, quite apart from beer and spirits, saw an impressive 65 bottles of champagne consumed to mark a third successive Test match victory. Slattery might well have been one of the least affected, as although he played as hard as he worked he enjoyed an enviable reputation for showing remarkably few after-effects the following day. Those who joined him on the training pitch having shared a bar with him the previous night were to suffer doubly, as his fitness regime was more than vigorous enough for even the clear-headed.

There were precious few in anything less than the most delicate condition after that third Test party, for the occasion was the sweetest any Lions in the republic had known. Slattery says: 'The third Test in South Africa was a big moment because the clean sweep was still there for us and there was no turning back. Victory would mean the tour was over before it was over. In '71 it was down to the last second of the last game. That was a great moment, a great feeling, too, but going 3–0 up in South Africa was more satisfying. I probably enjoyed '74 more than '71 because it was more emphatic. Plus one of the problems I found in New Zealand was that you had played the whole winter here, then you played the whole winter there and after that you came back to another winter here. That's hard going. Some players took a bit of time out but I didn't.'

Slattery loved touring, especially to France for some reason, but that aspect of rugby playing took its toll both physically and financially. The non-stop playing cycle he describes in New Zealand was matched by his schedule around the Lions tour to South Africa and the exertions left him with an illness that cost him his Ireland place for the better part of two seasons. That prompted him to reassess the role of rugby in his life and with touring expenses in 1977 offering little more compensation than the 75 pence per day doled out on his last trip, he turned his back on the Lions for good. He explains: 'After '74 I decided not to play any more Lions tours because they were too long. There were great moments and they were enjoyable to a point but I found them very repetitive and in '74 I decided I had done as much as I could do and went down a gear after that. In '71 I was only just starting work. In '74 I took time off without pay and after that I wasn't interested in doing it again. That was another consideration, but the biggest problem was the boredom. You go round in a circle for six weeks, you have good and bad places to go to and then you have to go round the same track again. But the second time round you know where you are going.'

Like Willie John McBride, Slattery was already one of rugby's biggest names by the time of his second Lions expedition in 1974. The same could not be said of the third Irishman to make the Test team that year, Dick Milliken, the Bangor centre who emerged on the tour from the long shadow of Mike Gibson to become a class international performer in his own right. Like Slattery in '71, Milliken had won his first cap for Ireland just a year before making the Lions party. Unlike Slattery, he got his chance early on and was able to grasp it with both hands, becoming recognised as the most improved player in the party and one of its unsung heroes. A broken ankle suffered soon after returning home would effectively end his international career the following year after just 14 caps.

In another parallel with Slattery's early experiences, Milliken too found himself pondering the political dimension of playing against the representatives of South Africa's reviled apartheid system. Like Slattery, and almost every other player who considered the question, he elected to play and recalls today: 'If I'm very honest it didn't bother me. I bought into the argument then that we were simply rugby players. Before we went out we were cooped up in a hotel for four or five days in London with demonstrations outside. A very famous author, Laurens van der Post, came to talk to us and he was very inspirational, but most of all I remember Tony O'Reilly speaking at the Ireland–England dinner that year. He said, "My advice to anyone given the opportunity to visit South Africa is to go with an open mind and open eyes." That, I think, was the way I approached it. At 23 with someone dangling the carrot of playing with people like that, it's very hard to take the moral viewpoint. I found that particularly true coming from somewhere like Northern Ireland at that time, when there was such strife and unrest. You could say, under the equal opportunities tradition, how could you tolerate what had happened to the majority population over the last 20 years? But you go and you realise there are good white South Africans and there are bad white South Africans, just as there are good black South Africans and bad black South Africans.

'In a funny sort of way, a lot of people thought that the fact that they were beaten really shook their self-belief in some divine right to be superior. In his book Nelson Mandela talks about being in Robben Island listening to the Lions beating the Springboks and that being a sort of inspiration to them. I don't think we appreciated that but I know we worked very hard to extend the hand of friendship to non-whites at every possible opportunity.'

That sort of contact was almost completely off the agenda for many of Milliken's predecessors, such as those of 1962. David Hewitt, another Northern Irish Lion, says of his experiences on that trip: 'I was aware of the situation there but didn't have enough knowledge at that time to ask questions and investigate it. We were subjected to a certain manipulation so we didn't see the worst excesses of apartheid but it was only looking back later that we really realised that.'

More than a decade on, Milliken and co. would get the same treatment and again would not realise right away the control the authorities exerted over the tourists. He says: 'We played a coloured team, a Bantu team, in Port Elizabeth. Quite illegally three or four of us went up into a township that night and met with community leaders and talked at great length with them about what they thought about us coming, what the issues were and what life was like for them. We thought naïvely that it was all arranged without the authorities knowing. We thought we were very clever organising this but we were told by the community leaders we met that the white authorities would know exactly where we were because they had spies in the townships who would report back.

'We weren't any more political than that but we wanted to try and find out what life was really like. We were quite sensitive to the issues but we weren't politically motivated. I would have to say the sheer temptation at 23 years of age to play rugby with such great players in such a fabulous climate, I would have had difficulty turning round and saying I wouldn't go, especially since the decision was taken by the four Unions to go. Once the tour was going you wanted to be part of it.'

When he set off, Milliken had no idea quite how big a part of the tour he would become. With the likes of Mike Gibson unavailable for the full tour, he had an idea that three-quarter places might be up for grabs but in only his second full season of international rugby did not consider himself as a Lions Test team starter. He says: 'Ireland shared the championship in '73 and won it in '74 but no one really emerged. I managed to score a try against Scotland in '74. They should have annihilated us really but we defended pretty well and after the match some of the Irish guys said to me: well, that must have catapulted you into contention. I hadn't really thought of it.

'Even when we made the squad, Ian McGeechan and I felt we were rather the number three and number four centres. There were two distinct pairings of a big one and a little one, the main one being Roy Bergiers and Geoff Evans, the big one being Roy, the little one Geoff, and then the second pair with me being the big one and Ian being the little one. I felt I was behind Roy and Ian felt he was behind Geoff. We both went out thinking we were making the numbers up.'

Milliken had come up through the Ulster scene playing alongside Mike Gibson in the centres, where his hard tackling and straight running made a useful foil for the deft touches of the master alongside him. The Queen's University graduate never considered playing with Gibson anything but a pleasure, yet when given a more senior role with the Lions he grew as a player and particularly as an inventive attacker whose pace, power and angles of running posed all manner of problems for the South African defences, who also struggled to get past his iron hand-off. He settled down quickly but most importantly struck up an instant rapport with McGeechan on and off the field, to the extent that the duo remain the closest of friends more than 25 years on.

Milliken says: 'I got off to a very good start, scored a try in my first match and two tries in my second match. Your confidence just surges then, it's all about self-belief, and whenever we played together we read things in a very similar way, clearly struck up a very good understanding early on and I think that went for us. Also Syd Millar was always very keen on making sure the midfield was defensively sound. Ian McGeechan was a pretty useful tackler for someone his size and I think Syd liked to pick guys who could get the defence right and then build from there.'

But he adds: 'I didn't know whether I was going to be picked until right up to the first Test; I don't think anyone did because there were really no dirt-trackers, everything was mixed up pretty well. I played my first match in the second match of the tour out in South West Africa, which is now Namibia, and I didn't play another Saturday match until the first Test because things were rotated so much. Gareth Edwards, Phil Bennett, J.J. and J.P.R. were probably the only backs who could count on their places with any certainty so there was plenty to play for. And once you get picked for first Test you're in the driving seat.'

That opening international was unlike anything Milliken had experienced, even before the Lions got on to the pitch. He says: 'I don't think that even the management thought we would win, and one of the scariest things for me was in the changing-room before the match. The thing that scared Ian and I most was seeing how nervous Willie John and Gareth Edwards were. They kept saying things like, guys you don't know what you're in for here. I played for Willie John with Ulster and Ireland so I knew him pretty well and this was a very nervous Willie John McBride and it was scary to see him so nervous.'

A 12–3 victory settled the butterflies, with Milliken's crash-tackling helping to keep the Lions' try-line intact, but his finest moment came in the next Test in Pretoria. Milliken scored six fine tries in his 13 appearances, including a crucial one against Transvaal created by a clever dummy in what was his best performance of the tour. More satisfying, though, was the score with which he rounded off the record 28–9 win at Loftus Versveld – even if not everyone saw it the same way. Gareth Edwards mounted a blindside break and found Milliken in support for the powerful Bangor man to bowl over the first would-be tackler and then bash his way through two more defenders to go over at the corner flag. He says of the moment: 'I remember being very hurt when John Reason of the *Daily Telegraph* said that Jan Ellis had more or less carried me over the line. I've seen the footage of it and I thought it was actually quite a good try. I had quite a bit of running to do but because I had become quicker and stronger on tour I was able to get in at the corner. That was just a great day. We had played a dour match in the first Test and were told once we got up to the high veld we would really find out what we were made of. To be part of that was unbelievable, to come out of that pressure you felt something a little bit special was emerging here, although we weren't quite sure what.

'And as we marched on the aura around us got bigger and bigger, adding to the psychology of it all. I was talking to a guy called Gerald Bosch [Springbok stand-off] after the second Test and he just couldn't hack it, he was intimidated, kind of thought these Lions were incredible, people like McBride, Slattery. They were just intimidated.'

Slattery's pace around the field meant that he and Milliken met up quite frequently in open play, where the flanker remembers the centre as 'the strong man we needed in midfield because we had Phil Bennett at fly-half' and he in turn recalls his colleague as being 'so quick over the ground that whenever you made a half-break he would be there on your shoulder'.

Those were two of the strengths that so scared the Springboks, but Slattery believes that the thing their hosts found most dispiriting was the fact that there were plenty more where they came from. Where South Africa had little strength in depth to turn to when the wheels fell off their wagon, the Lions had talent to spare in every position. And in that, he says, they laid down the blueprint for success for all later Lions to try to follow. He says: 'I think the day of the Test side is gone. The team is the full party now and you will only win if you have good players throughout, a full squad of players who are good enough to play in a Test. The strength of the '71 and '74 tours was that almost all the players could have played in the Test side. In 1974 Alan Old at fly-half looked like he was going to get the nod for the first Test but he got very badly injured and Phil Bennett played all four Tests. Mike Gibson was only available to come out as a replacement but when he did, Dick Milliken and Ian McGeechan kept a talent that special out of the team. That underlines the strength of the squad.'

# 16

## CIGARETTES AND ALCOHOL

SOMETHING WAS BADLY WRONG. Willie Duggan had not smoked a cigarette in eight weeks and had missed only four nights of training all season, while an appointment to speak with Moss Keane at 8.30 a.m. was to catch him at the start of his day rather than the end of his evening. 'We're coming to terms with our own mortality,' laughs Keane at the relative slowing down in the lifestyles of Irish rugby's most celebrated tourists. Happily, it is still possible to meet both men in a pub and Duggan's new-found dedication to training only comes now he no longer has to do it himself, instead taking the role of tracksuited poacher turned gamekeeper castigating the slackers from the sidelines at Kilkenny. The forsaking of the cigarettes is more of a surprise, though, as the dangling fag was as essential to his off-field style as a comb was superfluous. But looking on the bright side, he says, giving up the smokes has meant he doesn't get hangovers any more.

Cold sweats and splitting headaches were what Willie and Moss tended to leave their opponents with before they even reached the bar throughout the late '70s and early '80s. The pair toured New Zealand with the Lions in 1977, with Duggan excelling in all four Tests, although Keane's contribution was constricted by the effects of concussion that limited him to just one international. Only his on-field activities were curtailed, mind you, as off the pitch he lived up to his reputation as the life and lungs of the party, leaving a trail of empty beer crates, broken hotel doors and false fire alarms behind him as he wrought havoc across the country. Not for nothing did his team-mates christen him 'Rent-a-Storm'.

Both men played with a similar sort of elemental force and produced probably the best rugby of their career through their association with the Lions, Duggan on the 1977 tour itself, Keane in the years immediately following it. According to his contemporaries, this was the closest Duggan ever got to regular training and the effect was both immediate and far-reaching. Keane, meanwhile, fell ill on his return and was ordered off the booze by his doctor. Allan Martin, his first Test partner in the Lions second row, recalls: 'He had to stop drinking completely. That meant he came down in weight and for two years after he was a revelation. In every game he played he had more energy and was galloping all over the pitch. He was always more of a support forward than a lineout jumper so that made his game even better.'

Duggan was simply unique, an immense presence at the back of whichever scrum he packed down in, whether for Blackrock College, Leinster, Ireland or the Lions. Perhaps Keane sums him up best when he says: 'Willie was a very good rugby player and he was also an enigma. He never believed in training and his brain was unreal: he had a tremendous sense of space and time. A straight line might not always be the shortest route between two points for him. I think he also appreciated a lot the fact that there were only two phases of play then; five might have stretched him a bit!

The massive number eight with the coal-scuttle hands became his country's most capped player in his position through his dominance of the back of the lineout and the defence-scattering charges that were his hallmark in the loose. He may not have been the fastest of all breakaways – he was allegedly once seen mysteriously stamping on the pitch and explained himself by saying, 'I'm trying to get rid of this snail that's been following me around all game' – but a physical courage bordering on suicidal recklessness made his dishevelled figure the most welcome of all those arriving at a ruck or maul.

Donal Lenihan, the former Ireland captain and manager of the 2001 Lions team, rates Duggan, at one time the world's most capped number eight, as the best all-round forward he ever played with, 'particularly in terms of his sheer ruggedness and his ability to take it as well as give it', while others single out his physical and mental toughness as the attributes that set him apart. The electrician's willingness to play through the pain barrier was startling and became most evident on tour, where the games came thick and fast and team-mates could see the way he shrugged off the batterings he took at the closest of quarters. In 1977, marked out as the danger man of the Lions pack almost straight away, he took a vicious kicking in the game against Manawatu/Horowhenui yet stayed on to help mount a desperate fightback to save a match that appeared lost; then he turned out against the might of Otago for another immense forward test just four days later. No other member of the pack could beat his record of playing in 16 of the 25 matches in New Zealand and he made the bulk of those appearances while nursing a heavily strapped back problem that would pain, if not hamper, him throughout his career. Ollie Campbell recalls: 'In Australia in '79 his back was so bad that he was literally sleeping on the floor and struggling from match to match. I wouldn't say training session to training session because it would be a complete insult to even suggest that Willie went to a training session. He would play a match and basically be flat on his back until he would get up and play the next match. He was a genuinely hard man, one of those sort of players who you didn't really appreciate until he wasn't there.'

That was a rare event in itself, either in the starting line-up or in the thick of the fiercest action once the whistle blew. Duggan won his 41 Ireland caps – all but two at number eight – in ten seasons, over which he missed just seven internationals, a remarkable record for someone who put himself in positions where serious injury looked more of a certainty than a risk. On tour with the Lions, the New Zealanders paid him the compliment of comparison with the great, whole-hearted Irish back rower Bill McKay, who toured there with Karl Mullen's side in 1950, while the Maori All Blacks paid him another one by punching him, their only means of halting the tearaway tourist, into the middle of the following week. Duggan could always look after himself when the gloves were off and in the season before the tour he and Geoff Wheel had become the first players to be sent off in the Five Nations after a sparring session in Cardiff. But on this occasion at Eden Park the Maori managed to remove him from the equation without sacrificing one of their own players in exchange. Even that backfired, though, as Duggan's departure sparked one of the great comebacks, led by his enraged countrymen Keane, Mike Gibson and Phil Orr. Keane recalls: 'There were only a few Irish guys on the trip but I think we did our bit, certainly that day. New Zealand Maori were nearly out of sight at 19–6 early in the second half but we came back and won it, which was one of the biggest turnarounds of all time. Duggan got a belt and got carried off and I think that spurred us on.'

Two whirlwind spells of two tries in three minutes turned the tide against a side featuring the likes of Sid Going and All Blacks captain

Tane Norton, with Gibson and Orr among the try-scorers. Neither man had the happiest of tours, with Gibson, then 34 but still in his pomp, failing to make the Test team at all. Indifferent early form and a later hamstring injury were ostensibly responsible, but Duggan believes other factors were in play. He says: 'Something happened there on that tour between the management and Mike Gibson. In my opinion, Mike should have been on the Test sides.

Duggan holds Orr, who was considered unlucky to lose his place after the Lions' narrow defeat in the first Test at Wellington, in similarly high regard. He says: 'During that period, Ireland could not go out on an international field without Philip. The only thing I knew about front-row play was which prop was under pressure because it would all come back to me, and it rarely came back from his side.'

The deep-thinking Old Wesley loose-head, who was at one time the world's most capped prop and whose 58 caps are still an Irish record, was one of the finest technical scrummagers in the game at the time, but he lost his place to Fran Cotton on the grounds that the Englishman, who had two inches in height and a full stone in weight over Orr, offered more ball-winning options at the front of a lineout which was under severe pressure from the All Blacks. Kent Lambert, the Manawatu tight-head who would turn to rugby league at the end of the series, had also been one of the few players in Tests to match the massive Irishman in the tight but ironically was forced out of the second rubber with appendicitis, giving Cotton an easier ride in the front row and so allowing him to devote more energy to his vital lineout duties.

Orr, whose mathematical mind earned him the duty of drawing up room-sharing rotas on the tour – and with it the pleas to avoid Duggan's notorious snoring – took his relegation to the bench with equanimity but, like all the tourists, found the appalling New Zealand winter and the locals' apparent interest in nothing other than rugby increasingly dispiriting. For the man whose 49 consecutive Ireland appearances left him just one short of Sandy Carmichael's world record, a single word sums up the 1977 tour: rain. He says: 'It just rained all the time and you couldn't really get out, which wasn't much fun. It was the tour of the famous Fran Cotton mudbath photograph against the Junior All Blacks in Wellington. He was one in the lineout, I was three and in a matching condition.

'We also didn't see a great deal of New Zealand and there was much too much rugby. It would be nice to go and see New Zealand properly. I'm not a rugby fanatic and I like to get away from it but one of the problems of being on a Lions tour is that it is difficult to do that. It's relentless and the intensity of interest is incredible. I remember in one town waking up in the morning and switching on the radio – it was the morning of the match – to find that the station which was broadcasting was doing so live from the breakfast in our hotel. When you wake up on the morning of a match the last thing you want to do is be interviewed over your cornflakes. So everyone ordered breakfast in bed, which didn't go down too well with the public, but you can understand why we did it. That sort of pressure you didn't need.'

Orr and co. responded by turning the screw themselves in a scrum that immediately shaped up to be more than a match for anything the New Zealanders could throw at it and that was a key factor in building a provincial record blemished only by a single defeat. Duggan says of their might: 'It's my view New Zealand have never seen a pack of forwards like that, before or since. The eight guys were so physical but we all had rugby skills. We were able to match them up front for strength, aggression and will to win. It was the first time in New Zealand history that they had to use a three-man scrum at one point. When I saw it, to be honest I didn't know what to do about it. Foolishly I went into the scrum and the ball went out so fast it was away down the blindside and I had to get back to retrieve it. I knew what to do the second time, though.'

Duggan proved a major thorn in his opponents' side in New Zealand, as well as damaging his own when he fell on top of Phil Bennett in the first Test and badly damaged the out-half's shoulder. The All Blacks won that match 16–12 and owed much to their ploy of using Lawrie Knight and Ian Kirkpatrick to double-team Duggan at the back of the lineout and so hinder the quality of ball he could produce. Leaving out Derek Quinnell meant the Lions were unable to give the Blackrock eighth man a level playing field on which to compete, but once he was given the Welshman's support in the second match, the tables were turned as the Lions won 13–9 to level the series with Duggan a major force in both the lineout and the fierce mauls that established the tourists' superiority. The win was literally hard fought, with the All Blacks – by their own later admission 'out to get anything in red' – instigating the bulk of the violence that punctuated the contest and culminated in a mass brawl after Bennett, the recipient of late hits and cheap shots all afternoon, had been flattened long after the ball had gone by flanker Kevin Eveleigh. Duggan, along with Bill Beaumont and Gordon Brown, had been warned beforehand by pack leader Terry Cobner that the match would be won and lost in the lineout and the blame for defeat would be laid squarely at their door, and he responded with real vigour, relishing the game more and more the harder it got. He says of the action: 'The second Test was the most physical game of rugby I have ever played in; a real humdinger of a game. It was a game we had to win and when I say it was physical, it came to fisticuffs and whatever had to be done was done. It was what I would call a good old-fashioned game of rugby where the referee didn't get involved. I believe there shouldn't be a referee on the field. Let the lads sort it out themselves.'

New Zealand won the third Test easily, although Duggan was at least compensated with a try that rewarded his anticipation when he latched on to scrum-half Brynmor Williams's blindside break and muscled his way across the line. He had also demonstrated his eye for an opening in creating a clever try for J.J. Williams against Canterbury when he took advantage of the home team's delay in getting a replacement on for flanker Alex Wylie by exploiting the gap on the side of the scrum his departure had left. The All Blacks clinched the series in a desperately close final rubber, where Duggan was inches from glory in the dying moments as the Lions battered away to overturn their 10–9 deficit, being held up on the line as he exploded off the back of a scrum close in. He says of the epic confrontations: 'The first Test they won by an interception by Grant Batty, the second Test we won, and in the third Test we were annihilated. When I say that I mean they got a try in less than a minute and things went downhill from there. And in the fourth Test I got over in the last minute but couldn't get the ball down. Just before that they had scored a runaway try with a high kick and a mistake by two of our backs. Basically the whole Test series hinged on an interception and a silly mistake.'

Duggan had already put down a marker in New Zealand as he came of age with Ireland there in 1976, but really made his name with the 1977 Lions. By the end of his career he would also be as well known for his inimitable style as much as for his exploits in the heart of battle. All his contemporaries remember him with a cigarette in one hand and a beer in the other and as an unkempt tourist with a pathological dislike of training. Duggan says, 'I've heard all the things I did in my life and I wish I had done half of them,' but the most popular images, he has to admit, are not too far off the mark. David Irwin, the Ireland and Lions centre, says of his team-mate: 'If you could have got him fit he would have been the best number in the world, but his problem was that he didn't like to train.'

Duggan's main concession to healthy living was eating up to half a dozen raw eggs on the morning of a match, a habit he shared with Keane, who also swore by a large range of herbal medicines. But he admits: 'The main benefit of these things is between the ears. It's like fitness: if you think you're fit, you are fit. I always had the philosophy that if you had a horse running in the Derby would you take it out on the Thursday and beat it up for two hours, do the same thing on the Friday and expect it to win the race on the Saturday?

'If I was picking an Irish team, using the Duggan psychology, I would bring the 30 players out for a night and make sure they were well pissed before they went to bed at three in the morning. I would then have them up at eight, train the bejaysus out of them and then you would know who would last 80 minutes in an international. Fergus Slattery and John O'Driscoll would be well able to achieve that level.'

Some of Duggan's coaches went to even more extraordinary lengths to get him on to the training pitch, let alone actually run round it. Ollie Campbell says of his philosophy: 'Willie Duggan's often-quoted attitude to training was that it took the edge off his game. In Blackrock years ago they were absolutely fed up with Willie not turning up for training so the captain, God bless him, organised a coach for the whole team and they would drive down to Kilkenny and hold the training session there. You have one guess as to who did not make it to the training session. He slept in.'

Even when Willie did make it down to the ground, some of his team-mates often wondered if it had been worth it, although at least it usually meant they didn't have to worry about coming last in the exercises. Allan Martin remembers one particular occasion from the '77 Lions tour: 'Willie would sleep all day and be up all night. We stopped off on the way to Whangarei or somewhere and Willie of course had been up all night. He didn't really come to life before one in the afternoon and we were training quite a way before that. We were all there and ready when suddenly he appeared on the field wearing a Lions T-shirt he had tried to iron and which now looked like a rag with a big brown triangle burned into the back of it. He had a knotted hankie on his head, no socks and had left his boots at the hotel so was wearing some pair of Adidas running shoes he'd got from somewhere. I don't think the locals could believe it. This was the Lions, this was supposed to be a very professional outfit with everyone training hard. Then Willie appeared . . .'

In fairness, Duggan probably did not have much choice of kit that day. Martin recalls: 'Willie came on tour with just one bag; everyone else had two or three suitcases. We got to the hotel and he emptied his bag onto the bed. It contained one shirt, one tie, one pair of pants, one pair of shoes and one pair of socks. That was his tour kit for four months.'

That policy of sticking only to the bare essentials – which extended reputedly to not combing his hair for the entire length of a tour – left plenty of room for supplies of the cigarettes he drew on right up until he stepped onto the field. Duggan once famously asked a match official to hold his lighted cigarette as they stood in the tunnel before an international and then ran on to the pitch leaving him to face the world with a fag on the go, while Ollie Campbell remembers being able to identify which dressing-room toilet cubicle he was occupying by the cloud of smoke billowing over the door. Duggan explains: 'I always smoked before I went out because I was of a nervous disposition. I had to try to relax. Wouldn't it be marvellous playing today, you could have three cigarettes at half-time.'

Campbell also remembers Duggan once finding something else to distract him in the tense final moments before a big game in Dublin, although not everything was as it initially seemed. He recounts: 'At Lansdowne Road I went to the toilets about half an hour before the game and there is Willie at the basin, seemingly cleaning his boots. Willie cleaning his boots just before an international? What's going on? Willie was so insulted that I would have thought he was cleaning his boots that he went to no end of trouble to absolutely make it crystal clear that he was not cleaning his boots. The previous international we had played two weeks earlier had been in very bad, muddy conditions, and five minutes previously had been the first time since that match Willie had taken his boots out of the plastic bag he carried them in. And they had hardened, all caked in mud and he couldn't get his feet into them. So he was simply softening his boots so he could get his feet into them.'

If Duggan was to be surpassed as a character among the Irish Lions of his age, there was only one man to do it: Maurice Ignatius Keane, Moss for short and, in Ollie Campbell's words, 'probably the most popular Irish rugby player of all time. At his surprise fiftieth birthday party at Lansdowne about 200 invitations went out and 400 people turned up. That's how popular he is; an incredible character and competitor, and no dumb Kerryman either. He's a very shrewd, highly intelligent man. There isn't a mean bone in his body and he is just a funny man. People would just do anything for him. He's a genuine living legend. If he heard you say that he would cringe but it's true.'

Moss wasn't necessarily the favourite of all the people all the time, though. David Irwin recalls how he and the rest of the backs used to dread the Friday night before home internationals when Keane would drag the entire team round to Sean Lynch's bar off St Stephen's Green for 'a few pints', as they tried to escape with just the one while Moss sank his usual six or seven. And Donal Lenihan believes that while not everything said about Moss and Willie was always strictly true, so too were some of the things they used to say about themselves, particularly the fear of flying that meant they had to visit the airport bar whether they liked it or not. He says: 'The greatest excuse Moss and Willie ever had was when they dreamed up the idea that they were bad travellers and hated flying, so everywhere we went it was taken for granted that they would have to have five or six pints beforehand or they wouldn't be able to travel. I think their advice was that any young player should get a fear of flying in early if he wanted to enjoy himself.'

However, others, including Keane himself, insist it was genuine. Allan Martin claims that in dashing to the airport on receiving his last-minute Lions call in 1977, Moss became so nervous that he crashed his car and left a message for his mother saying 'The car's at the airport, it's written off, see you in four months.' Keane himself says he has now conquered his fear but adds that he and Duggan were not helped by several touring incidents that left even the calmer travellers among the party keen to go by bus in future. He says of one occasion on that Lions tour: 'The pilot on the flight from Hamilton, in Waikato, did a figure of eight over the top of the pitch but without telling anyone what he was going to do. I was sitting beside Ian McGeechan, who knew more about flying than most of us, and he thought the plane was in trouble. They had had a close call with a flock of birds in 1974 and McGeechan thought the same thing was happening again. So you can imagine what the likes of Willie and I were like. When we arrived in Wellington, Willie threw a bottle at the pilot. He wasn't too impressed.'

Keane was initially only on standby for the tour, as he had been in 1974, but was called into the squad just days before they were due to meet up after Geoff Wheel was ruled out by a medical. The tour hierarchy then got their first taste of the Keane sense of humour when they rang with the good news. Ronnie Dawson had tipped him off about his selection minutes earlier so Moss was able to take the exciting news of his surprise inclusion with a deadpan, 'Oh yes. So what else is new?'

The civil servant from the Department of Agriculture had to use his entire annual holiday allocation to go on the tour and then take unpaid leave for the other ten weeks of its duration, but was a fine addition to the party. He says of his arrival: 'It was a surprise because I was a sub in '74 and I wasn't needed then so I presumed it would be the same this time. Certainly I didn't expect to get called so early. I actually sent a card to Geoff Wheel's doctor thanking him very much for finding something wrong with his heart.'

Keane had a well-earned reputation as one of Ireland's most big-hearted players, admired by all for his commitment to his team-mates on and off the field. If his club Lansdowne had a game on the Sunday after an international Keane would invariably turn out even if he had been playing for his country the previous day. He didn't win 52 caps, appear in a Test for the Lions, help Ireland to a Triple Crown and play a leading role in Munster's finest hour, the 1978 defeat of the All Blacks at Thomond Park, by simple heart, however. Keane could also play a bit. Tough, durable and a handful in the scrum and lineout, he proved himself by appearing in six of the Lions' first nine games leading up to the first Test, before a punch in the tourists' only non-Test defeat knocked the middle out of his trip. Following the first international he played in only three of the next 11 matches, although he did end up with a total of 12 games and one try to his name. His appearance in that first Test was as much a tribute to his commitment as to his ability, as he now admits. 'I shouldn't have played,' he says. 'On the Tuesday before the Test we played against New Zealand Universities and I was taken off with concussion. Nowadays you have to have three weeks out for concussion; back then I had four days. So I can't really remember too much about the Test itself. After that I had two and a half weeks out and it tore the heart out of the tour for me, really. I played seven games out of the first ten and then drifted off, not playing for the two and a half weeks. So it was good and bad. Billy Beaumont came over as a replacement for Nigel Horton and he got the other three Tests after that.'

Even on the sidelines, though, Moss proved almost as valuable to the side, with his antics keeping spirits up on what became one of the most depressing of all Lions tours, beset by foul weather, non-stop abuse from the home crowds and levels of press hostility never seen before. As Duggan says of his friend: 'Moss was fantastic fun. He would create fun in the most desperate situations.' Willie also reckons that there were so many players from Wales on that tour that he came home with a Welsh accent, but there was little chance of the Welshmen picking up Keane's broad Kerry tones in return. Literally, as Allan Martin recalls, saying: 'Moss is fabulous company once you begin to understand what he's saying. Even with four months on tour with him, it wasn't until the last week that I could work out what he said.'

And he adds: 'No one could live with him when it came to drinking. One Easter he was invited on tour to France with Crawshay's Welsh. Now Crawshay's tours are very, very sociable, and so is Moss. He played the first game but got a bit of a knock which he knew would keep him out of the other two, so he went on a bit of a binge. The only problem was that he was such a star they asked him to kick off in the next game. So he goes out onto this mudheap of a pitch in his best, brown, pin-striped suit, takes a swing at the ball and slips. His legs went straight up in the air and he landed flat on his back in a huge puddle. He didn't bother changing, though; he just went off and carried on.'

Both Keane and Duggan could always be relied upon to carry on regardless, whatever the circumstances, both on and off the pitch. The last word, as ever, should go to Willie, who speaks for both men when he says: 'I think I was always known as a good tourist. I always tried to enjoy myself in victory or defeat.'

# 17

## OLLIE IN WONDERLAND

AT FIRST GLANCE it does not make for an obvious career highlight: a series in which the Lions are whitewashed 4–0 for only the second time in their history; in which their captain is subjected to relentless character assassination by his own press; and one in which you operate on starvation rations as far as goalkicking opportunities are concerned; finish one Test match as a borderline hypothermia case; and play through the pain barrier with serious injuries that will end your career prematurely the following season at the age of just 30. Yet for Ollie Campbell, to be a Lion in New Zealand in 1983 was to be in rugby heaven.

Campbell did not play his best rugby in the Land of the Long White Cloud. He did not break any points scoring records there, but when he was forced to retire less than 12 months later he could do so a happy man, having lived out his childhood fantasies. As a schoolboy at Belvedere College, his fields of dreams were much further than a bus ride to Lansdowne Road away; they lay on the other side of the world. 'The first international my dad brought me to was Ireland against the All Blacks in Lansdowne Road in December 1963, when I was nine, and New Zealand hammered Ireland 6–5 with Don Clarke, Kelvin Tremain, Colin Meads, Stan Meads, all that sort of ilk. And in many ways I've had a love affair with New Zealand rugby ever since. I would have a couple of hundred books here and I would say 85 to 90 per cent of them are books on New Zealand. I grew up reading about New Zealand tourists, about New Zealand players, about Invercargill, about Dunedin, about Otago and its rucking, about Christchurch and Canterbury and Auckland and Eden Park, and windy Wellington and Athletic Park. I just grew up submerging myself and if put to a test I would probably know more about New Zealand rugby history, sketchy as it would be, than I would about Ireland rugby history.

'So, disappointing as the tour was, to be in these places, to be playing in places like Pukekohe, that you had only ever read about before, to be in the Invercargills, the Aucklands, the Wellingtons, the Christchurches, the Dunedins, as cities and as rugby grounds, it was a romantic tour for me in that sense. It obviously would have made it all the more romantic had we actually been playing better but in every other respect it was Ollie in wonderland.'

When Campbell hung up his boots in 1984 it was widely believed that the rigours of the New Zealand tour had exhausted him and contributed heavily to the sudden nature of his international demise, a suggestion he is quick to dismiss. 'I wasn't tired,' he says, 'I was energised by what I had experienced in New Zealand. Their rugby was different from anything I had experienced before; at times, particularly in the second and final Tests, it was just wave after wave after wave. It was like standing on the beach trying to keep the tide back; eventually it just goes over you.

'New Zealand was everything I had imagined it to be. My whole rugby, in terms of the way I wanted to play, was changed. It was the totality of the way New Zealand played rugby, it was almost not forwards and backs as traditionally we would have. And in the biting wind and rain in Dunedin in the third Test, at one stage in getting up off the ground having made an attempt at making a tackle, I heard the forwards talking among themselves, criticising each other and saying the backs cannot do anything with that sort of ball. The ball is in play and here you have the All Black forwards chatting amongst themselves as they are running in support, "The backs cannot do anything with that ball, we've got to do better." This was foreign. It's right but it was such an education. A real eye-opener.'

And he adds: 'The hamstring problem I had there was the beginning of the end for me and that's why it was so frustrating that the end of my career was only just around the corner, because I felt that I really had just about reached my peak. I think I probably had three or four years of my best rugby ahead because of the experience of New Zealand. And I know in a number of matches I played after that the energy I had in playing and in encouraging teams not to constantly set up rucks and mauls, my whole game I felt, went up two or three notches. Unfortunately, it never really got the chance to be proved in terms of games because after that I really was beginning to struggle with the hamstrings and eventually I couldn't even do a warm-up lap without pulling them.'

Frustratingly, Campbell will forever associate the torn hamstrings that truncated his glittering career with his Lions experience. Not with any sense of resentment that they cut him down in his prime but rather that they prevented him from making the touring contribution he would have liked and which could have tipped the balance the Lions' way. He says: 'Regrettably, my Lions memories are of what might have been: frustratingly close to reasonably successful tours but in actual fact two unsuccessful tours. One incident probably summed up my Lions career. After I had been injured in South Africa in 1980 I came on as a replacement in the second Test and within about two minutes we had a penalty on about the 22, five yards in from the left touch-line. I struck it absolutely beautifully and it just shaved the outside of the post. That probably said it all, that I was so close to being successful yet at the end it just slipped through the fingers like sand.'

Campbell's best years for Ireland came between his two Lions tours when he was the points-scoring machine at the heart of the teams that won the Five Nations championship and Triple Crown in 1982 and shared the championship with France the following year, smashing the previous goalkicking records along the way. His fame with the boot, however, masked the quality of his all-round game, the solidity of his tackling, the soundness of his touch-kicking, his underrated ability as a runner with the ball and the timing of his passing, the last the skill that created so many chances for his three-quarters and which was instrumental in winning him the long-running selection debate over whether he or the mercurial Tony Ward should wear the out-half's jersey. Donal Lenihan, who won the deceptively fragile-looking number ten priceless possession in the Irish lineout in those years, says of his value: 'Ollie Campbell was outstanding in every way. Unusually for a number 10 he thrived on defence and just loved tackling fellows. You rarely get that in out-halfs, especially in those days. Without doubt he was the reason Ireland were as successful as they were in the early '80s.'

Perhaps even better placed to judge were the men in the centres, represented by David Irwin who says of the Ward–Campbell question: 'If you put me on the spot I preferred to play outside Ollie, just because of his all-round game. For a charity match, maybe Wardy, but otherwise Ollie. Ollie would be more of a team pleaser, Wardy would be more of a crowd pleaser. That's probably unfair because there was only a slight difference between them, but as a centre you would find that Wardy would jink past ten players and give you the ball and you would get emptied. With Ollie you knew as a centre that he would not give you the ball unless you had time to do something with it. There were never any hospital passes and you always had confidence in him to make the right decisions. He was a true professional in an amateur age. As an out-half he had everything. He could place-kick, he could punt, he moved the ball well, he could tackle, he could run, he was very aware of what his options were. But Ollie was so gentlemanly about the whole thing, there were no sour grapes, whoever played.'

In fact, the affair became something of a running joke to the men involved as it took on almost absurd proportions and followed them right across the globe, to Australia with Ireland and South Africa with the Lions. The debate once saw Campbell accused of not passing to Ward when they lined up together at out-half and inside centre respectively in an Old Belvedere centenary match, and long after they had retired a joke went round that Ollie was trying to steal Tony's girlfriend after he was spotted dining with her father, a well-known rugby man. Campbell had been first to win his cap but disappeared without trace after a nightmare début against the Wallabies in 1976. Ward made an instant impact when given his chance in 1978 and the star status he was quickly afforded – including coronation as European player of the year – ensured that the return of Campbell on tour to Australia the following year would split opinion right down the middle. The red-haired goal-kicker admits he is still in debt to coach Noel Murphy for taking what was a massive gamble in throwing him into the team for the first Test against Australia in Brisbane. At the time, though, he did not immediately comprehend that he was back at number 10. He says: 'My memory of it is simply that the team was read out. I had no warning that I was chosen at out-half other than from Tony Ward, but even then I didn't realise what he was saying to me at the time. We had driven down from Brisbane to Surfers' Paradise and a school there where the team was going to be announced, and in the dressing-room at this school where we were togging out, literally within about 30 seconds of the team being announced by Jack Coffey, the manager, Tony Ward just sidled up to me and whispered, "Congratulations, you're in." Now it had never crossed my mind that I would be in instead of Tony because there had been a fair bit of chat that I might get in at centre. So all I waited for was confirmation of hearing my name being read out. I couldn't have told you the name before, the name after, any other name, just confirmation of mine. I did not know I was in instead of Tony until the training session. My immediate presumption was that I was in at centre and it was only when we actually started running the back line that I realised.'

Campbell repaid that faith by setting new Irish points-scoring records as the tourists pulled off a remarkable 2–0 series win. His place in the side was cemented and when Murphy was appointed coach to the Lions of 1980, there was little doubt as to who would be his first choice at outside-half. Of course, where the Campbell–Ward saga was concerned, nothing was ever that straightforward. That tour was probably the worst for injuries the Lions have ever known and Campbell was among the first onto the casualty list. He says: 'I had hamstring trouble from the first couple of training sessions, so I wasn't available for the first two games. That was probably the beginning of the problem that cut my career short. Once I got them right I didn't have any trouble with them for a year or two but at the time I had a big problem. I don't know what initially caused it but I know what exacerbated it – the actual treatment I got. I got all the wrong treatment. The one thing you don't do with hamstrings is stretch them. You might when it's a well heated stretch to the point of pain but the advice I was given was to stretch it as much as I could.

'Noel then came to me a couple of days before the third match, against Natal, and said that really, if I wasn't fit to play in this match they would have to consider sending for a replacement and me going home. So what choice did I have? I played. In the dressing-room before the match I couldn't touch my toes but somehow managed to get through the game – I've no idea how – and even, if I may say, set up the winning try. It was 15–15 going to full-time, I made a bit of a break and we scored a try. But I also made probably the jammiest place-kick of my career, and simply because of my hamstrings. The ball did not get off the ground. It was very embarrassing. I got through it but the next day, because of all the treatment I had been given and all the wrong advice in terms of stretching and stretching and stretching and stretching, all the blood had actually congealed at the back of my knee. It was like a wooden leg. Somehow I was kept on and it actually healed quite quickly but I missed another fortnight to three weeks.'

That meant Campbell would not be ready for the first Test, and the first of the eight replacements the tour would call upon began to fly out. Among them, of course, was Tony Ward. The Garryowen out-half made as instant an impact as his rival had in Australia 12 months earlier and straight away the Irish debate was back on again. Campbell winces jokingly at the memory: 'I have to be honest, at that stage he was the one guy I particularly did not want to see, having sort of seen him off the previous year. But suddenly Wardie is being flown down. And he plays the first Test, and he scores a record number of points. I'm like, "Ah, let me go home."'

But he adds: 'I think I faked it pretty well, though. I managed to give him a pretty warm welcome, but if only he knew! And then, my God, for the sake of the cause, going out and being Wardie's ball boy for his kicking practice the day before the first Test. No greater sacrifice and all that! And Wardie actually pulled a thigh muscle in that session and I was hoping against hope it wasn't too trivial, but unfortunately it was. The next day, 18 points later, I'm thinking, "Ah, why don't I just get out of here, take my hamstrings and go home?" Yes, there were other outside-halfs it would have been more pleasant to have seen at that stage, definitely.'

Gareth Davies was given the nod for the second Test but the injury jinx struck again and Campbell got on for the final 15 minutes, although that early missed penalty meant the Test was the only one of his appearances in which he did not score. As a goal-kicker under the pressure of joining a Test match still in the balance, though, he was not given a welcome calculated to ease the nerves. He says: 'I remember coming on in that second Test in Bloemfontein, it's 15–16 with about 15 minutes to go. This is very tight stuff, we're 1–0 down in the series and I come on for my first Lions Test match. So what sort of thing would you expect from the first centre, Ray Gravell? Good luck, well done, give it to me, I'll take it up, just get it down in their half? Anything in that sort of vein you would think. But what Grav actually said was: "Ollie, how do you think I'm playing? Do you think I'm playing well enough to get selected for the third Test?"'

'On another occasion, he used to room with John O'Driscoll a lot, and he woke up one morning and asked John how he had slept. Not how John had slept, but how he, Ray, had slept! It was all a great introduction to the whole raison d'être of the Lions. Previously, Ray Gravell was someone that you see on the TV, that you play against. He's six foot one and he's fourteen and a half stone, he's strong, physical, fast. Phew, this guy knows no fear, and that's when you are playing against him. It's only when you are touring with him that you see the human side. The same guy was actually very unsure of himself. He was so emotional before games. Grav used to play tapes of a well-known Welsh nationalist singer and before matches he would be going round the dressing-room singing at the top of his voice all these Welsh songs. He would get sick or he would make himself sick before every match. The national anthems are played and he has tears rolling down his face. Before we played Northern Transvaal – the fifth Test – Ray Gravell cannot find his gumshield so he is not playing. So while he is making himself sick in the toilets and singing Welsh nationalist songs, the other 14 Lions are searching bags, looking into shoes for his gumshield. We eventually found it and Ray was playing again but until then he was not playing. So the Ray Gravell you saw playing for Wales in Cardiff Arms Park was not the Ray Gravell you saw living with him for three months in South Africa. He was one of the guys who gave you an insight into what the Lions was all about.'

The Lions lost the series 3–1, winning the fourth Test 17–13 with Campbell kicking two penalties and a conversion to round off his top-scoring haul of 60 points. But with five points the biggest Springbok winning margin, he feels that the tourists were desperately close to winning the series, having been beaten by a late try in the first Test, let slip a lead in the second and lost to a soft, sucker punch of a try in the third. He says: 'It was nice to win the final Test but it was irrelevant really at that stage. But before that, after three games it really could have been 2–1 to us, 2–1 to them or 3–0 to us; in actual fact it was 3–0 to them and the tour was over. The first Test was the crucial one, as the Lions of '97, '74 and '71 all showed. The '89 Lions lost the first Test and won the series but generally the first Test is the one. The whole tour takes on a whole different dimension if you can win the first Test. Unfortunately, in both 1980 and 1983 we lost matches that I feel we should have won but at least could have won, and in both series we were suddenly under pressure. I will never forget the day after that first Test in '83. It was just such a disappointment. We knew we had had a chance and we hadn't taken it. And against the All Blacks you don't get a second chance. Suddenly, we were heading for a long tour.'

Where the 1980 side remained competitive despite the decimation by injuries, their successors in '83 fell away in the final Test, by which stage a casualty list of similar proportions meant that anyone who could walk had to play. Campbell only just came into that category as his old problem had flared up again. He says: 'We were struggling from the start and never really got our game going. We never flowed, never really got a pattern going and we had so many injuries that at the end of the tour it was almost the 15 men standing played. It's not an exaggeration. On the Tuesday before the last Test I tweaked a hamstring again, probably for the first time since 1980, and there was no way I should have played in that game. But there was just no choice. So we had become a little bit of a ragball outfit at that stage and it was humiliating to be beaten 38–6.'

That tour was the second big learning experience of Campbell's career; the first one had earned him the chance to become a Lion and coincidentally also involved New Zealand. He explains: 'Probably the biggest single influence on the way I played was a very quick clip I saw of the '71 Lions, maybe in 1979 or 1980. It was a quick clip of Barry John taking a flat ball outside the end of a lineout and my eyes just lit up. It changed the way I played. I would have stayed in the pocket up to then but that one scene changed my appreciation of angles and the gain line, of taking the ball flat rather than deep. Barry John would have been one of my idols anyway but that one clip had a huge influence on the way I played.'

The Lions had been pipped by New Zealand in the first Test, having trailed 13–12 in the last minute before Allan Hewson fielded Campbell's huge diagonal kick out of his own 22, put up in a desperate attempt to keep the ball in play to delay the final whistle and give his three-quarters a glimmer of hope to chase, and glossed the scoreline by kicking a long dropped goal for 16–12. The second Test saw one of the greatest of all New Zealand second-half performances after they turned into the Wellington gale with an apparently inadequate 9–0 half-time lead. But Campbell, the student of All Black rugby and the Lions' resident Athletic Park authority, knew the job was still less than half complete. He says: 'I remember us getting together at half-time and there was almost a relaxation as if to say we had done it. I said, guys, we have not done it. New Zealand teams playing in Wellington against the wind have played some of their best rugby ever, and as it turned out we hardly saw the ball in the second half and the final result was 9–0.'

The Blacks did not concede a single penalty within Campbell's wind-assisted range in the entire 40 minutes and the series went on to Dunedin with the Lions needing to win both remaining Tests to square the contest. What awaited them at Carisbrook almost defied belief and made the conditions suffered by the 1977 Lions look tropical in comparison. Campbell says: 'They were without a shadow of doubt the worst conditions I ever played rugby in. I have never in my life been so cold and I do not know how we ever finished that game. It was horrendous. There was water all over the pitch but the water was only part of the problem; it was the cold. So you had absolutely freezing, freezing water.

'In the dressing-room before the match we were handed these wetsuits we could wear beneath our gear. I tried one on and it was actually very tight and felt uncomfortable. My view was, look, I've played in bad conditions before, so I went out togged out normally: socks, knicks, jersey, as you would play in in any other match. But as soon as we ran out, off the red carpet and onto the pitch, the instant my foot hit the grass water came over it. The cold! So before the match even started we're, "Woah, we're in trouble here." Twenty minutes into the game I was just numb, absolutely numb from head to toe. Afterwards we found out that most, if not all, the New Zealanders had these wetsuits and what they had also done, and this was very clever, was put plastic bags over their socks and then put their boots on. And Allan Hewson, and maybe Stu Wilson as well, actually wore mittens with the fingers cut off. You would think, hmm, maybe a little bit cissyish – if you could ever call a New Zealand rugby player a cissy – but it did the trick.

'I just didn't realise how cold it was going to be. The wetsuits were like proper divers' suits but with the arms cut off. But it just didn't seem necessary, it didn't seem to be that cold. But before we even kicked off it was horrendous. After the match I just didn't move from under the shower for what seemed like hours. I had my dinner and I was in bed that night by about ten o'clock. It was just not a pleasant experience. But having said all that, we only lost 13–8. So it was a similar pattern to South Africa in 1980: very close first Test, very close second Test, very close third Test. But in New Zealand we fell off after that, we just ran out of players, really.'

As well as his four Test appearances, Campbell played in seven of the 14 provincial games and was again top scorer, more than doubling his South African tally with 124 points. All but four of those came from the boot but the lone try he added was arguably the best of the tour and showcased his attacking skills on a dry pitch in Hamilton. Campbell scooted round on the blindside in support of Roy Laidlaw's improvised break, took the ball 30 yards from the Waikato goal-line and proceded to jink and dummy his way past a succession of defenders to claim the touchdown, which converted as part of a 24-point haul, one short of the individual Lions record for a single match. That was not the highlight of the tour for Campbell, as he took greater satisfaction from his goalkicking record achieved without the benefit of thin air that South African rugby offered. He says: 'I never noted my percentage success or failure rate but [New Zealand sports writer] Keith Quinn noted it during that tour and I had just short of a 75 per cent success rate. I don't know what Neil Jenkins' is, probably well into the 80s, but certainly at that time with, I have to point out, the leather ball, I would be very, very proud of that.'

That pride might also conceal an element of relief, as the master goal-kicker had been struck by the rugby equivalent of the golfer's dreaded 'yips' just weeks before setting off on tour. He says: 'Before going on tour I actually had the only time in my career when I lost my rhythm. Between the end of the Five Nations and the start of the tour I completely lost it. It had never happened before and I didn't know what to do. I got very anxious about it and in the end I just left it, I didn't kick a ball for a couple of weeks. It was a hell of a gamble, I didn't kick until we got down there to New Zealand and it just came back as quickly as it had left me.'

Campbell's kicking was all the more impressive for the circumstances under which he played. His captain, Ciaran Fitzgerald, says of the out-half: 'Ollie was important to us and there was a huge expectation on him going out there. But he was very, very closely marked in every game and the conditions were very, very difficult as well, much more difficult than here. He had to overcome all that and all the changes we had to make at scrum-half didn't help his situation either.'

Despite those mitigating factors, to which can be added the injury he was carrying in the fourth Test, Campbell was among those charged with not playing up to his best form on the tour. The irony is not wasted; as a group the Irish have usually found in the Lions a stage on which they were able to reveal the true talents that often struggled to shine in collectively weaker Ireland sides. Campbell is in a tiny minority of Irish Lions who earned higher praise for their displays for their country. And they said Tony Ward was the unconventional one.

# 18

## In the Line of Fire

IN 1983, THE RACE for the captaincy of the Lions team to tour New Zealand was between just two men. One had taken over the leadership of his national side at a time when they had just lost seven matches on the trot and immediately steered them to the Five Nations championship and their first Triple Crown in 33 years, following up in the campaign preceding the tour itself by sharing the championship with France. The other had far greater international experience but was playing in a side that ended up with the wooden spoon that season and had captained only at club level, where he had done well but had still been twice overlooked for the honour of leading his nation. In theory, the selectors' decision to plump for the former candidate should not have attracted too much comment. In reality, it sparked an astonishing adverse reaction in the media, culminating in a barrage of hostile coverage being directed at the captain before the tour even got underway and which did not let up at any point in the subsequent two and a half months. The target of the newspaper tirades was Ciaran Fitzgerald, the respected captain of Ireland but now the derided, pilloried leader of the Lions. His rival for the job had been Peter Wheeler, the Leicester skipper and England hooker, who had been heavily touted by the English media ahead of his opposite playing number in the Irish pack. When Wheeler was not just turned down for the tour captaincy but excluded from the squad altogether, the knives were out for Fitzgerald. The charge was upgraded to allege that he was neither the best captain nor even one of the two best hookers available to the selectors and the situation eventually placed the New Zealand media in the novel position of joining the Irish in defending the Lions captain against the attacks of their English counterparts.

Fitzgerald conducted himself with remarkable dignity and restraint in the face of hostility of a level rarely faced by any Lions leader, and certainly never from what was supposed to be his own side. Ronnie Dawson, another Irish hooker and captain, had been placed in a similar situation in 1959 when he was a controversial choice ahead of Wales's stalwart Bryn Meredith but never had to endure anything on this scale. But in 1983, several factors combined to put Fitzgerald on the rack. On tour his committed play and off-field good humour earned him the respect of his hosts, but while his team were losing the media from home were able to continue laying blame at his door. He led what was seen as one of the weaker Home Unions parties, selected from what manager Willie John McBride considers 'the worst Five Nations I had seen in a long time', and then saw the Test team disrupted by a succession of injuries in key positions, as well as by an itinerary which McBride and Jim Telfer, the coach, considered too short to build and harden a real team in advance of the international matches. And he was unluckier still to play in one of the few positions in which the Lions had talent in abundance. Scotland's Colin Deans was the other hooker in the party and would prove himself arguably the finest northern-hemisphere player in his position over the length of his near decade-long career, so there was always going to be legitimate disagreement over whether Fitzgerald would have made the Test team without the aid of the captaincy.

It was also possible to argue that Peter Wheeler, another high-class performer in both the technical disciplines and the loose, was unlucky to miss out. But only two hookers could be accommodated and a spell out injured had already placed a question mark against Wheeler's name on the selectors' short-list before Fitzgerald and Ireland scored a conclusive 25–15 victory over his English wooden-spoonists in the final round of the Five Nations. Tough choices were made, as they always are when it comes to picking 30 players from the combined resources of four entire nations, Deans and Fitzgerald got the nod and the captain heard the first rumble of the imminent avalanche of criticism that would soon engulf him.

In fact, according to many of those on the tour, the media onslaught completed a vicious circle itself. The ferocity of the attacks from day one unsettled the tourists and affected their morale, which then contributed to their failure in the Tests, which in turn fuelled more criticism in the press, further damaging team spirit, and so on. Donal Lenihan, who was credited with inspiring the comradeship that carried the 1989 Lions to a series victory in Australia, was selected in '83 as well and says of Fitzgerald's problems with the press: 'Touring New Zealand is a difficult assignment in the best of circumstances but, regardless of what was said, when you get off on a negative note like that it does have an effect on the tour party. It certainly did not help the morale of the squad.'

The Irish members were surprised not only at the level of abuse directed at their captain but also by the fact that anyone would question his playing and leadership abilities at all. Lenihan says: 'I'd be biased but I had played for Ireland with him for three years and we won the championship and shared the championship in 1982 and 1983. He was an excellent captain of Ireland and he was fully deserving of being selected as captain of that tour.'

No one disputed either that the captain faced one of the hardest of all Lions leader's jobs in trying to rally his troops under the constant personal sniping he faced. Lenihan insists that, 'If you're away from home for three months and this thing is being thrown at you week in and week out, it's bound to affect you,' while David Irwin, the durable Instonians and Ireland centre, reflects: 'I think the pressure did affect him, although whether he would admit that I don't know. Peter Wheeler in one sense had more experience but at the time it would have been hard to argue with Ciaran's leadership qualities over the previous two years as captain of Ireland. When you lose games people look for excuses and I thought he came in for some unfair stick from the English media. They were picking on everything they could find, particularly how he threw the ball into the lineout.'

If he did come close to cracking, Fitzgerald will never let his detractors know. He insists that under all the circumstances morale remained high throughout and considers the tour to have been a personally rewarding one. And he says of the captaincy question: 'The controversy meant we got off to a difficult start. The New Zealand media were a little bit amazed that the media coverage from this side was digging at their own. It was a bit of a distraction at the beginning but once we got into it, it wasn't as noticeable.

'I wasn't really surprised to get the captaincy because I knew I was going to be in there with a chance because of our record over the previous two seasons. I knew Peter Wheeler and I were the likely candidates and I reckoned I had as good a shot at it as he had. I think the thing that stood out most was our team performances so I probably had a slight edge on him there. I was very surprised by the criticism that followed, though, by the level and the intensity of it.

But I think if it was going to affect me it would have been more likely to if it was a more gradual process, one that was a build-up to at least being judged on when you started to play. But the intensity of it from the start without even having kicked a ball down there was surprising. The New Zealand guys found themselves in an unusual position in that they were coming out writing positive things about a Lions captain, which they would never do. If it had been less intense it might have affected me more, but it was so intense so quickly that it was "something's wrong here". My view was that it wasn't based on the way I was playing, so so be it.'

Others inside the tour felt later that Fitzgerald had been putting on a brave face. Ollie Campbell, a veteran of the previous tour and the senior back whose out-half talents carried the bulk of the tourists' hopes, says: 'I think Ciaran had a far more difficult job than Bill Beaumont because Billy was everyone's choice as captain in 1980. But once it isn't unanimous and there's any sort of division, of opinion even, whoever is the captain is going to struggle a bit. It would be fair to say that Fleet Street certainly thought that Peter Wheeler should have been not only first-choice hooker but also captain of that tour. So that made it very difficult from the start for Ciaran.'

But he adds: 'One of the regrets I have is that I'm not sure we actually realised in New Zealand quite how hard a time Ciaran was getting, although I'm sure we knew he was under pressure to some extent. One of my other regrets is that there were nine Irishmen on that particular tour and we should have actually taken responsibility among the rest of the Lions and, whether publicly or privately, said to Ciaran that he was the captain as far as we were concerned and it didn't matter what anybody else thought. One of my regrets is that we didn't do that because he was probably under a lot more pressure than we realised at the time. He was under siege. Then early in the tour people started picking on him for his throwing in. So he must have been under a lot of pressure.

'Ciaran had been our captain in '82 and had taken over from Fergus Slattery who had been captain from '79. I don't think there was any question of Ciaran's leadership qualities. But there was a huge difference from being the accepted captain of your country to being questioned as the captain of the Lions. It must have been very difficult.'

Irwin, who was no stranger to adversity himself, having spent three weeks in an Argentinian jail for lending Willie Anderson some moral support when he found himself in trouble with the law on a

Penguins tour in 1980, insists that the complaints against Fitzgerald's leadership and performances had little substance. He says: 'I thought he played well on tour and I thought the only thing he might have done differently was that the Scottish players said they never really got to know Ciaran in that he was very much part of the management and not a big enough part of the team socially. I think he wasn't a particularly social personality and that came across as not wanting to socialise.'

That distance was, in fact, deliberate as Fitzgerald elected to take a watching brief early on in order to make the most of the short lead-in he had to the Test matches. He says of his approach: 'Lots of things are different when you are with the Lions and not your national side because you're trying to find a niche in the management team and playing structure with guys who are all different and who all respond to different things. Initially, my own style would have been one of trying to assess the guys themselves and what would make them operate and what they responded best to. At the start of the campaign I would be watching to get some information on the players and how they gel, and I suppose you are probably looking at combinations of players rather than the best individuals because you've got to realise you're not going to have time to build units and sub-units, you just have to make the best of what's there in the time frame that's there. So you've a lot of watching, listening and assessing to do at the start and then you've just got to take over and go with what you have, and try and cement the plan and say that's it.'

And he adds: 'With a national side there's already a ready-made identity there, guys probably aspire all through their careers to play for their country and wearing the national jersey is a huge source of pride. It's a build-up over a number of years through making it to the fringes and then the squad and the team itself, there's a gradual preparation. With the Lions you're talking about a much shorter time frame in terms of team preparation, you're talking about a number of weeks before the first game. I think in our case we had a fairly equal division betwen the countries and trying to contrast the different styles and different schools of thought is very much a fast-forward operation in terms of finding the best playing style and getting the guys to think alike. That's different from a national team. On the other hand, you're probably dealing with guys with much higher levels of skill and fitness, much better ability, so you can do things you normally wouldn't do.

'Then there's the tremendous thrill of being involved with an élite squad and environment. From my point of view it was totally professional, you were playing rugby, training for rugby and nothing else, thinking about rugby and nothing else. Your whole being for that period was dominated by rugby, whereas at home you were juggling all sorts of other responsibilities, domestic and professional, with your training and playing. So it was a huge thrill to devote three months of your life to something you've always wanted to do and I found that very, very beneficial on a personal level.'

Finding his niche in the management structure was also another issue, where Fitzgerald's natural inclination to place himself at the centre of training sessions, as he did with Ireland, ran the risk of clashing with Telfer, whose fierce determination and perfectionist streak often made it difficult for others to get a look in. McBride describes his coach as 'a tough taskmaster' but wishes he had 'talked with the players rather than at them', while Irwin remembers: 'Jim Telfer was very hard, to the point of being obsessed with getting things right. He had a lot of respect for anyone who laid themselves on the line for him. I tended to be that sort of player, as did Trevor Ringland. He came across as a hard taskmaster but he had a soft spot for some.'

Fitzgerald's own take on the situation is: 'My style as a captain was more hands on than many other styles. I've always been very used to the preparation side of it. Jim Telfer would have been different in that he would have been used to the captain playing a different role with Scotland, for example. They were just things that had to be accommodated.'

These difficulties were rarely reflected in Fitzgerald's play on tour as he led from the front with the fire and fervour that had fuelled his country's Five Nations revival. With Ireland he had been known for his big-match temperament and he turned in some of his best displays in New Zealand in the Tests themselves. He was at his belligerent best in the third rubber – the Lions' strongest showing in the series – and actually scored a try in the 9–0 second Test defeat when he pounced on a spilled garryowen, only to be denied the score by referee Francis Palmade who had blown up too early for Allan Hewson's initial knock-on. Set against that, though, was a sub-par display of throwing-in during the first Test, when the media pressure was still unsettlingly fresh and the playing stakes were highest. Fitzgerald says of the impact of that 16–12 defeat: 'The crucial Test was the first. We had a number of scoring opportunities we didn't take, particularly in the second half, when we dropped the ball a couple of times. If we had scored we would have won the match, and had we won that first Test they would have changed what was a fairly seasoned team, because there was already a lot of clamour down there to do that and defeat would have added to the presssure. There's never a shaky New Zealand side, but there was an element of doubt in the make-up of that one and that Test win eroded all doubt that was there, and probably put some doubt into our camp, as losing does, and started some people looking for alternatives. That first Test was probably our best shot but it didn't happen and we lost all four.'

Crucial to that record was the loss of three key players in the opening rubber: scrum-half Terry Holmes, prop Ian Stephens and flanker Jeff Squire. The loss of Holmes was crucial, as it was the start of a succession of scrum-half disasters that befell the side and hindered the back line in their search for some continuity and consistency. Before the tour set out, the Irish joint-champions had been expected to make a major contribution to the backs as Campbell was first choice out-half and his team-mates full-back Hugo MacNeill, wing Trevor Ringland and the centre pairing of Irwin and Michael Kiernan were all strong contenders for a Test jersey. All five did indeed win their caps but the regular reshuffles meant they never all played at the same time. All but Kiernan started the first Test and Irwin was surprised to be paired with Bob Ackerman as his partnership with the nephew of Lions great Tom had stood out in Ireland's championship success. He says: 'There were certain combinations that might have been kept together but we were chopping and changing all the time. We had a lot of injuries and we had different half-backs, different centre partnerships, different wings, so there were no established partnerships in the back line. I played the first Test with Bob Ackerman and the second with Michael Kiernan. In the third Test they played John Rutherford and Michael Kiernan and then went back to myself and Michael in the fourth. Among the half-backs Terry Holmes wrecked himself, Roy Laidlaw wrecked himself, Nigel Melville flew out and he wrecked himself and in the end Steve Smith had to fly out.

'Also, there were no distinct midweek and Saturday sides because of the way the itinerary had been drawn up, meaning some of the midweek games were very hard. So we had real difficulties with consistent selection and at that level it will show. The New Zealand back line had just two changes in the whole series.'

Irwin, an aggressive, hard-tackling three-quarter, did much of the spadework in the Lions midfield, being ever dependable in defence and unfussy in attack. He proved one of Ireland's most durable of players in his ten-year, twenty-five-cap Test career, having recovered from a broken leg the year before his Lions tour and later from the terrorist bomb blast that ended the career of Nigel Carr and also injured Philip Rainey. With the Lions in '83 his replacement for the third Test by Rutherford, moved out from his usual position of stand-off, suggested that the honest Ulsterman could not offer the same standard of invention and flair, but he nevertheless finished as top try-scorer among the centres and his total of six from eleven matches was beaten only by English wing John Carleton, a string to his bow he still feels was overlooked by many observers who were fixated on the stylish exploits of the England man. He says: 'We played some terrific stuff because the intention was to vary our game quite a bit, spreading it wide, taking it up the middle, Ollie kicking or whatever. We certainly didn't go out to play 10-man rugby, we went out to spread the ball wide and we did that. We had some great games before the first Test, particularly where we were up against some of the New Zealand Test players. I was pretty pleased with myself because I came out of the tour as second top try-scorer, which I thought the English press particularly never gave me credit for. One example was over the classic move, a simple out-half loop. I did it at all levels and no matter who we were playing against it worked. With me being quite big at inside centre I would have taken my opposite number out and then passed the ball on, but on this occasion I did a dummy and when Ollie came round I didn't give it to him, I went straight through and then gave it to Ollie who scored. When I saw the tape, Nigel Starmer-Smith is going, "Great loop by Campbell", not a single mention of me! He was always licking up to the big names.'

At the head of the party, Fitzgerald found few faces looking to curry favour with him, but he knew at least that back in Ireland his stock remained as high as ever. His Lions disappointment was initially compounded when he lost the Irish captaincy and was briefly dropped the following year, but the former schoolboy boxing champion was quickly back off the ropes to reprise the inspirational resilience he had brought to the side on his initial elevation to the leader's role. He returned to lead the team to another championship and put himself alongside Karl Mullen as Ireland's most successful skipper. Unsurprisingly, his achievements with his countrymen provide sweeter memories than his variable experiences with the Lions. He says: 'Being successful with your country would always be the highlight of your career, and from my point of view winning Triple Crowns with Ireland would be the high point, because they don't win them that often. On a personal level, the recognition of being selected as captain of the Lions was a nice achievement, but doing well with Ireland means most to me.

'The best thing about '82 would have been the fact that we did it even though up to '81 Ireland had lost nine matches on the trot. I took over the captaincy in '82 and it was the fact that we won the Triple Crown against that sort of backdrop that made me most proud. It was similar in '85, too. In '84 I had been dropped and Ireland had lost their matches and the next year, with a whole new team of young lads, Ireland won the Triple Crown against the odds. In sport it's the things you win when you're not expected to that are the great achievements. In team sports, going through the mill with people is a great experience because you share special memories when you come out the other end. There's no greater satisfaction, the personal reward is far greater than just the recognition. Inside it's deeper, it means a lot.'

# 19

# DR O'DESPERATE
# AND MR HYDE

WHEN YOUR PARTNERS IN crime are Willie Duggan and Fergus Slattery, it takes something fairly spectacular to get yourself noticed, either on or off the pitch. Happily, and occasionally frighteningly, John O'Driscoll managed both, perfecting his party piece of dangling from the window ledges of South Africa's high-rise hotels and playing the starring role in what Syd Millar rates as one of the greatest of all Lions forward packs. Perhaps the greatest measure of O'Driscoll's worth to both Ireland and the Lions during the late 1970s and early '80s is that his greatest admirers are those with whom he stood shoulder to shoulder in the Irish eight and who maintain that he remains among the most underrated of his country's Lions. 'John never, ever got the recognition he deserved,' insists Duggan. 'That guy did so much work that wasn't seen but was appreciated by the guys who played with him. John O'Driscoll should have played on for a further two seasons after we finished but the selectors wrongly had him in our age bracket.'

O'Driscoll was the junior partner in the Irish back row which helped win the Triple Crown and championship in 1982 and whose three members all toured with the Lions, although remarkably never on the same occasion. Slattery was first to receive the call, travelling in 1971 and '74, then it was Duggan in '77 and finally O'Driscoll in 1980 and '83. All three men saw their international careers ended in the same season, though, as the Irish selectors culled the 'Dad's Army' side whitewashed in 1984. O'Driscoll had three and four years respectively on Duggan and Slattery but paid the price for having become synonymous with the other two as a unit. That may have cost him anything up to a further dozen caps to add to the 26 he won in the six years from 1978, but it is also a fine tribute to his skill and strength that he remains worthy of automatic equal billing with two of the game's all-time greats. Donal Lenihan says of the trio: 'They were the best forwards I was involved with in Irish rugby, collectively and individually,' while David Irwin remembers chiefly the way they combined as an irresistable force. He says: 'I think back to the 1991 World Cup quarter-final [when the Irish led the Wallabies through a late try from Gordon Hamilton only to lose to an even later one from Michael Lynagh] and if Ireland had gone into that lead with Duggan, Slattery and O'Driscoll in the team, Australia would never have seen the ball again. They had such experience and they knew exactly how to tie a game up.'

A disciplined presence on the blind-side flank, O'Driscoll was a calm, steadying influence on the fiery Irish pack, the sturdiest of defenders, a strong operator at the tail of the lineout either in support of Duggan or as a jumper in his own right, and proved himself an intelligent foil for Slattery and Duggan in their charges around the paddock. He first came to prominence as the captain of London Irish during the late '70s but made his breakthrough as one of the new generation who won both Tests in Australia in the final year of that decade. The season that followed confirmed his arrival as his unfancied Exiles reached the RFU Cup final at Twickenham. He became an ever present in Ireland's Five Nations campaign and capped the lot with an invitation to tour South Africa with the Lions.

Like Slattery six years earlier, O'Driscoll prospered on the firm pitches of the republic and although both his Lions tours ended in defeat, this near miss was the more pleasurable experience. He says: 'I enjoyed 1980 most because we played well and should have won the series, whereas in 1983 we were quite well beaten. We had two very different teams and in '83 the All Blacks were very strong. I also preferred playing in South Africa because I liked the hard grounds. Playing in New Zealand was like playing at home. I liked going out training in a T-shirt and going back and having a swim afterwards. South Africa and Australia are more relaxed off the field because of the climate and in South Africa you could get away from rugby. Everybody is interested in rugby but you can still get away from it. In New Zealand everyone thinks about rugby all the time and there's no way to escape or be off-duty.'

Where the Lions faded away in the closing stages of the 1983 tour, O'Driscoll and his team-mates of 1980 rallied to take the fourth Test against the Springboks and avoid a first ever 4–0 whitewash there. 'The last Test is always quite difficult,' he says. 'The key to that win in South Africa was that everyone came into it with a lot of enthusiasm and not tiredness because we felt we hadn't done ourselves justice in the previous Tests, even though we had won all the provincial matches. Coming into the final Test 3–0 down did not reflect the way things had gone, whereas in New Zealand in '83 we couldn't really argue with being three down after three Tests. Then we weren't playing well so we struggled in the last Test.'

He is too modest to mention it himself but the winning try in the 17–13 Pretoria win was scored by one John O'Driscoll, his gallop to the posts sitting alongside the muscular touchdown he secured in the second Test to make him the only Lion to score twice in the series. That try in Bloemfontein was a barnstorming effort that saw him shoulder aside several tacklers on his way to the line and was typical of the physical style that impressed his hosts. The Lions were an awesome force up front on that tour, with O'Driscoll prominent in the mauls and in serving up quality lineout ball under the heaviest Springbok fire. Rodney O'Donnell, the St Mary's full-back on the trip, says of his countryman: 'John O'Driscoll became a world-class wing-forward on that tour. The South Africans had a hell of a lot of respect for him after that, although any tour he went on he came on in leaps and bounds. He was a very quiet individual, too! John O'Desperate, Ray Gravell used to call him.'

With good reason, too. Noel Murphy, the coach in 1980, describes O'Driscoll as someone 'you feel is a shy, quiet type when you first meet him, but he's got a tremendous fun element in him', and does so with a fair degree of understatement. Ollie Campbell's 'Jekyll and Hyde' character assessment is widely considered nearer the mark. As well as inspecting hotel rooms from the outside and keeping pace with the likes of Slattery and Duggan, the Manchester dermatologist earned infamy for committing the cardinal sin of missing training after his friend Gravell spiked his drinks – which were already strong enough for most anyway – during a notorious 'Sunday school' session, and was rarely lost for a wind-up at his team-mates' expense. Campbell recalls his own suffering at the doctor's hands, both with Ireland and the 1983 Lions in New Zealand. He says: 'In 1981 we played Tony Ward at out-half and me in the centre. I hadn't really played anywhere other than out-half since I was nine years of age so I was feeling uncomfortable. John and I always used to go for a stroll round Stephen's Green on the morning of the match and he knew I was concerned. Just as we came back towards the Shelbourne he said, "For what it's worth, I think they're right to play you in the centre." I said, "John, thanks very much. But what makes you say that?" He said, "Well, we need an out-half who can tackle," and walked off, crossed the road and went into the Shelbourne, leaving me standing there absolutely dumbfounded. I didn't move for about five minutes. Talk about reassurance.'

And he adds: 'You wouldn't want to be sensitive, either. In 1983, John presented me with a milk bottle in honour of my milk-coloured legs. We were playing Counties in Pukekohe and I kicked five out of five, including the longest penalty I ever got. It was from our own ten-yard line and it actually cleared the crossbar by six feet and landed beyond the dead-ball line. John said to me afterwards that despite all that the only thing people were talking about was my white legs. It was a very dark and dreary day and there were these two white beacons standing out, he reckoned.'

Another sufferer from the attentions of Dr O'Desperate and Mr Hyde was his 1980 room-mate in South Africa, Rodney O'Donnell, who is generally regarded as the most superstitious of all rugby players, Irish or otherwise. He would drive Murphy wild with his refusal to get on the team bus unless he could be last, his insistence on not stepping on lines – including those painted on the pitch – and his refusal to stay in, or even next door to, any hotel room not just numbered 13 but bearing a multiple or combination of those figures or any which added up to a total of 13. Campbell and John Robbie once forced him to stay in his room all day on Friday 13th by taping lines all over the corridor floor between his room and the lift and the dreaded digits on his door itself. O'Driscoll was another to join in the fun. He says of his room-mate: 'He was absolutely definite about these superstitions. Willie [Duggan] always had to be last onto the pitch but Rodney simply would not go out unless he was last. Willie is very strong-willed but eventually he came out followed by Rodney because when it came down to it Rodney would say it's not meant to be for me to play today, so Willie had to give way or be responsible for us playing with 14 men.

'Rodney also had this ritual of getting into bed which involved him having to put all the pictures and mirrors straight, put the phone on the hook the 'right' way round and fix the curtains in a certain way. This would take a good quarter of an hour and then he would have to jump into bed without touching either the top or bottom sheet. I used to wait until he was all settled in and then get up and move a picture slightly to make it crooked. He would then have to get up to straighten it and go through his whole routine again, after which I would wait another 20 minutes and then get up and move the picture again.'

O'Donnell took it all in good part, as he still does, saying today: 'They had nothing else to do, they were boring old farts the lot of them, nothing to do but check up on me!' But he adds: 'John, Ray and myself got on so well and I have fond memories of touring with the lads, especially John O'Driscoll.'

The South African adventure ended with O'Donnell facing far more serious difficulties than merely being the butt of his team-mate's pranks. In the penultimate match, against Griqualand West, he broke his neck in tackling Springbok powerhouse Danie Gerber. He would never play again, but had it not been for the prompt intervention of O'Driscoll, who dissuaded the sponge men from moving him immediately, the outcome could have been far worse. O'Donnell says: 'I was very, very lucky I wasn't paralysed. Whenever doctors see the X-rays they all say that. Somebody must have been smiling on me. I was full-back and they made a break down the side and literally the man tried to steamroller right through me. My head hit him in the chest and was compressed into my shoulders; it nearly went into my chest. The C6 and C7 vertebrae were dislocated and fractured so I was very lucky. I was operated on out there and I needed another operation when I got back to fuse them, using bone from my hip. I then had a couple of months on my back in bed recuperating.

'I got capped in 1979 in Australia and a year later, on 16 June, I was retired from rugby at 23. It was the worst thing that ever happened to me. Capped at 22 and finished totally a year later, and lucky to have my life, lucky not to be a quadriplegic. People say I was very unlucky but really I was very lucky indeed. You've got to be rational about it.'

The idea of a rational Rodney might raise a smile from the team-mates who saw his superstitions in action, but all parties now blame Murphy, tongue in cheek, for the mishap. The fault, recalls Campbell, lay with the coach's refusal to let O'Donnell wear his usual lucky shorts, 'which were a size 32 even though he needed a 34. Rodney wouldn't wear a 34 because three and four add up to seven which was one of his unlucky numbers. And, of course, on this occasion the only spare knicks were a 34.'

O'Donnell confirms all the details – as well as Murphy's guilt: 'I did have a usual pair of shorts and Noisy wouldn't allow me to wear them because they were torn. I was hiding from him in the dressing-room but he caught me going out. But I look back now and . . . yes, I still blame him!'

Coincidentally, his team-mates had already fretted for the full-back's safety, albeit in another regard entirely. O'Driscoll says: 'Rodney was an incredibly brave player. That was a very nasty accident and it was very hard for him not to be able to play again, but really with a fracture dislocation like that he was lucky not to be paralysed.' And he adds: 'Even before that we used to fear for him. He used to get up really high to take the high balls and in those days the laws didn't protect you when you were in the air, so he was often spun over and landed on his head. It was ironic that he suffered his injury not through something like that but in making a tackle.'

O'Driscoll's second Lions tour was disrupted by injury, although thankfully nothing remotely as serious as O'Donnell's. A rib injury sustained in his first match, against Auckland at Eden Park, limited him to just two Tests and six provincial matches, although he did captain the side in two of the latter contests. 1980 had seen the Lions' worst ever run of injuries and '83 was not far behind. This time six replacements were called for, as opposed to eight on the previous trip, but amid the disruption the changes at least gave Donal Lenihan the chance to join a tour he had initially been cruelly deleted from at the eleventh hour. The Cork Constitution lock, then in his third season of international rugby and one of Ireland's fastest rising stars, had been named in the original party and was expected to mount a strong challenge for a place in the Test team. He joined up with the squad, but in medical tests prior to departure was discovered to be in need of a hernia operation and found himself catching the plane back to Cork instead of to Auckland.

Seven of the Ireland side that shared the Five Nations Championship with France that year made the party – Campbell, Hugo MacNeill, Trevor Ringland, Michael Kiernan and David Irwin from the backs and O'Driscoll and captain Ciaran Fitzgerald among the forwards – and Lenihan was able to help bring the total up to nine when he and Ginger McLoughlin flew out as replacements for the Welsh duo Bob Norster and Ian Stephens. Time was too short for either man realistically to challenge for a Test place but Lenihan made impressive progress in double-quick time and ran Maurice Colclough mighty close in the run-up to the fourth international.

Munster's most-capped forward will be hoping his Lions luck improves as manager of the 2001 tour to Australia, as fortune might have been far kinder to him in the red of the four Home Unions. Having missed out in '83 he was then denied another tour – and possibly the captaincy – in 1986. This time politics stopped the proposed trek to South Africa and instead a special match was held at Cardiff Arms Park in which the Lions took on the Rest of the World to celebrate the centenary of the International Board, losing 15–7. In a move that suggested he might have been awarded the leadership of the cancelled tour, Lenihan was named captain of a side coached by Ireland's Mick Doyle and which included his compatriots Ringland, Brendan Mullin, Des Fitzgerald and Nigel Carr, with Michael Kiernan on the bench. Full Lions status was awarded to those taking part but the occasion did not have the charge of the real southern-hemisphere McCoy. Doyle, never one to hide his feelings, says of the cancellation: 'I detested apartheid but I felt cheated. I felt they had taken the soft option, used rugby as an easy choice. Why didn't they stop trading with South Africa instead of stopping a rugby tour? If they were really serious about it they would have severed all ties. And then, of course, the next year we saw the Cavaliers going there and that was the start of professionalism.'

Lenihan, by now among the northern hemisphere's finest scrummagers and lineout jumpers, found consolation in his Ireland career, captaining his country on 17 of his 52 international appearances and leading them through the inaugural World Cup of 1987. After the loss of the Lions tour the previous year, the advent of the new competition raised the spectre that the tourists would become lost in the enlarged rugby calendar whose centrepiece was now the individual nations' pursuit of the William Webb Ellis trophy rather than the four-yearly clash of the hemispheres. 1989, and the victory in Australia over a Wallaby side that would win the World Cup two years later was vital in securing the institution's future, and Lenihan played one of its most important roles, even though he did not appear in a Test.

In 1997 as the Lions stood on the verge of only their second series win in South Africa, coach Ian McGeechan told his troops: 'The only successful Lions teams have been so because of the players who didn't play in the Test team.' As coach of the 1989 side in Australia he must surely have had in mind the contribution of Lenihan to that trip as captain of the midweek side that forged so strong an identity that they went down in history as 'Donal's

Doughnuts', so dubbed because they 'filled the hole in the middle of the week'. The contrast with the subsequent mission to New Zealand, which subsided into rancour and recrimination as several dirt-trackers went 'off-tour' in the closing stages, is educational and Lenihan's ship is seen as the model for all future tours in building essential comradeship throughout the whole squad.

Donal, who inherited his sharp handling skills from his father Ger, a well-known Gaelic footballer in Cork, says of his Doughnuts: 'It began after [coach] Roger Uttley started roaring at me in training one day, using the word "doughnut" and Gareth Chilcott took it from there and it gathered its own momentum. But we created our own identity, made a laugh of it all I suppose, and people were made special awards for getting in the midweek team as opposed to the Saturday team. I think it is very important when you're away like that that everybody takes part in the whole thing, and I've no doubt it brought the whole tour party together.'

Not only that but Lenihan's second string altered the entire course of the tour on one inspirational afternoon immediately after the first Test defeat. The building society manager recalls: 'We had won all our matches going into the first Test and really just didn't perform on the day. There was a feeling of devastation after the first Test and only a week to put things right. Then we played ACT on the Tuesday or Wednesday and were 20 points down but came back to win the match 41–25. Everybody was there, all those who had played in the Test, and they all came to the side of the pitch and clapped off the midweek team. That game changed the whole mood of the tour and got everybody ready for the second Test. At that stage ACT was the hardest midweek game we would play and it really encapsulated the whole tour, everybody played their part. There were periods in the '93 tour when the midweek team seemed to fall apart a bit and I think that had an effect on the overall performance of the tour.'

In the same way, the form and commitment of the midweek team in '89 geed up the Test side to take the last two internationals and the series itself, although the ferocity with which they fought back in game two sparked a row over alleged acts of violence and led Wallaby skipper Nick Farr-Jones to warn that the final rubber 'could erupt into open warfare'. Lenihan says of the trouble: 'There were probably two isolated incidents which created that image, because overall it wasn't a dirty tour in any way. Our opening game was against Western Australia and the Western Australian team was made up mainly of New Zealanders – there were ten or eleven in their squad – and two or three of us ended up getting stitched. After that game the question came up of whether we were going to continue being patched up after every game or whether we were going to stand up to these fellows. Then there were the two incidents in the second Test. Nick Farr-Jones and Robert Jones got stuck into each other, which was just one flare-up in a game that was blown up out of proportion, and then you had the other incident where Dai Young stamped on Steve Cutler. That looked bad at the time but those two moments put a bad gloss on the whole thing and Australia tended to focus on them as the tour went on. It was certainly a very hard, physical Test series, but overall one or two incidents blew the thing out of proportion. In the modern game where you have citings and television replays, a lot of things that went down in rugby ten years ago would not be tolerated now. Anyway, they were used to playing New Zealand three or four times a year so they were well capable of looking after themselves.'

Lenihan, who retired from playing with neck and shoulder injuries in 1992, became Ireland manager only in 1998 but the year before had at last tasted Lions glory as a selector of the squad that won the series in South Africa. That experience taught him that only the bare essentials of the 1989 success apply in the new professional age. 'It's a totally different game now,' he says. 'For next year's tour the ground rules were set by the last tour of '97. The one thing I would take from '89 is that, regardless of rugby being professional, if you don't get the attitude right in terms of people coming together from the four different countries and everybody being focused on a common cause and pulling together playing for the one jersey, then you're wasting your time. I've never been on a successful team where people didn't enjoy each other's company or work hard for each other. It doesn't just happen, you can't just be a bunch of talented individuals; if you don't pull together and work for each other you're wasting your time. That is the same for an amateur or fully professional tour.'

The difference between the two is in the detail. Lenihan explains: 'Players now expect higher standards because they are looked after very well at international level by their own countries. I firmly believe the Lions is all about the best and from that point of view they've got to be looked after even better than they are with their national sides. Everything, in terms of making sure the itinerary is right and there is the best preparation for individual games and particularly the Test series, must be done so that the players don't have to worry about anything other than the playing of the game. And from the players' point of view, everyone must be seen to be given a fair chance of making the Test side. There are a lot of talented individuals and if you go on a Lions tour you are probably pretty much sure of your place in your own international set-up, therefore it's important that every player is seen to be treated equally and given the same opportunity as everyone else of making the Test side.'

Coming up with those winning combinations is the hardest task facing the tour management in the modern age when shorter tours mean fewer warm-up matches in which to try and to test before getting down to serious business in the international series itself. This is not a brand new problem, though, as Willie John McBride and Jim Telfer considered the itinerary of 1983 to have too short a run-in to the Tests for them to build a competitive team. And three years earlier, Murphy and Millar admitted they would have fared better had they introduced Shannon flanker Colm Tucker sooner than the third Test, but had been unable to because there were insufficient early opportunities to have a good look at how he operated within the various back-row permutations available. O'Driscoll, who played alongside the Munsterman, has no doubt they would have been right to have taken the plunge, saying: 'The back-row balance was much better when Colm came into it for the last two Tests. He was a tough player and I think the hard grounds suited him as well. The mobility of the back row improved when he came in at wing-forward and Jeff Squire went to number eight. Derek Quinnell was fine but as a pack, mobility-wise, that made a difference.'

Because of that oversight, and through no fault of his own, Tucker remained one of the bit-part Irish players in the Lions story, a minority group as the majority of the nation's tourists have made key contributions to their success. Of course, not everyone can stand beneath the spotlight, but the Irish have made a better attempt than most. As well as the record number of captains and their provision of so many coaches and managers, close on three quarters of those who made the trips from the four provinces appeared in Test teams. Of those who failed to make it, some were key members of the understudy sides, while others missed out through injury.

In the latter group, as Rodney O'Donnell puts it, 'The Lions have been a little bit expensive for Ireland over the last few years.' Quite apart from his own abbreviated career, he is referring to the loss of scrum-half Colin Patterson and stand-off Paul Dean, whose careers were ended by injuries suffered on the tours of 1980 and '89 respectively. Mick Doyle rates Dean, who was 29 when he suffered the knee injury that finished him off in the very first match of the tour, as the finest player he ever coached, 'The best I ever saw for getting the ball out from the scrum-half to the wings; he could give his centres anything up to an extra 15 yards of space to work in.' Patterson, the skilfully assured little Instonians scrum-half, was in only his third season of international rugby when he suffered what was then reckoned to be the worst knee-ligament injury ever seen, but at least he got the chance to show off his class in three Lions Tests, and his catastrophe allowed another Ireland great to make his bow in the red jersey as John Robbie, the smooth-passing, inspirational Greystones stylist – rated by Ollie Campbell as the greatest performer his playing days ever saw and the greatest captain his country never had – stepped in for the final tie. Elsewhere, Barry Bresnihan made rugby history by becoming the first replacement in a representative match when replacing the injured Mike Gibson in the opening match of the 1968 tour to South Africa, and the likes of Tom Grace, Stewart McKinney and Johnny Moloney made their contributions to the success of 1974. Most recently, Nick Popplewell quietly earned his spurs by propping the Lions scrum through all three back-breaking Tests in New Zealand in 1993, where Mick Galwey, having been in a hospital bed with his career in the balance at the season's start, was one of the dirt-trackers to retain his pride and commitment to the finish, as well as seeing his driving skills get him banned from every go-kart track in the islands.

One thing they all had in common was that regardless of the playing circumstances, they all enjoyed themselves and their experiences as Lions. And that, says John O'Driscoll, must remain at the heart of tourists' raison d'être if they are to continue to prosper. Happily, the question of their survival no longer seems an issue. O'Driscoll says: 'I think the professional era is taking the enjoyment out of playing and rugby is an awfully hard way to make a living if you're not enjoying it. There has always been an opportunity to be paid for playing rugby – go to rugby league – but people have stayed in union for the enjoyment factor. Lions tours are part of that and in South Africa in 1997 the players were clearly enjoying it. In other competitions I'm not sure that they are and in a game like rugby you have to be enthusiastic when you go on to the pitch.

'The Lions are a unique institution, something the players aim for, and it's very good for the ethos of the game to play together after so many years of playing against each other. I would have liked to have played in a World Cup but not at the expense of being a Lion. A World Cup is only once every four years and ultimately only one country is going to be happy. If your country isn't going to be competitive in the World Cup during your career, it is wonderful to have the opportunity to play for a Lions team.'

# 20

## Buzz Lightyear and the
## Demon Barber of Durban

THE NIGHT BEFORE THE Lions took on South Africa in the first Test match of the 1997 series, captain Martin Johnson lay awake in his hotel bed long into the early hours, more nervous than he had ever been and too tense to turn off and go to sleep. He was confident his men could beat the Boks in their own back yard, but in the fluttering pit of his stomach he knew they would have to dig deep, maybe deeper than they had ever done before, to accomplish a mission many pre-tour pundits had rated impossible. But even in the darkest hours of the Cape Town night he could never have imagined quite how deep and quite how quickly they would have to dig.

The atmosphere at a packed Newlands crackled with anticipation and the Lions knew they needed a good start to take the heat out of both the home crowd and their team. They didn't get it. The tourists kicked off, straight into touch to concede a Springbok scrum on halfway. The moment of truth had arrived. The Lions had dropped only one provincial match on their travels but had been playing against Currie Cup sides shorn of their South African squad members, who were holed up in a cloistered training camp, no doubt wrestling crocodiles and eating razor blades for breakfast. This allowed the Lions to experiment with a variety of combinations but left no one any the wiser as to how they would fare in the crucible of the Tests. The initial omens were not good. The two packs crouched nose to nose on the centre spot, referee Colin Hawke raised his arm between them and then they hit. The Boks had already broken one scrummaging machine in training and were hell bent on doing similar damage to these northern hemisphere upstarts. The Lions eight hopped backwards alarmingly on impact and landed in a mangled heap, picking themselves up to see Henry

Honiball's kick dribbling into touch two metres from their own corner flag. More pressure. Then they lost their own throw and South Africa were awarded a put-in right in the heart of the danger zone. This time the scrum did not go backwards. Instead, it went down, South Africa were handed the simplest of penalties and the Lions were 3–0 behind before they had even touched the ball.

Against the backdrop of that disastrous start, the Lions pack faced the biggest test of both technique and character they had ever known, and within the eight perhaps the three Irishmen in the side were under the greatest pressure of all. In the front row Paul Wallace, a surprise, comparatively lightweight choice to prop against the 19-stone bulk of Os du Randt, had conceded that initial penalty when he dipped to the ground under the yoke of the mighty Ox, while alongside him hooker Keith Wood had seemingly justified pre-tour concerns about his variable lineout delivery with that initial lost throw. And behind them at lock, Jeremy Davidson, the baby of the team at 23, knew that as one of the principal lineout jumpers he would join Wood in shouldering the blame for defeat should their supply of touchline possession not improve. Many former Irish Lions have spoken about the character of their countrymen and the can-do attitude that makes them so suited to the demands of these tours, but few have ever responded to adversity as positively and decisively as this trio did in 1997. The series may have been won by the bankability of Neil Jenkins' goalkicking, by Matt Dawson's audacious dummy and try in the first Test and the blast of arctic cool with which Jeremy Guscott dropped the clinching goal in game two, but the work of the Irishmen and their colleagues in the fierce forward exchanges had just as crucial a bearing on the outcome of the contest.

Heroic, tireless defence, as well as some woeful South African goal-kicking, played a significant part in the triumph, yet Davidson, who went into the tour a near unknown but emerged as the players' choice as man of the series, is in no doubt as to where the most serious damage to Springbok hopes was done. 'We were more capable in the lineout than the scrum,' he says, 'but we won because we held the best scrum in the world, although we were under a bit of pressure in the first Test. That first scrum was a real shock to the system. When you hit a scrum you feel the pressure and when we hit we were just literally blown backwards. I just felt everything falling back on top of me and thought, "Oh f★★★, this is going to be a tough one." But we all dug in and it went OK, but that was a bit of a shock.'

That was lesson one for the Lions, but they learned from it almost immediately. The forwards had been working overtime in training to prepare for the South Africans' scrummaging, famously being ordered by coach Jim Telfer to pack down 42 times in one 46-minute session, but had essentially become cocky by the time they reached Newlands. Wallace says: 'I think because we had been scrummaging very well against the other sides we had an awful lot of confidence and thought that if we could get a good square hit we could take them on at their own game, just with the big hit. It did rather bounce back in our faces. It's pure physics, really. If you're going to hit a pack that size you're going to come off second best, so after that we just used our advantage in being a shorter front row. We changed our tactics, went a bit lower and kept working. Because they were so tall it was very difficult for them to scrummage lower so we took our advantage from that. In the southern hemisphere their scrummaging style is that they like to hit and hold, while over here we scrummage a little bit lower and keep the pressure on a little bit longer and probably work a bit more in the scrum. I don't think they had the fitness in their front row and front five that we had and as the game went on we wore them down.'

Wallace particularly got under the skin of his opposite number as much as he got beneath his shoulder in the tight as the giant du Randt became increasingly frustrated at his inability to pin a man three stones lighter than him into a corner in the scrum. Matters came to a head in the third Test when referee Wayne Erikson lectured the duo at some length, scolding Wallace for not packing straight and du Randt for collapsing the scrum when the Irishman had him on the ropes, before the front rows erupted into an all-in brawl while play carried on across the other side of the field. Wallace, with the assistance of Davidson's cavalry, even won this one too as it was du Randt who ended up on a yellow card for throwing the opening punch.

The Saracens man's lucky escape came as no surprise to those who know him, as the shamrock on his international jersey might as well be a four-leafed clover. Wallace was a last-minute addition to the Lions squad when Peter Clohessy badly strained a back muscle in the first training session before the party even flew out of England and has similarly stepped out with Lady Luck throughout his rugby life. Donal Lenihan, his Ireland manager, explains: 'Wallace is the greatest man ever for taking his chance; every opportunity he has got in his career, as an Under-21, on the development tour with Ireland, winning his first cap, he always got in because somebody else got injured. And he always took his chance.' But he adds: 'Unfortunately for him, he's been paying for his success in South Africa ever since. He's just played too much rugby and also every time we have a South African referee he seems to penalise him at every scrum to get him back for what he did in '97. Every time we see we have a South African referee we say there's no point in picking Paul Wallace.'

Wallace's luck may have changed, but his countryman Eric Miller will curse the fact that this has remained exactly the same since he toured with the Lions in '97. Illness and injury have limited the young back rower's progress since then, just as they did on that expedition itself. The 21-year-old was, with Davidson, one of the revelations of the tour and was picked at number 8 for the first Test, only to be stricken by flu and have to step down in favour of England's Tim Rodber. Coaches Ian McGeechan and Jim Telfer had plumped for the Leicester youngster after being struck by his handling skills, work rate and forthright charges off the back of the scrum, and they felt that he could handle the physical challenge of the Boks while having an edge over his opposite number, home captain Gary Teichmann, in getting to the breakdown. Sadly, he never got the chance to prove them right. Rodber stayed in the team for the second Test and when Miller got his cap as a replacement four minutes from the end of that match he pulled a thigh muscle running onto the field and then tore it in training the following week to rule himself out of contention for the final showdown. Lenihan, who as one of the tour selectors had long marked him out as Lions material, felt for him. 'Eric Miller was outstanding on that tour,' he says. 'I think his performance against Orange Free State in the week between the first and second Tests was one of the best individual performances of that tour. I remember speaking to him literally an hour after the first Test and he didn't know whether to laugh or cry over the fact that they'd won the match but he had missed it. He was asking my advice over what he should do and I said, look, all you can do is go out and give the performance of your career and it's up to the people selecting the team after that. To be fair to him he did that and if he hadn't got injured he probably would have made the third Test when Rodber went down with the flu.'

The bug that rampaged through the camp, and was at its height in the hours preceding the final Test, also numbered Davidson among its victims, although it would take more than a prolonged bout of vomiting at 1.30 on the morning of the match to keep the mustard-keen London Irishman out of the side. That sort of commitment had pencilled him in as a potential Test competitor from early on, although his willingness to play while injured gave his masters cause for concern. So, too, did the cartoon chaos inflicted upon his own team-mates in training by the man whose lantern jawline saw him nicknamed after the Buzz Lightyear character in the animated film *Toy Story*. The trail of destruction he wrought included standing on the heads of Rob Wainwright and Gregor Townsend, treading on Wallace's knee and catching Neil Back full in the eye, while in practice before the second Test it was feared he had ruptured his own knee ligaments when he fell awkwardly on the hard ground. The diagnosis of a simple strain ended the panic, but even the worst would not have deterred Davidson from declaring himself available. He says: 'At that stage of your career – out in South Africa with the Lions, one Test up and preparing for the second – if there's any doubt whether you can play or not you're going to drive yourself to carry on and go the whole length of the tour unless its something very serious. Everyone involved was pushing themselves to the limit at that particular time and I didn't really get many injuries on that tour, I only got one which kept me out of the Natal game, so I was happy enough.'

Only John Bentley played more games than Davidson, who appeared in eight of the ten provincial matches and all three of the Tests, and at one point the coaching staff were worried about the danger of him becoming stale through being overplayed, although they probably would have needed an elephant gun to halt him. The energetic Ulsterman says: 'I never ever thought of that. Getting selected for the Lions when you're a young player is the complete pinnacle of your career. I knew that the Test series was behind it all but I just wanted to take every opportunity I could. I never thought I would be able to play with my childhood heroes. I would watch people like Will Carling and Jerry Guscott playing on television and then there you are meeting up with Jerry Guscott in the Lions hotel. It was a bit of a shock to the system but I always just looked at the next game every time and I think that might have helped me. Some people maybe looked too far ahead and looked to the Test series and were disappointed if they got injured or whatever, but I just took it game by game, which I think was a good way to do it.

'I did get an awful lot of games at the start because they were trying to see what level a player I was. Because I was a young international player I didn't really have a big brand name like a

Rodber, a Dallaglio or a Guscott. Two or three games and you know Guscott is ready for the big match against the Springboks, you know you can throw him in there. So they played some of the younger players a bit more so they could have a look at them and see whether they were up to it or not. Before the first Test I played midweek against South Africa A and I think that was another big test for me and I came through it reasonably well.'

Davidson's mobility and lineout skills earned him the nod for the first team ahead of England's Simon Shaw, who had started out as favourite to lock the scrum alongside Johnson. The newcomer's work in the loose – already good enough for him to win his first three Ireland caps as a blind-side flanker – caught the eye of South Africa's World Cup-winning coach Kitch Christie, who cited his selection as the sort of visionary move that turned the series, and the fact that he was considerably lighter than Shaw gave him the crucial advantage of being easier to lift in the line. Davidson was largely exempt from criticism over that first lost throw in the opening minutes of the Test series as the ball had been aimed at Johnson only for Hannes Strydom to muscle in on possession. That gave the Lions captain a taste of what was in store for him as the Springboks targeted him as their guests' main threat in that phase of play. Knowing he would be double-teamed, the Leicester and England man turned to his second-row partner for support. Davidson did not let him down, taking everything that Wood threw at him and providing a primary-phase platform from which the Lions could engineer scoring chances. Lenihan says: 'When the Test side was announced, people couldn't believe that Wallace and Davidson were in. But if you talk to people like Jim Telfer, they just couldn't believe Jeremy Davidson's hunger for work and for knowledge. At the end of the day he worked so hard in training and played so well in the matches prior to the first Test that they just had to pick him.' And he adds: 'The best tribute to him was during the Tests, and in the first and second Tests in particular, when Martin Johnson, the captain and pack leader, called 80 to 90 per cent of the lineout ball to Davidson. Johnson is a player you have to have huge respect for, so when you see someone like him having that sort of confidence in a young fellow like Davidson it tells you all you want to know about him.'

Davidson's lack of experience – he had played only two full seasons with Ireland – placed the main question mark against his selection but he performed in the Tests with the confidence of someone with Johnson's 30-odd cap pedigree, particularly when the responsibility for lineout ball came to rest upon his broad shoulders. He says: 'In the heart of a game like that you're over the moon to get that amount of lineout ball. If you go out there for the Lions against the Springboks you've got to have a bit of confidence in yourself, you've got to be able to back yourself in the lineouts and I knew I was capable of winning whatever ball was called to me, and luckily enough the captain called me a lot. It's not often a captain does that, but it shows you what a good captain Martin Johnson was. Getting so much ball helped me play a bit better. As a second row, being called a bit of ball gets you into the game, gets you feeling a part of the team and you play that much better because of it. It also helped having Keith there, because he's a good friend whom I've played with for years, and it was good to have Paul Wallace there in front of me as well. The people around you give you a lot of confidence, especially if you know them very well.'

Davidson's team-mates had just as much belief in him and so Johnson again called his number as the second Test clock ticked down to the final four minutes on a scoreboard showing the teams locked at 15 points apiece. Wood pinpointed his Ireland mate, who brought the precious pill safely back to earth, and Dawson launched Townsend towards the line. He was held up short, the pack piled in and rucked the ball back to Dawson. With his stand-off buried, Guscott was the first man out and the only one required as he popped over the hero's dropped goal. Davidson says of his moment: 'We knew we needed to get up there, we needed possession, we needed to get the ball back in our hands and we needed to score because time was running out. The throw was called to me and I just wanted to get it for the team. I've got a picture of the dropped goal and you can just see one of my feet sticking up out of the ruck before it. There was nothing on for Jerry but to drop the goal, although I didn't see it because I was at the bottom of that ruck. I've watched it on video many times since and it still gives me shivers down the spine.'

The spine of any rugby team starts in the centre of the front row, with the hooker. And for added backbone in that position the Lions could have had no better number two than Keith Wood, formerly and latterly of Garryowen but a Harlequin of London at the time of the Lions tour. The Ireland talisman was following in the footsteps of his late father, Gordon, who propped the tourists' scrum alongside Ronnie Dawson and Syd Millar in New Zealand in 1959, patenting the trick the 1997 side used against bigger opponents by employing his solid frame and lack of height – he stood 5'9" tall – to negate his opponents' advantage through an ever lower angle of attack. The three Irishmen also pulled off the same strategy to beat Wood Jr to a victory over the Springboks when they formed the bedrock of the Barbarians team that defeated South Africa in 1961. With his unusual interests stretching to underwater photography, Gordon was one of the most popular off-field personalities of the 1959 tour, although his team-mates remember him having to cut down on opportunities to indulge his passion for brown sauce as he battled against his weight throughout his career. Keith presumably inherited his penchant for playing as a three-quarter in open play from his father, who was a schoolboy wing, although Tom Kiernan notices some significant differences between the generations. He says: 'There are no similarities between them. Gordon was much slower and really in the true prop's mould, very much like Syd Millar, but he was also a very good number two lineout jumper.'

Keith's confidence in throwing to anyone further away than his father's old position in the line was just about the sole worry the coaching staff had about the only Irishman fancied to make the Test team when the party flew out of Heathrow. But the ultra-professional environment generated on tour improved that part of his game immeasurably as Telfer turned to video analyst and technical specialist Andy Keast to pinpoint Wood's difficulties on film. Several screenings highlighted the need for a steadier body position on releasing the ball and Davidson can testify to the success of the ensuing quick fix. Where Wood was most valuable, though, was in roaring his team-mates on, squeezing the last ounce of effort from the scrums, and in running with the ball in broken play. Wallace says of the man alongside him in the front row: 'Woody's greatest strength is around the park; he's very mobile and a great runner with the ball. On the Lions tour sometimes he might have been criticised for being a bit loose but I think he played the best rugby of his career. He was at the bottom of every ruck, he would be taking the ball on, he had a great all-round game.'

Reluctantly, Joost van der Westhuizen might have to agree. The Springbok scrum-half appeared to find Wood's charges through the fringes and his combative persistence an immense irritant, slamming the ball into the prostrate Munsterman's stomach when he did eventually beat him to score a try in the second Test, and later in that game attempting to trip him as he barrelled round the side of a ruck, kicked ahead and set off in pursuit of the grubber. Had van der

Westhuizen either connected or been spotted by referee Erikson he might well have been sent off. But he might also have saved the series as Wood's follow-up of his own kick forced the lineout from which Guscott scored the winning points. The Limerick dynamo, looking like Alexei Sayle on speed as he fizzed about the pitch, had earlier displayed his skill with the boot when he chipped the Natal defence perfectly to set Townsend up for a try. But that he saved his most significant contribution for the series' key moment might have been expected. McGeechan and Telfer felt he came close to losing the plot in the second Test as the pressure began to get to him, but Lenihan was always confident he would come through. 'Wood is a world–class forward,' he says, 'there's no question or doubt about that. And the higher the quality of the opposition, the better Wood is. He could go out and play against Japan and he would be good, but he mightn't be outstanding. But put him in against South Africa, Australia, or New Zealand and his game just takes off. He's unbelievably hard and he trains harder – I don't mean he does more but he physically trains harder – than anyone I've ever seen. He just doesn't hold back. When you consider the serious injuries he had to his shoulder earlier in his career, I think he's just getting better and better.'

Wood, singled out by Bob Dwyer as a potential great on his Ireland début against the Wallabies in 1994, dislocated the joint after just seven minutes of World Cup action the following year and faced a fitness race to make the Lions tour after missing most of the previous Five Nations with another shoulder problem. He made light of the injury but again his punishing style of play took its toll when he was invalided out of contention for the final Test. Yet Wood had already made his contribution to the tour's success, off the field as well as on it. He was one of seven senior players whom McGeechan and Telfer would consult on strategic and tactical matters, and presided as judge over the traditional players' court. Judge and executioner as it turned out, for when McGeechan submitted to the forfeit he had earlier pledged if the Lions won the series, it was Wood – presumably the best qualified of the follically challenged – who had the honour of taking the razor to the coach's hairline in a moment that for Davidson somehow encapsulated his entire Lions experience. He says: 'It only started sinking in how well we had done when Keith Wood shaved Ian McGeechan's head. We had made such sacrifice and commitment that somebody in his fifties was going to shave his head. I remember thinking then, my goodness, we have done something special.'

# 21

# WALTZING O'DRISCOLL

FOR THE BRITISH and Irish, sporting heaven is unlikely to be furnished in green and gold, swathed in barbecue smoke and have a panoramic view of the Great Barrier Reef. With the Ashes now eligible for Australian citizenship on residency grounds and seemingly every sport under antipodean domination – from swimming to the hybrid International Rules code that matches Gaelic football with Aussie Rules – six weeks of slog around the rugby backyard of the world champions sounds more like penance than paradise. Especially when those world champions are out to claim the only honour they have never won and to give their most successful coach a send-off in keeping with his winning record. Of course, in the end, and despite – or maybe because of – the fact that its outcome hung in the balance until the final play of the final match, that was how the 2001 British and Irish Lions tour of Australia turned out. All the pain for no ultimate gain. Yet before the disappointment of Melbourne and the heartbreak of Sydney, heaven had a Brisbane postcode, as a full hour of Pommie nirvana unfolded with the Lions laying waste to the Wallabies at the Gabba. The ecstasy before the agony. In front of a delirious, astonishing 20,000-strong army of travelling support, the red jerseys scored four tries without reply to lead their hosts 29–3, ultimately running out 29–13 winners to set up hopes of series victory.

Yet even in the immediate aftermath of victory, Keith Wood, captain of Ireland and touchstone of the Lions front-row, counselled caution. 'You still have at the back of your mind that nobody will give a shit about the Gabba if we lose the next two Tests,' he said.

Relentless competitor that he is, Wood no doubt consigned his Australian experience to the slender file marked 'failure' within seconds of the final whistle blowing in Sydney. But, for Irish rugby in particular, the glee of the Gabba should not be banished from memory quite so quickly or so easily. Alongside England's Jason Robinson, the three principal architects of that monumental win were the three Irishmen in the XV: Wood, Brian O'Driscoll and Rob Henderson.

With their overall efforts across the three Tests, that trio achieved individual consolation for collective series defeat. Wood cemented his reputation as the best hooker in the game, O'Driscoll confirmed himself as the brightest new star in the rugby firmament and Henderson proved to the world that he was more than just a joker and a crash-ball merchant. As with the Lions at large, they enjoyed their finest hour in that Brisbane bonanza: among the highlights were O'Driscoll scoring a try of true class and genius; Henderson scything clear to set up the score that put the tourists out of sight, and Wood turning in a performance of such all-round quality and ambition that nobody laughed when he attempted a drop goal from 40 metres in the closing stages.

Ironically, it was O'Driscoll who had the most to prove when he collected his jersey from Willie John McBride, the greatest Lion of them all, as the team prepared for battle. Ironic because for much of the previous 18 months, from the moment he exploded into the national consciousness with his hat-trick for Ireland against France in Paris, the 22-year-old centre had been built up as the greatest gift to Irish back play since Mike Gibson hung up his boots. Yet by the time of the first Test, O'Driscoll somehow had it all to prove. Wood had been in rumbustious, rumbling nick from day one; Henderson had posted Day-Glo notices of his new-found form with every game he played; only O'Driscoll had yet to reveal himself, to step forward out of the crowd.

Before the party set off, McBride himself had identified the series as the acid test of the young Dubliner's ability, of his right to be bracketed with the game's outstanding performers. 'Let's see what he does on this tour and then we can judge,' said the tourists' most respected sage. The whole tour, he might have emphasised, as not everyone could wait that long. After the first couple of weeks, the Australians and much of the media decided they had seen enough and that they were not impressed by the view. By the first Test's end, as the Lions' number 13 exited the arena clutching the man-of-the-match award, opinions had been radically revised. The visiting crowd sang 'Waltzing O'Driscoll' to the tune of 'Waltzing Matilda'. The hosts now knew their man was the genuine article.

At least one of the Australian players was already aware of that, having recognised the talent, if not the name, down the coast in Sydney two years earlier. Matt Burke, the Wallaby full-back, was asked if he had been impressed by any of the Ireland players his Waratahs team had just defeated heavily. 'I don't know who he is,' he replied, 'but it was the number 13 and he had a great game, looked a great talent.'

That was only O'Driscoll's second appearance in the Ireland shirt and he lasted a mere 30 minutes before going off injured. But his jolting acceleration and slashing breaks had made an instant impression. Two years on, in Brisbane, being left on his backside by O'Driscoll's high-speed shuffle merely confirmed Burke's earlier assessment.

Nevertheless, that was where he ended up as the final victim of O'Driscoll's 50-yard epic that killed off the first Test as a contest just 55 seconds into the second half. Fatally, Nathan Grey and Jeremy Paul had presented the young Lion with the glint of a gap on halfway. O'Driscoll's eyesight is poor enough for him to struggle to read the scoreboard at Donnybrook from out on the pitch, but he enjoys 20–20 vision when it comes to spotting an opening and has the speed off the mark to convert possibility into yardage in a twinkling. Grey and Paul were left groping blindly in his wake as the UCD man streaked towards the last line of defence, Burke – who he left mesmerised and on the seat of his pants with a flamboyant side-step that bought him safe passage to the try-line. And this, remember, against a defence that won the World Cup at a cost of just one try all tournament.

O'Driscoll's was a phenomenal score by any measure, but the critical point at which it was taken and the impact it had on the contest made it all the more special. Lenihan says of the moment: 'When you put it into the context of the situation, it was even better than it looked. We had been under a lot of pressure going into the first Test and were in a reasonably strong position at half-time, but for him to score that try at that stage of the game quite simply closed out the first Test. Compare the effect that had to what happened in the first ten minutes of the second half of the second Test. We were in a similar position at half-time, emphasised the same things in the dressing-room but this time we gave away 15 points in 10 minutes and that was the second Test closed off for Australia.

'The try was a totally individual one and to see three or four

Australians flailing vainly after him gave the team and the crowd a huge lift at a very important stage of the game.'

O'Driscoll had confirmed the attacking potency he had showcased in Paris, but what impressed his handlers most was the complete nature of his performance in a game in which he created another try for wing Daffyd James and made 14 tackles to help repel one of the game's most powerful attacks. Lenihan says: 'What impressed me most about O'Driscoll was his all-round contribution. People already recognised him as a player of blistering pace with a very good sidestep and the ability to beat anyone one-on-one. But if you looked at his overall game his defence was outstanding throughout and his work effort in cleaning out ruck and maul was excellent. He did that throughout the tour to show he was an all-round player and it's very unusual in the modern game that you get a midfield player who is equally adept in defence and attack.'

Before Brisbane, O'Driscoll would not have blamed the Australians for running him down; prior to the two Saturday games preceding the opening Test he was equally unimpressed by his early efforts. 'Even the coaches were scratching their heads in the beginning,' admits Lenihan of a start that was less than auspicious. This nine-handicap golfer was not helped by being asked to play full-back for the first time in his life as the tour kicked off in Perth, a move which Lenihan says was planned before the squad left England but, due to the abject nature of the opposition (the part-timers of Western Australia were flayed 116–10), turned out to be 'a waste of time that didn't prove anything at all'. The management considered O'Driscoll a certainty for outside centre when they selected the squad and so had wanted to see if he could fill in at full-back to allow them to pick a replacements bench without specialist cover for the role.

O'Driscoll's main problem was rust, and he was fortunate that Lenihan was sufficiently aware of his situation to buy him time on a whistle-stop tour where opportunities were so limited that one mediocre performance could kill a player's Test chances stone-dead.

The manager explains: 'People just didn't understand that it was always going to take the guy two or three weeks to get into the pace of the thing, because he had only played 14 games all season because of injury, the foot-and-mouth crisis and the fact that Leinster didn't qualify for the later stages of the European Cup. Before the tour, his last representative game was against France in February. All he had played in between were a few all-Ireland league games in April, which were totally inadequate preparation for the level of rugby he would have to play in Australia.'

But he adds: 'He played very well against Queensland without being outstanding, but when the pressure was on for his Test place against New South Wales he was brilliant. He was in the opposite situation to most of the others in that he had had too few games in his season as opposed to too many.'

Lenihan brackets O'Driscoll with Wood as a big game player who thrives in pressure situations – hence his heavy stamp on the accelerator when the crunch came against New South Wales Waratahs seven days before the first Test. Back at the Sydney Football Stadium, the player his team-mates refer to as 'God' was as revelatory as on his first visit there in 1999, this time previewing the sort of try with which he would sear his name into Lions lore the following week.

O'Driscoll had scored one scorcher against Queensland but here, amidst a performance of perpetual motion, he took a pass from Robinson one-handed and burst through a sliver of space to bear down on full-back Duncan McRae. A textbook sidestep, and the scoreboard could add another five points to the visitors' total.

That sequence of spiralling success and ambition through Queensland, NSW and the Wallabies themselves in Brisbane comprised the prime of O'Driscoll's tour. He created the platform for the Lions' lone try of the second Test with a brave, superbly timed leap and take of his own high kick and always looked dangerous in possession, but was increasingly targeted by the Wallaby defence and was never again afforded the platform of the first rubber by a pack that was no longer on the front foot. A late, high hit from Daniel Herbert hampered him in the second encounter and he was one of many players carrying injuries through the decider, but he had already proved his quality and worth, with the promise of plenty more to come.

Lenihan says: 'For 22 years of age, in terms of attacking play he is the most exciting back in the northern hemisphere. If he was selected to play for Australia or New Zealand tomorrow he would be totally comfortable in that sort of company. He will develop physically over the next two or three years and I don't think we will see the best of him until then, when he will be a seasoned international with another 20 or 30 caps under his belt. But from what we have seen so far he would be in the running to make any World XV.'

If O'Driscoll made it into that theoretical global side he would find Keith Wood there waiting. The billiard-ball bonce of the Harlequins hooker cracked around the baize as invigoratingly as it had in South Africa four years earlier, but with an even greater degree of measure and effectiveness in its work. Lenihan summarises: 'He proved he is the number-one hooker in the world as a result of this Test series.'

Of the highlights, there were the statistical and – more memorably – the visual; the exhibitions of footballing skills and vision beyond those of any of his rivals in the number 2 jerseys of the Test scene: the long-range, Zinzan Brooke-style drop goal attempt in Brisbane (15 yards short but 'by the time I get home this summer it will have shaved the underside of the bar,' he said), and the inch-perfect chip with which he sent in James for a try in the 42–8 dismemberment of Queensland. Classic Woody all round.

The tour saw the son of late Lions prop Gordon Wood record his first win over the country his father whitewashed in 1959, but also saw him lose his unbeaten record in the red jersey on his 10th outing. Most significantly, though, he was able to add the captaincy of the side to his leadership of Ireland when he led out the first tour selection against Western Australia in Perth. Wood had been many people's choice as skipper of the entire party and, despite losing out on that honour to England's Martin Johnson, he remained a strong voice in the dressing-room and on both the pitch and training-ground.

Lenihan says of the captaincy debate: 'He was a genuine contender for the captaincy but Martin had always been the number-one choice and the foot-and-mouth postponements meant Keith lacked the opportunities others had to state his case. I don't think missing out on the captaincy was a problem for him because he appreciated that Martin was always the favourite, but more importantly he had a lot of respect for him. That went both ways because Martin recognised his leadership qualities and Keith still had a big influence on the touring party. A lot of the coaches who wouldn't have worked with him before didn't realise quite how good a leader he was until they saw him at close quarters on a regular basis.'

Wood trains as hard as he plays and the physical commitment he offers has meant that in recent years he has had to reduce his workload with Munster and then Harlequins, to ensure he can play every game he enters at full throttle throughout. On what was, in terms of training regimes, the most demanding Lions tour of them all, however, self-preservation was not an option. Unlike some members of the party, who went public on their dislike of the apparent excesses and harshness of the preparation work, Wood was prepared, if not to grin, then at least grit his teeth and bear it.

He said: 'We were told at the start, and I remember talking both to Donal and Robbo [assistant coach Andy Robinson], that we would train very hard. And I have to say that I was grumpy that we were training an awful lot because it was bloody hard work.'

But he added: 'If you get an opportunity to go on a Lions tour you do everything you bloody can. And if you're shattered at the end of it you better make certain you go away on holiday. You better make certain that you talk to your club or your province and make certain they look after you, because this is a once-in-a-lifetime opportunity, and you try and do whatever the hell you can to get in the Test team, to win in the Test team, to win the Test series. You have to do whatever you can.'

Wood may not have been the leader of the Lions but he set the example in his energy and commitment around the park, making 14 tackles – a remarkable figure for a front rower – in the first Test alone, one of which was a spectacular hit on Grey that knocked the ball free before the Wallaby inside-centre had returned to earth. His work was noted gratefully by manager Lenihan: 'His contribution on the field in the basics of scrum and lineout were their usual high standard but his work-rate went up to another level and his tackling also moved to a level we hadn't seen before, as did his footballing skills. In the first Test he kicked the length of the field and had a dropped goal attempt from 40 yards. He has the skills others do not have and he has the footballing brain to use them. This tour saw him at the height of his playing ability.'

The only area of the game in which the Lions faltered where Wood was a key component was in the lineout; the eight turnovers conceded in the third Test conceivably costing them the series. In such situations, the hooker normally takes the flak, although that knee-jerk reaction masks the array of factors that govern a lineout's operation. The throw can be spot-on, but if the timing of the jumper's leap is wrong, if the call is the wrong one, or if the opposition's countering strategy is from the top drawer, then the ball can be lost. Often, only those in the middle really know what has gone on. Against Australia – the best lineout operators in the game – and with just four weeks to create a smooth restart machine, perhaps the odds were always against the Lions in this department. Wood took a measure of blame for the turnovers but some of the calls the team made, particularly in defence, were eyebrow-raisers of Roger Moore proportions.

Whatever his culpability, it was surely far outweighed by his all-round contribution to the cause. Lenihan says: 'This Lions side and Australia are two of the very few teams who compete strongly at lineout time. Eales and Harrison, in the third Test, put a huge amount of pressure on our lineout and had really done their homework. In that situation your lineout throwing really has to be spot-on. Keith would admit there were lapses but that was due to the pressure Australia put on us collectively more than anything else. But his contribution to the set piece was outstanding.'

Wood's excellence was expected, as was O'Driscoll's, despite his quiet start to the tour. The surprise package of the trip, alongside Jason Robinson's fast-track ascent to the summit of attacking wing play, was Rob Henderson, who headed for Munster after the tour presumably on the grounds that now he had foresaken the charms of the Teddington Tandoori there was nothing left to stay in London for.

In the age of po-faced, mineral-water-and-an-early-night professionalism, Henderson had for years been painted as the last bearer of the cigarette-lighting flame of Willie Duggan and Moss Keane. Legend has it that while at London Irish he once went from an all-night party to Sunbury (stopping only for a straightener in his local en route), where he scored an outstanding individual try against Northampton. At that stage of his career, if Hendo had told his teammates he needed to get lighter, they would have assumed he had forgotten his matches.

Eventually, he decided a change of image was required, a move generally considered to have come after his omission from the Ireland World Cup squad in 1999. In fact, Henderson had already put himself on the straight and narrow, and privately was seething over a selectorial decision he saw as being based on reputation alone, as he considered himself to be fitter than he had ever been. The following January, he was close to turning his back on the international scene when he could not even make the combined Test and A team squad at the beginning of the Six Nations. He watched Ireland play England in an Irish bar in West London.

But five days after that nadir, his luck began to change. A clutch of injuries unexpectedly gave him a place on the bench for the next match. Girvan Dempsey had to come off during the first half and Henderson was suddenly back in the big time and playing well. Determined not to let his chance slip, the Teddington Tandoori famously came off his Friends and Family telephone list, beer took a back seat and he started working over the summer with a fitness trainer he picked at random out of the Yellow Pages. Four sessions a week and within the year he was four kilos of muscle heavier and three quarters of a second quicker over 100 metres. Ten tries in fourteen league games for Wasps – including three against Gloucester as an emergency fly-half – plus a hat-trick for Ireland against Italy in the Six Nations and some dogged defending against France, booked him his place on the plane as he thrived in the company of O'Driscoll.

Henderson was happy to pedal the self-deprecating line that he was enjoying success by association. The duo have a genuine understanding, he reckons: 'The understanding is that I give him the ball and he scores.' But the Dover-born inside-centre, whose mother hails from Wexford, showed in his performances without 'God' at his side that he was more than just a sidekick. His Italian job was pulled-off solo and his debut Lions hat-trick against the Queensland President's XV earned him headlines in his own right, and convinced the player himself he had at last arrived at the top table. He said afterwards: 'You can talk about various occurrences in your career, like your first cap or your first try for your country, but your first full start for the Lions and then to score three – it surpasses everything, I think. The record books will show that I actually have a Lions hat-trick and no one can ever take that away from me.'

Henderson is still built for the midfield wallop, but as he has been given the freedom to become more than a human battering-ram he has sought space rather than contact and unveiled previously hidden talents for tactical kicking, as well as showing a nifty turn of foot through a gap and increasingly deft timing of his offload. The 40-yard break he made in the first Test to set up the Scott Quinnell try that had the Lions home and hosed by the hour mark, was a classic of its type.

At the other end of the field, his defence – 18 tackles made in the first Test; none missed – remains as concrete as ever. Lenihan says of his efforts: 'Defensively he's always been very solid but he thrives on playing with O'Driscoll. If teams try to double bank on O'Driscoll he will utilise any space that then opens up. He made a couple of really telling breaks like that in the first Test, one of those leading to

Quinnell's decisive try. Through injury he wasn't as effective later on but he showed he is a lot more than just a take-the-ball-up, bashing centre. He has a kicking game and a genuine ability to get behind defences.'

He adds: 'Hendo also showed a lot of character. He used his demotion from the World Cup squad as a spur to get his act together and went out to Australia probably fitter and stronger than he had ever been. Even then, he was still a guy going on tour who a lot of people thought should not have got the selection ahead of Scott Gibbs, but [he] became a central member of the tour party on and off the field.

'He used the tour as the pinnacle of his career and as a measure of how far he had come over the previous 12–18 months. He took a very positive attitude into the tour and was the revelation of the first Test. That was the best rugby he has played and if he can take the positives out of that, he and O'Driscoll could play together up to the next World Cup as a very potent combination at international level.'

On a tour that had little respite from its relentless workload, Henderson's upbeat persona brought some much-needed light relief to the party, although the room-mates he drove to sleep in the bathroom with his ear-shattering snoring ('it's not a problem for me; I'm asleep') might disagree. Malcolm O'Kelly also paid homage to Willie Duggan by turning up at Dublin airport with little more than his toothbrush and, in the words of O'Driscoll, 'looking like he's out of the scratcher about 15 minutes', although this turned out to be not because he thought more than one shirt a fortnight an extravagance, but because he knew a mountain of free clothing from sponsors awaited when the squad met up in England.

That was one change from the days before professionalism, but not the only one that had occurred since the Lions, and manager Donal Lenihan, last toured Australia in 1989. Even when he flew out on a fact-finding mission in the summer of 2000, nothing Lenihan saw prepared him for the reality of life with the Lions, twenty-first-century style. He says of the experience: 'This Lions tour was bigger than anyone could have envisaged beforehand. It was phenomenal to see the support at the first Test in the Gabba and the lengths that the Australians then went to to try and negate the Lions' support. There were 120 journalists travelling, plus all the television coverage; it just goes to show how far the Lions have come in the professional era. The interest in the tour was unprecedented from a rugby perspective. Back in Ireland it was like the Jack Charlton era in football in terms of the numbers of people going to pubs and clubs to watch the matches.'

In light of the fact that Lenihan led the best-remembered of all dirt-trackers – 'Donal's Doughnuts' of 1989 – it was no small irony that the management were accused of neglecting the midweek team, several members of which went public with gripes of not being given a fair crack of the whip to stake their claims for a place in the Test team. Lenihan attributes the difficulties of keeping everyone happy to a combination of the character of the professional beast and of a tour whose intensity required a large squad to cover for injuries but whose itinerary could not be extensive enough to keep everyone playing.

He explains: 'It was a hugely intense tour and totally different to anything anyone had experienced before. On a national tour, eight or ten of the thirty-five would be development players and happy to play in one or two matches. Here, every single one wanted to play in every game and because of that their competitive nature really comes out. The fact that not everyone can and will play is hard for them and I think the nature of the professional era has accentuated that more than ever.'

The professional age has also altered the backdrop against which Lions tours are played out and Lenihan was disappointed by the reception the Lions received in the domestic press Down Under. He says: 'The most disappointing aspect was some of the media coverage from the Australian perspective. They were very worried after the Queensland match because we had played so well in the first three games. There was then a constant barrage of coverage claiming that we were illegal or focusing on the '89 tour and the violence of that series, complete with endless pictures of all that, which we saw as totally irrelevant to the situation.

'We were constantly in a battle, which was a pity because I think the Lions tour did a huge amount for rugby in Australia, which we must remember is still a minority sport there. The Lions brought rugby in Australia to the fore like no other tour in the past and it was a pity these side issues were detracting from that, although, let's be fair, some of our players didn't help in that regard. But all the side issues detracted from the quality of the rugby, what the travelling support did for the Australian economy, and what the tour itself did for rugby in Australia.'

The Test defeats may initially detract from the positives the series created for its players, but in the long run its benefits for the Irish eight who returned as Lions tourists should become crystal clear. Lenihan says: 'The younger guys have been given a platform and to be fair to England, they have raised the bar in terms of professionalism and attitude – among both their players and coaches – and I think our players will have learned a lot from that. For Ronan O'Gara to go on a tour like that in only his second season of international rugby will prove a big learning curve for him. He learned a lot from working with Jonny Wilkinson and from coming under the influence of Dave Alred in terms of his kicking. He will only benefit from that in years to come.'

# Appendix 1

# Lions of Ireland

## THE TEST LIONS OF IRELAND, 1910-1997

| NAME | BIRTHPLACE | CLUB | TESTS | TOURS |
|------|-----------|------|-------|-------|
| Bob Alexander<br>*Born 24 September 1910*<br>*Died 19 July 1943* | Belfast | NIFC | 3 | 1938 |
| George Beamish<br><br>*Born 29 April 1905*<br>*Died 13 November 1967* | Dunmanway,<br>Co. Cork | Leicester | 5 | 1930 |
| Vesey Boyle<br><br>*Born 2 July 1915* | Dublin<br>Univ. | Dublin | 2 | 1938 |
| Norman Brand<br>*Born 5 January 1899*<br>*Deceased* | Belfast | NIFC | 2 | 1924 |
| Barry Bresnihan<br>*Born 13 March 1944* | Waterford | UCD | 3 | 1968 |
| Niall Brophy<br>*Born 19 November 1935* | Dublin | UCD | 2 | 1962 |
| Ollie Campbell<br><br>*Born 5 March 1954* | Dublin<br>Belvedere | Old | 7 | 1980/<br>1983 |

| NAME | BIRTHPLACE | CLUB | TESTS | TOURS |
|---|---|---|---|---|
| Tom Clifford | Tipperary Munster | Young | 5 | 1950 |
| *Born 15 November 1923* *Died 1 October 1990* | | | | |
| George Cromey | Ahoghill, Co. Antrim | Queen's Univ. | 1 | 1938 |
| *Born 8 May 1913* | | | | |
| William Cunningham | Dublin | Lansdowne | 1 | 1924 |
| *Born 27 March 1900* *Died 1959* | | | | |
| Jeremy Davidson | Belfast | London | 3 | 1997 |
| *Born 28 April 1974* | | | | |
| Ronnie Dawson | Dublin | Wanderers | 6 | 1959 |
| *Born 5 June 1932* | | | | |
| Mick Doyle | Castleisland, Co. Kerry | Blackrock College | 1 | 1968 |
| *Born 13 October 1941* | | | | |
| Willie Duggan | Kilkenny | Blackrock College | 4 | 1977 |
| *Born 12 March 1950* | | | | |
| Jimmy Farrell | Dublin | Bective Rangers | 5 | 1930 |
| *Born 7 August 1903* *Died 24 October 1979* | | | | |
| Ciaran Fitzgerald | Galway | St Mary's College | 4 | 1983 |
| *Born 4 June 1952* | | | | |
| Alexander Foster | Londonderry | Queen's Univ. | 2 | 1910 |
| *Born 22 June 1890* *Died 24 August 1972* | | | | |

| NAME | BIRTHPLACE | CLUB | TESTS | TOURS |
|---|---|---|---|---|
| Mike Gibson | Belfast | Cambridge Univ. NIFC | 12 | 1966/ 68/71 |
| *Born 3 December 1942* | | | | |
| Bob Graves | Valentia, Co. Kerry | Wanderers | 2 | 1938 |
| *Born 23 January 1909* *Died 14 October 1990* | | | | |
| Noel Henderson | Drumahoe, Co. Derry | Queen's Univ. | 1 | 1950 |
| *Born 10 August 1928* *Died 27 August 1997* | | | | |
| Rob Henderson | Dover, Kent | Wasps | 3 | 2000 |
| *Born 27 October 1972* | | | | |
| David Hewitt | Belfast | Queen's Univ. NIFC | 6 | 1959/62 |
| *Born 6 September 1939* | | | | |
| David Irwin | Belfast | Instonians | 3 | 1983 |
| *Born 1 February 1959* | | | | |
| Moss Keane | Currow, Co. Kerry | Lansdowne | 1 | 1977 |
| *Born 27 July 1948* | | | | |
| Ken Kennedy | Rochester, Kent | CIYMS London Irish | 4 | 1966 |
| *Born 10 May 1941* | | | | |
| Michael Kiernan | Cork | Dolphin | 3 | 1983 |
| *Born 17 January 1961* | | | | |
| Tom Kiernan | Cork | Cork Constitution | 5 | 1962/68 |
| *Born 7 January 1939* | | | | |

| NAME | BIRTHPLACE | CLUB | TESTS | TOURS |
|------|-----------|------|-------|-------|
| Jack Kyle | Belfast | Queen's Univ. | 6 | 1950 |
| *Born 10 January 1926* | | | | |
| Ronnie Lamont | Belfast | Instonians | 4 | 1966 |
| *Born 18 November 1941* | | | | |
| Mick Lane | Cork | UCC | 2 | 1950 |
| *Born 3 April 1926* | | | | |
| Sean Lynch | Dublin | St Mary's College | 4 | 1971 |
| *Born 22 September 1942* | | | | |
| Willie John McBride | Toomebridge, Co. Antrim | Ballymena | 17 | 1962/ 66/68/ 71/74 |
| *Born 6 June 1940* | | | | |
| Bill McKay | Waterford | Queen's Univ. | 6 | 1950 |
| *Born 12 July 1921* *Died 15 October 1997* | | | | |
| Harry McKibbin | Belfast | Queen's Univ. | 3 | 1938 |
| *Born 13 July 1915* | | | | |
| Ray McLoughlin | Ballinasloe, Co. Galway | Gosforth Blackrock College | 3 | 1966 |
| *Born 14 August 1939* | | | | |
| Hugo MacNeill | Dublin Univ. | Oxford | 3 | 1983 |
| *Born 16 September 1958* | | | | |
| Jim McVicker | Ballymoney, Co. Antrim | Collegians | 3 | 1924 |
| *Born 1 October 1896* *Died 18 December 1985* | | | | |

| NAME | BIRTHPLACE | CLUB | TESTS | TOURS |
|------|-----------|------|-------|-------|
| Blair Mayne | Newtownards Univ. | Queen's | 3 | 1938 |
| *Born 11 January 1915* | | | | |
| *Died 14 December 1955* | | | | |
| Syd Millar | Ballymena | Ballymena | 9 | 1959/ 62/68 |
| *Born 23 May 1934* | | | | |
| Eric Miller | Dublin | Leicester | 1 | 1997 |
| *Born 29 September 1975* | | | | |
| Dick Milliken | Belfast | Bangor | 4 | 1974 |
| *Born 2 September 1950* | | | | |
| George Morgan | Dublin | Clontarf | 1 | 1938 |
| *Born 24 March 1912* | | | | |
| *Died 15 April 1979* | | | | |
| Bill Mulcahy | Rathkeale, Co. Limerick | UCD | 6 | 1959/62 |
| *Born 7 January 1935* | | | | |
| Karl Mullen | Courtown, Co. Wexford | Old Belvedere | 3 | 1950 |
| *Born 26 November 1926* | | | | |
| Brendan Mullin | Jerusalem, Israel | London Irish | 1 | 1989 |
| *Born 30 October 1963* | | | | |
| Andy Mulligan | Kasulu, Tanzania | London Irish | 1 | 1959 |
| *Born 4 February 1936* | | | | |
| Noel Murphy | Cork | Cork Constitution | 8 | 1959/66 |
| *Born 22 February 1937* | | | | |

| NAME | BIRTHPLACE | CLUB | TESTS | TOURS |
|------|------------|------|-------|-------|
| Paul Murray<br>*Born 29 June 1905*<br>*Died 1 June 1981* | Dublin | Wanderers | 4 | 1930 |
| Jimmy Nelson<br>*Born 16 September 1921* | Belfast | Malone | 4 | 1950 |
| Rodney<br>O'Donnell<br>*Born 16 August 1956* | Dublin | St Mary's<br>College | 1 | 1980 |
| Brian O'Driscoll<br>*Born 21 January 1979* | Dublin | UCD | 3 | 2000 |
| John O'Driscoll<br><br>*Born 26 November 1953* | Dublin | London<br>Irish | 6 | 1980/83 |
| Henry O'Neill<br><br>*Born 1 July 1907*<br>*Died November 1994* | Portstewart, Co.<br>Londonderry | Queen's<br>Univ. | 5 | 1930 |
| Tony O'Reilly<br><br>*Born 7 May 1936* | Dublin | Old<br>Belvedere | 10 | 1955/59 |
| Phil Orr<br>*Born 14 December 1950* | Dublin | Old Wesley | 1 | 1977 |
| Colin Patterson<br>*Born 3 March 1955* | Belfast | Instonians | 3 | 1980 |
| Cecil Pedlow<br>*Born 20 January 1934* | Lurgan | CIYMS | 2 | 1955 |

| NAME | BIRTHPLACE | CLUB | TESTS | TOURS |
|------|-----------|------|-------|-------|
| Oliver Piper<br>*Born 14 February 1884*<br>*Deceased* | Neath, Wales | Cork Constitution | 1 | 1910 |
| Nick Popplewell<br>*Born 6 April 1964* | Dublin | Greystones | 3 | 1993 |
| Tom Reid<br>*Born 3 March 1926*<br>*Died October 1996* | Limerick | Garryowen | 2 | 1955 |
| Trevor Ringland<br>*Born 13 November 1959* | Belfast | Ballymena | 1 | 1983 |
| John Robbie<br>*Born 17 November 1955* | Dublin | Greystones | 1 | 1980 |
| Fergus Slattery<br>*Born 12 January 1949* | Dun Laoghaire | Blackrock College | 4 | 1974 |
| Tom Smyth<br>*Born 12 December 1884*<br>*Died May 1928* | Antrim | Malone | 2 | 1910 |
| Robin Thompson<br>*Born 5 May 1931* | Belfast | Instonians | 3 | 1955 |
| Colm Tucker<br>*Born 22 September 1952* | Limerick | Shannon | 2 | 1980 |
| Sam Walker<br>*Born 21 April 1912*<br>*Died 27 January 1972* | Belfast | Instonians | 3 | 1938 |
| Paul Wallace<br>*Born 30 December 1971* | Cork | Saracens | 3 | 1997 |
| Tony Ward<br>*Born 8 October 1954* | Dublin | Garryowen | 1 | 1980 |

| NAME | BIRTHPLACE | CLUB | TESTS | TOURS |
|------|-----------|------|-------|-------|
| Gordon Wood | Limerick | Garryowen | 2 | 1959 |
| *Born 20 June 1931* | | | | |
| *Died 18 May 1982* | | | | |
| Keith Wood | Limerick | Harlequins | 5 | 1997/ |
| *Born 27 January 1972* | | | | 2000 |
| Roger Young | Belfast | Queen's Univ. Collegians | 4 | 1966/68 |

*Born 29 June 1943*

**Abbreviations:**
CIYMS: Church of Ireland Young Men's Society
NIFC: North of Ireland Football Club
UCC: University College, Cork
UCD: University College, Dublin

## IRISH LIONS TOURISTS BY YEAR

(Test appearances in brackets)        ★ indicates replacement

### 1910 v South Africa (series lost 1–2)
Tom Smyth (captain; 2,3), Alexander Foster (1,2), Oliver Piper (1), Arthur McClinton, William Ashby, William Tyrrell
Total: 6

### 1924 v South Africa (lost 0–3 with one draw)
Norman Brand (1,2), William Cunningham★ (3), Jim McVicar (1,3,4), Mick Bradley, Jammie Clinch, William Roche
Total: 6

### 1930 v New Zealand (lost 1–3) and Australia (lost 0–1)
George Beamish (1,2,3,4/1), Jimmy Farrell (1,2,3,4/1), Henry O'Neill (1,2,3,4/1), Paul Murray (1,2,4/1), Michael Dunne
Total: 4

### 1938 v South Africa (lost 1–2)
Sammy Walker (captain; 1,2,3), Bob Alexander (1,2,3), Harry McKibbin (1,2,3), Blair Mayne (1,2,3), Vesey Boyle (2,3), Bob

Graves (1,3), George Cromey (3), George Morgan (3)
Total: 8

### 1950 v New Zealand (lost 0–3 with one draw) and Australia (won 2–0)

Karl Mullen (captain; 1,2/2), Jack Kyle (1,2,3/1,2), Bill McKay (1,2,3,4/1,2), Tom Clifford (1,2,3/1,2), Jimmy Nelson (3,4/1,2), Mick Lane (4/2), Noel Henderson (3), Jim McCarthy, George Norton
Total: 9

### 1955 v South Africa (drew 2–2)

Robin Thompson (captain; 1,2,4), Tony O'Reilly (1,2,3,4), Cecil Pedlow (1,4), Tom Reid (2,3), Robin Roe
Manager: Jack Siggins
Total: 5

### 1959 v New Zealand (lost 3–1) and Australia (won 2–0)

Ronnie Dawson (captain; 1,2,3,4/1,2), Tony O'Reilly (1,2,3,4), David Hewitt (1,3,4/1,2), Noel Murphy (1,2,4/2), Syd Millar (2/1,2), Bill Mulcahy (4/1), Gordon Wood (1,3), Andy Mulligan* (4), Mick English, Niall Brophy
Total: 10

### 1962 v South Africa (lost 0–3 with one draw)

Syd Millar (1,2,3,4), Bill Mulcahy (1,2,3,4), Niall Brophy (1,4) Willie John McBride (3,4), David Hewitt (4), Tom Kiernan (3), William Hunter
Assistant manager: Harry McKibbin
Total: 7

### 1966 v New Zealand (lost 4–0) and Australia (won 2–0)

Mike Gibson (1,2,3,4), Ronnie Lamont (1,2,3,4), Ken Kennedy (1,4/1,2), Noel Murphy (2,3/1,2), Willie John McBride (2,3,4), Ray McLoughlin (4/1,2), Roger Young (1/1,2), Barry Bresnihan*, Jerry Walsh
Manager: Des O'Brien
Total: 9

### 1968 v South Africa (lost 0–3 with one draw)

Tom Kiernan (captain; 1,2,3,4), Mike Gibson (1, 2,3,4), Willie John

McBride (1,2,3,4), Barry Bresnihan (1,2,4), Syd Millar (1,2), Mick Doyle (1), Roger Young (3), Ken Goodall★
Coach: Ronnie Dawson
Total: 8

### 1971 v New Zealand (won 2–1 with one draw)
Mike Gibson (1,2,3,4), Sean Lynch (1,2,3,4), Willie John McBride (1,2,3,4), Mick Hipwell, Ray McLoughlin, Fergus Slattery
Total: 6

### 1974 v South Africa (won 3–0 with one draw)
Willie John McBride (captain; 1,2,3,4), Dick Milliken (1,2,3,4), Fergus Slattery (1,2,3,4), Mike Gibson★, Tom Grace, Ken Kennedy, Stewart McKinney, Johnny Moloney
Coach: Syd Millar
Total: 8

### 1977 v New Zealand (lost 1–3)
Willie Duggan (1,2,3,4), Moss Keane (1), Phil Orr (1), Mike Gibson
Total: 4

### 1980 v South Africa (lost 1–3)
John O'Driscoll (1,2,3,4), Ollie Campbell (2[R],3,4), Colin Patterson (1,2,3), Colm Tucker (3,4), Rodney O'Donnell (1), John Robbie★ (4), Tony Ward★ (1), Phil Orr★
Manager: Syd Millar
Coach: Noel Murphy
Total: 8

### 1983 v New Zealand (lost 0–4)
Ciaran Fitzgerald (captain; 1,2,3,4), Ollie Campbell (1,2,3,4), David Irwin (1,2,4), Michael Kiernan (2,3,4), Hugo MacNeill (1,2,4[R]), John O'Driscoll (2,4), Trevor Ringland (1), Donal Lenihan★, Gerry McLoughlin★
Manager: Willie John McBride
Total: 9

### 1989 v Australia (won 2–1)
Brendan Mullin (1), Paul Dean, Donal Lenihan, Steve Smith
Total: 4

**1993 v New Zealand (lost 1–2)**
Nick Popplewell (1,2,3), Vince Cunningham★, Mick Galwey, Richard Wallace★
Total: 4

**1997 v South Africa (won 2–1)**
Jeremy Davidson (1,2,3), Paul Wallace (1,2,3), Keith Wood (1,2), Eric Miller (2 [R])
Total: 3

**1997 v South Africa (won 2–1)**
Jeremy Davidson (1,2,3), Eric Miller (2[R]), Paul Wallace (1,2,3), Keith Wood (1,2)
Total: 4

**2000 v Australia (lost 1-2)**
Rob Henderson (1,2,3), Brian O'Driscoll (1,2,3), Keith Wood (1,2,3), Jeremy Davidson, Tyrone Howe★, Ronan O'Gara, Malcolm O'Kelly, David Wallace★
Manager: Donal Lenihan
Total: 8

# APPENDIX 2

# LIONS RECORDS

## LIONS CAPTAINS SINCE 1910

| YEAR | | CAPTAIN |
|------|------|---------|
| 1910 | South Africa | Tom Smyth (Ire) |
| 1924 | South Africa | Ronnie Cove-Smith (Eng) |
| 1930 | New Zealand, Australia | Doug Prentice (Eng) |
| 1938 | South Africa | Sammy Walker (Ire) |
| 1950 | New Zealand, Australia | Karl Mullen (Ire) |
| 1955 | South Africa | Robin Thompson (Ire) |
| 1959 | New Zealand, Australia | Ronnie Dawson (Ire) |
| 1962 | South Africa | Arthur Smith (Sco) |
| 1966 | New Zealand, Australia | Mike Campbell-Lamerton |
| (Sco) | | |
| 1968 | South Africa | Tom Kiernan (Ire) |
| 1971 | New Zealand | John Dawes (Wal) |
| 1974 | South Africa | Willie John McBride (Ire) |
| 1977 | New Zealand | Phil Bennett (Wal) |
| 1980 | South Africa | Bill Beaumont (Eng) |
| 1983 | New Zealand | Ciaran Fitzgerald (Ire) |
| 1989 | Australia | Finlay Calder (Sco) |
| 1993 | New Zealand | Gavin Hastings (Sco) |
| 1997 | South Africa | Martin Johnson (Eng) |
| 2000 | Australia | Martin Johnson (Eng) |

## MOST CAPPED LIONS PLAYERS

| PLAYER | CAPS | LIONS TEST CAREER |
|--------|------|-------------------|
| Willie John McBride (Ire) | 17 | 1962–74 |
| Dickie Jeeps (Eng) | 13 | 1955–62 |
| Mike Gibson (Ire) | 12 | 1966–71 |
| Graham Price (Wal) | 12 | 1977–83 |

| | | |
|---|---|---|
| Tony O'Reilly (Ire) | 10 | 1955–59 |
| Rhys Williams (Wal) | 10 | 1955–59 |
| Gareth Edwards (Wal) | 10 | 1968–74 |

## MOST CAPPED LIONS BY POSITION

| POSITION | PLAYER | CAPS | TEST CAREER |
|---|---|---|---|
| Full-back | J.P.R. Williams (Wal) | 8 | 1971–74 |
| Wing | Tony O'Reilly (Ire) | 9 | 1955–59 |
| Centre | Mike Gibson (Ire) | 8 | 1966–71 |
| | Jeremy Guscott (Eng) | 8 | 1989–97 |
| Out-half | Phil Bennett (Wal) | 8 | 1974–77 |
| Scrum-half | Dickie Jeeps (Eng) | 13 | 1955–62 |
| Prop | Graham Price (Wal) | 12 | 1977–83 |
| Hooker | Bryn Meredith (Wal) | 8 | 1955–62 |
| Lock | Willie John McBride (Ire) | 17 | 1962–74 |
| Flanker | Noel Murphy (Ire) | 8 | 1959–66 |
| Number eight | Mervyn Davies (Wal) | 8 | 1971–74 |

## MOST CONSECUTIVE LIONS CAPS

| PLAYER | CAPS | OPPOSITION |
|---|---|---|
| Willie John McBride (Ire) | 15 | 1966 NZ 2,3,4; 1968 SA 1,2,3,4; 1971 NZ 1,2,3,4; 1974 SA 1,2,3,4 |
| Mike Gibson (Ire) | 12 | 1966 NZ 1,2,3,4; 1968 SA 1(R),2,3,4; 1971 NZ 1,2,3,4 |
| Graham Price (Wal) | 12 | 1977 NZ 1,2,3,4; 1980 SA 1,2,3,4; 1983 NZ 1,2,3,4 |

## MOST POINTS IN LIONS TESTS

| PLAYER | POINTS | TESTS | TEST CAREER |
|---|---|---|---|
| Gavin Hastings (Sco) | 66 | 6 | 1989–93 |
| Phil Bennett (Wal) | 44 | 8 | 1974–77 |
| Neil Jenkins (Wal) | 41 | 3 | 1997 |
| Tom Kiernan (Ire) | 35 | 5 | 1962–68 |
| Stewart Wilson (Sco) | 30 | 5 | 1966 |
| Barry John (Wal) | 30 | 5 | 1968–71 |

| Jonny Wilkinson | 36 | 3 | 2000 |
| --- | --- | --- | --- |

## MOST POINTS IN ALL LIONS MATCHES

| PLAYER | POINTS |
| --- | --- |
| Andy Irvine (Sco) | 274 |
| Phil Bennett (Wal) | 215 |
| Bob Hiller (Eng) | 214 |
| Barry John (Wal) | 188 |
| Ollie Campbell (Ire) | 184 |
| Gavin Hastings (Sco) | 167 |
| Mike Gibson (Ire) | 114 |
| David Hewitt (Ire) | 112 |
| Tim Stimpson (Eng) | 111 |
| Neil Jenkins (Wal) | 110 |

## MOST TRIES IN LIONS TESTS

| PLAYER | TRIES | TESTS | TEST CAREER |
| --- | --- | --- | --- |
| Tony O'Reilly (Ire) | 6 | 10 | 1955–59 |
| J.J. Williams (Wal) | 5 | 7 | 1974–77 |
| Malcolm Price (Wal) | 4 | 5 | 1959 |